Public Utility
Economics
and
Finance

Public Utility Economics and Finance

Keith M. Howe
Associate Professor
Iowa State University

Eugene F. Rasmussen
Chief Economist
Iowa State Commerce Commission

PRENTICE-HALL, INC., *Englewood Cliffs, New Jersey 07632*

Library of Congress Cataloging in Publication Data

Howe, Keith M.
    Public utility economics and finance.

    Includes bibliographies and index.
        1. Public utilities.   2. Public utilities—United
States.   I. Rasmussen, Eugene F.   II. Title.
HD2763.H65   338.4'33636'0973   81-21023
ISBN 0-13-739300-8   AACR2

Editorial/production supervision and interior design by Margaret Rizzi
Cover design by Zimmerman/Fayster Design
Manufacturing buyer: Ed O'Dougherty

Printed in the United States of America

10 9 8 7 6 5 4 3 2 1

ISBN 0-13-739300-8

Prentice-Hall International, Inc., *London*
Prentice-Hall of Australia Pty. Limited, *Sydney*
Prentice-Hall of Canada, Ltd., *Toronto*
Prentice-Hall of India Private Limited, *New Delhi*
Prentice-Hall of Japan, Inc., *Tokyo*
Prentice-Hall of Southeast Asia Pte. Ltd., *Singapore*
Whitehall Books Limited, *Wellington, New Zealand*

Contents

----------------------------- **3** -----------------------------

Legal Concepts
of Public Utilities

_____ **6** _____

A Critique of Public
Utility Regulation   158

_____ **7** _____

Pricing—The Regulation
of Consumer Demand   180

---------------------------------- **4** ----------------------------------

Traditional Issues
in Regulation   62

---------------------------------- **5** ----------------------------------

Independent Regulatory
Commissions   146

8

Capital Budgeting
and Finance

238

Preface

Our interest in public utility economics stems from several sources. First, among the important characteristics of what we term public utilities is the pervasive regulation by a regulatory authority. The unique relationship between the public utility and the regulatory commission has come under increasing attack from several quarters in recent years, with calls for regulatory reform and closer monitoring of utility performance. Second, the economic significance of these industries is seldom recognized. Public utility industries, for example, account for over one-third of all new capital expenditures and nearly forty percent of new security issues. Moreover, this broad group of industries is vital to the growth and effectiveness of our economy. It is indeed difficult to envisage a developed economy running smoothly with a slow and unpredictable transportation system, an ineffective communication system and unreliable sources of power and water. Third, the very nature of public utility industries is continually evolving and dynamic, reflecting in some cases profound change in the underlying economic and political institutions. For these reasons and others, we find that the area of public utility economics and finance is especially worthy of our attention. The particular blend of economic theory and institutional arrangements which circumscribe this area make it both interesting and challenging.

We believe that a text used for instruction and reference achieves its highest value by carefully setting forth relevant principles. This public utility economics text relates regulatory and economic principles, current principles which will not become quickly outdated. The student—whether undergraduate, graduate, or practitioner—can relate these principles to problems and issues whose nature might not even be foreseen today. Of course, yesterday's and today's issues and problems can educate one in the application of these principles; thus, numerous applications are also presented. But an exclusive reliance on the precise solution of prior problems and issues is apt to cause regulatory myopia, while reliance on general regulatory and economic principles can promote foresight. Public utility students, of whatever group, are encouraged to seek out the symptoms of today's and tomorrow's problems and issues and devise appropriate solutions. But this should not be random activity. A basic understanding of the principles of regulation and economics will help the student to focus on the relevant problems and issues as well as to suggest their solutions.

As public utility economics has undergone significant change in recent years, the materials for classroom use, particularly at the undergraduate level, are scattered and uneven in quality. Thus, a primary purpose of this text is to bring together many of these materials at a fairly uniform level and to highlight the principal concepts and practices in this area. The book is organized to facilitate a junior or senior level course (or graduate course if supplemented by readings) in public utility economics and finance, and to provide a suitable reference for the public utility practitioner. While the only suggested prerequisite for this text is a principles of economics course, it is believed that additional courses in economics and a first course in finance would be helpful.

We wish to acknowledge the individuals who helped in the preparation of this book. First, we would like to express our deep appreciation to our wives, Stephanie Howe and Elizabeth Rasmussen, for their assistance and support of this effort. Thanks are also due to the many dedicated and conscientious people with whom the authors have been associated at Iowa State Commerce Commission, University of Missouri, University of Nebraska, Lake Forest College and Illinois Bell Telephone Company. In particular, we are indebted to Richard M. Beary, Roger P. Bey, Joseph Collins, Basil L. Copeland, Jr., Adam K. Gehr, Jr., Gerald Groper, Rosemary Hale, Murray Herlihy, David Huettner, Hugh A. Latimer, Phillip B. Malter, Charles W. Marberry, James Maret, Walter Primeaux, Jr., James Spiker, Leo Steffen, Jr., and Don Charles Uthus. The support of the Graduate School, University of Missouri–Columbia, is acknowledged. Finally, we wish to extend a special thank-you to Professor John R. Felton at the University of Nebraska–Lincoln, who guided our early study of public utility economics and who continues to offer his encouragement.

Where views and opinions are expressed in the book, they are those of either or both of the authors and do not necessarily reflect the views of the Iowa State Commerce Commission. Moreover, in an undertaking of this type, particularly a first edition, there will almost surely be errors of some type. The authors assume responsibility for these errors without implicating any of the individuals or institutions which have aided in the preparation of the book. Finally, the authors would greatly appreciate receiving any suggestions, comments or corrections which may be beneficial in future editions. Of course, they will be acknowledged.

Keith M. Howe
Iowa State University
Ames, Iowa 50011

Eugene F. Rasmussen
Iowa State Commerce Commission
Des Moines, Iowa 50319

Public Utility
Economics
and
Finance

1

Introduction

The bulk of American business activity is conducted according to what is generally called the free market or private enterprise system. In this scheme, government influences the operation of the private, competitive sector in numerous ways, but its role is considered to be supportive and secondary, not controlling. But the public utility sector, though not as large as the private market sector, is subject to pervasive government regulation. Governmental prescription, not the competitive market, largely dictates performance in the public utilities area. Our focus in the following chapters is on the economics of public utilities and on the various institutions that control this area.

This chapter defines public utilities along traditional lines in terms of their distinguishing characteristics and types of service. It includes a summary of the regulatory process and a statistical review of public utility industries to show their relative significance. The chapter concludes with a brief description of subsequent chapters and the orientation of the text.

_____ WHAT IS A PUBLIC UTILITY? _____

CHARACTERISTICS

No single characteristic distinguishes the public utility from other firms. However, the several conditions that follow, when considered in combination, do serve to identify the public utility. First, public utilities are frequently natural monopolies, and vice versa. A natural monopoly exists when one firm can supply the entire market at less cost than can two or more firms. Utilities such as electric, gas, water, and telephone are physically connected to their customers. This connection inhibits the ability of new utilities to compete with an established utility. This spatial monopoly is an important consideration limiting competition. In this setting, new suppliers generally have cost disadvantages arising from duplication of facilities. Utilities located some distance away typically require more costly facilities, such as transmission lines and mains, to transport services into the area. Second, the prices these industries charge for services are determined by government regulation. The state has determined that uncontrolled laissez-faire capitalism is undesirable in some industries. Obviously, prices of other products and services are controlled by government—rent control and agricultural price supports, for example—but such controls are usually of short duration and are often concerned with maximum or minimum prices, not with the exact price. Third, the utility must supply all who want service when they want it at the regulated price; the utility cannot turn away customers who are willing to pay the prescribed price. Fourth, utilities are given franchises as exclusive suppliers within the franchise area. Moreover, public utilities need formal approval from the appropriate governmental authority to offer new service, or to extend, change, or abandon a particular service.

Not as specific as those above, the fifth condition is that the utility is subject to additional regulation not required of other firms, including regulation of accounting practices and procedures of security issuance, as well as extensive reporting of business activities. A sixth condition, which is often added though difficult to define in practice, is that the utility must provide a service that is essential in some sense to modern living.

As a related matter, the means of providing utility services are classified as social overhead capital, capital that produces services which are not consumed directly, but are a primary requirement in direct production of goods.[1] Public utility facilities are frequently grouped along with transportation, education, and public health as social overhead capital. Social overhead capital is comprised of expensive, long-lived, and lumpy fixed capital investments. A shortage of primary social overhead capital can inhibit secondary and tertiary investment by consumers in durables and by industry in plant and equipment. (The concept of social overhead capital is developed more fully in Chapter 2.)

---

[1] Campbell R. McConnell, *Economics*, 3rd ed. (New York: McGraw-Hill, 1966), p. 743.

[2] James C. Bonbright, *Principles of Public Utility Rates* (New York: Columbia University Press, 1961), p. 4.

Types of Services

A second way of identifying the public utility is by specifying the services public utilities provide. As the well-known public utility economist James Bonbright put it, there are basically two categories of public utilities:

(1) those enterprises which supply, directly or indirectly, continuous or re-peated services through more or less permanent physical connections be-tween the plant of the suppliers and the premises of the consumer; and

(2) the public transportation industries.[2]

Important among those of the first group are utilities supplying electricity, gas, telephone and telegraph, and water. The second group includes airlines, motor freight carriers, railroads, water carriers, petroleum pipelines, and local transit systems. This latter group is usually given short shrift in public utility economics texts because this group is somewhat diverse and may not approximate the monopoly model as well as the first group. We too will emphasize the electricity, natural gas, and telephone industries. Water utilities are frequently publicly owned and usually are subject only to local regulation, not state commissions. Privately owned water utilities do exist, but they play a relatively small role in this sector and therefore will receive much less attention than other utilities. The telegraph industry is currently a relatively weak and less important industry and will be omitted from our discussion. Also, in recent years the postal service has been regulated according to utility principles. Although these industries are normally thought of as public utilities today, there is no assurance that this will be true in the future, since the conditions prompting public utility status change over time.[3]

Textbook writers and many economists tend to look upon the electric, gas, and telephone utilities as essentially the same in terms of economic characteristics. However, students of utility regulation must recognize at the outset an important difference between the telephone and the other utilities: the gas and electric utilities are basically one-product industries; the telephone is a multiproduct industry. Indeed, the typical Bell System company offers some 3000 tariffed items. Therefore, it is possible that major economic and regulatory issues bearing on these two groups could vary.

---

[3] An interesting alternative viewpoint is expressed by the economist Walter J. Primeaux, Jr., who argues that the electric utility currently does not possess the prerequisite conditions for a natural monopoly and therefore its monopoly status as a public utility ought to be reexamined. See Walter J. Primeaux, Jr., "Some Problems with Natural Monopoly," *The Antitrust Bulletin*, 24 (spring 1979), 63–85.

THE ROLE OF REGULATORY COMMISSIONS

Enterprises deemed to be public utilities by state and federal legislatures and the courts are put under the control of regulatory commissions. These commissions are charged with the responsibility of regulating prices and ensuring adequate service at a minimum cost to consumers, consistent with a reasonable return to public utility owners. In the furtherance of this objective, commissions typically exercise control over entry, quality and conditions of service, and price.

THE IMPORTANCE OF PUBLIC UTILITIES

IMPORTANCE FOR THE U.S. ECONOMY

The broad group of industries we have called public utilities is vital to the growth and effectiveness of the business community. The services provided by these industries permit us to have a modern life style that in their absence would be impossible. Indeed, it is nearly impossible to envision the functioning of a developed economy with a slow and unpredictable transportation system, an ineffective communication system, and unreliable sources of power. Yet the importance of these industries in a statistical sense is not generally appreciated. A selected set of statistics is presented below:

1. *Percentage of Corporate Profits:*
   Of the $140.9 and $148.5 billion in corporate profits of domestic nonfinancial industries in 1978 and 1979, respectively, approximately 14 percent were contributed by the transportation, communication, electric, gas, and sanitation industries combined, with $20.3 and $18.9 billion in profits for these two years.

2. *Value Added by Industry as a Percentage of 1978–79 National Income* (without capital consumption adjustment):

Communication	2.3%
Electric, gas, and sanitation services	1.9
Transportation	3.9
	8.1% of national income

   The proportion of national income accounted for by public utilities is less than the proportion of profits attributed to utilities. This phenomenon is accounted for by the greater capital needs of the utilities.

3. *Percentage of New Plant and Equipment Expenditures, 1978–79:*

	1978	1979	Total 1978–79	% of Total 1978–79
All industries	$153.82*	$177.09*	$330.91*	100.00%
Electric	$ 24.79	$ 27.50	$ 52.29	15.80%
Gas and other	4.70	5.07	9.77	2.95
Communication	18.16	20.56	38.72	11.70
Railroad	3.32	3.93	7.25	2.19
Air transportation	2.30	3.24	5.54	1.67
Other transportation	2.43	2.95	5.38	1.63
Total	$ 55.70	$ 63.25	$118.95	35.95%

* Billions of dollars.

4. *Percentage of Total Corporate Securities Issues, 1978–79:*

	1978	1979	Total 1978–79	% of Total 1978–79
Total securities issued including bonds, notes, preferred and common stock	$46.62*	$51.10*	$97.72*	100.00%
Utilities	$12.25	$13.65	$25.90	26.50%
Communication	3.64	4.67	8.31	8.50
Transportation	1.76	2.79	4.55	4.66
Total	$17.65	$21.11	$38.76	39.66%

* Billions of dollars.

Source: U.S. Department of Commerce, *Survey of Current Business*, April 1980.

One is immediately struck by the relatively large annual capital investment and the financial market dominance of the public utility. For public utilities, a large percentage of new investment is financed with new security issues, with the remainder being financed internally, primarily by retained earnings, depreciation, and deferred taxes. Other firms finance a substantially lower percentage of their new investment with new security issues.

THE UTILITIES' OPERATING EXPERIENCES

Some noteworthy operating experiences have occurred in the last decade and a half. From 1967 through 1979, the production of utilities outpaced the industrial production of American industry generally.[4] The number of phones in service at the end of 1979 had risen 72 percent over 1967.[5] Electric

---

[4] U.S. Department of Commerce, *Survey of Current Business*, April 1980, pp. S-2, S-3.

[5] *Survey of Current Business*, April 1980, p. S-21. U.S. Department of Commerce, *Business Statistics*, 1975, p. 123.

and gas rates rose somewhat faster than the consumer price index generally from 1967 through 1979.[6] Yet telephone service price growth was less than the pace of the consumer price index.[7] Average hourly earnings per worker in the transportation and public utility industries were $7.57 and $8.17 in 1978 and 1979, respectively, higher than the $5.69 and $6.16 for private nonagricultural payrolls generally.[8]

By 1977, electric operating revenues had risen to 3.87 times the 1967 revenues.[9] In the investor-owned electric utility industry, capital costs increased from $109 per kilowatt of new generating capacity in 1967 to $275 per kilowatt in 1977.[10] At the same time average fuel costs rose from 25.7 cents in 1967 to 129.7 cents per million BTUs in 1977.[11] The thermal efficiency of converting fuel into electricity remained virtually constant, with only 33 percent of the energy in fuel burned being available as electricity.[12]

From 1969 through 1978 natural gas deliveries rose a total of 18 percent, though after 1973 gas supply growth slowed, increasing by only 4.5 percent.[13] Total gas reserves from 1969 through 1978 declined 48 percent, while total pipeline miles increased 18 percent.[14] Gas operating revenues in 1978 for major class A and B pipelines were still 3.58 times 1969 revenues.[15] Primarily because of the increased cost of gas from producers, operating and maintenance expenses rose even faster than pipeline revenues. Operating and maintenance expenses, 71.5 percent of gas operating revenues in 1969, had risen to 80.4 percent by 1978.[16] After peaking in 1972, total natural gas retail sales volumes declined. Residential sales remained static, and commercial sales increased, but industrial and other sales declined.[17]

---

[6] *Survey of Current Business*, April 1980, p. S-6.

[7] Bureau of Labor Statistics, U.S. Department of Labor, *Monthly Labor Review*, 103 (May 1980), 88.

[8] *Survey of Current Business*, April 1980, p. S-13.

[9] U.S. Department of Energy, *Statistics of Privately Owned Electric Utilities in the United States, 1977* (Washington: U.S. Government Printing Office, January 1979), p. 34, and Federal Power Commission, *Statistics of Privately Owned Electric Utilities in the United States, 1972* (Washington: U.S. Government Printing Office, December 1973), p. xxvi.

[10] U.S. Department of Energy, *Steam-Electric Plant Construction Cost and Annual Production Expenses, 1977*, December 1978, p. xii.

[11] Ibid., p. xvi.

[12] Ibid., p. xxv.

[13] U.S. Department of Energy, *Statistics of Interstate Natural Gas Pipeline Companies— 1978, Classes A & B Cos.*, October 1979, p. 37.

[14] Ibid., p. 38.

[15] Ibid., p. 29.

[16] Ibid., p. 30.

[17] American Gas Association, *Gas Facts 1978* (Arlington, Va.: American Gas Association, 1979), p. 83.

TABLE 1.1 Financial Ratios of U.S. Corporations 1975

	LIQUIDITY RATIOS		LEVERAGE RATIOS			ACTIVITY RATIOS	
	Current Ratio	Acid Test[a]	Debt Ratio[b]	Interest Coverage[c]	Fixed Charge Coverage[c]	Total Assets Turnover[d]	Inventory Turnover
Communications	1.42 times	1.10 times	42%	1.99 times	2.54 times	0.44 times	15.81 times
Electric, gas, and sanitation services	0.93	0.64	47	1.70	1.26	0.40	11.24
Transportation	1.05	0.92	38	1.50	1.01	0.89	30.63
All industries	0.99	0.84	21	2.10	0.91	0.69	9.32
Agriculture, forestry, and fishing	1.02	0.65	54	1.94	0.54	1.26	11.33
Total mining and energy	1.41	1.22	22	21.22	6.20	0.99	18.90
Total construction	1.38	1.02	34	2.13	0.56	1.87	11.42
Total manufacturing	1.75	1.10	27	4.10	1.38	1.33	7.28
Wholesale and retail trade	1.60	0.86	31	3.62	0.70	2.94	9.13
Total services	1.13	0.97	46	2.04	0.93	1.39	28.24

[a] Current ratio adjusted to remove inventory.
[b] Debt to total assets ratio.
[c] Before income taxes.
[d] Business receipts to total assets.

SOURCE: Internal Revenue Service, *Statistics of Income—1975, Corporation Income Tax Returns* (Washington, D.C.: U.S. Government Printing Office, 1979).

The telephone industry had a more sanguine history of operations. From 1967 through 1979, operating revenues per telephone more than doubled.[18] Slightly less than 90 percent of 1979 telephone operating revenues were evenly divided between station revenues and message toll revenues. Both local and toll telephone services are dominated by AT&T and the Bell System. Independent telephone companies account for less than 20 percent of the telephones in the United States.[19]

THE UTILITIES' FINANCIAL AND ASSET EXPERIENCE

Utilities have unique financial and asset experiences relative to other American industries. For comparison, Table 1.1 presents three types of financial ratios—liquidity, leverage, and activity ratios. The reader should keep in mind that in 1975 there was a major recession that followed major increases in energy prices. Electric, gas, and sanitation services had the lowest liquidity ratios, while communications had one of the highest. Since local telephone revenues, but not toll revenues, are billed in advance and other public utilities bill in arrears, the difference is understandable. Construction, manufacturing, and wholesale and retail trade exhibit a greater reliance on inventories than do the other industries.

Transportation, communications, electric, gas, and sanitation services tend to use more debt financing, as indicated by the leverage ratios. The greater use of long-term debt and greater amounts of cash flow from depreciation by these three industries appear as smaller differences between "Interest Coverage" and the "Fixed Charge Coverage."

The greater capital intensity of the transportation, communications, electric, gas, and sanitation services industries shows up in the low "Total Asset Turnover" ratios. Inventories are a relatively less important asset for these industries, resulting in higher inventory turnover ratios than for construction, manufacturing, and trade.

A SCHEMATIC DIAGRAM
OF THE PUBLIC UTILITIES

The political and economic institutions that are important in public utility economics are shown in Figure 1.1. A brief explanation of the relationships among the various participants follows:

1. Creditors and owners provide money capital to finance rate base—working capital, land, and plant and equipment—and in turn, receive interest payments and dividends.

---

[18] *Survey of Current Business*, April 1980, p. S-21, and *Business Statistics*, 1975, p. 123.

[19] U.S. Independent Telephone Association, *Phonefacts 1979* (Washington: U.S. Independent Telephone Association, 1979), p. 1.

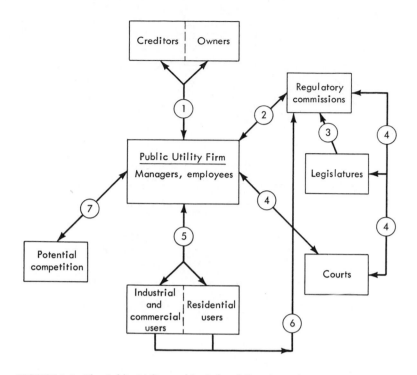

FIGURE 1.1   The Public Utility and Its Related Constituencies

2. Regulatory commissions regulate and control; they set rates so as to provide a reasonable return to the capital suppliers of the utility and ensure adequate service. Public utility managers provide information and request permission for change in services, corporate policy, and rates.

3. Legislatures give the mandate to regulate and set the general provisions of this regulation.

4. The acts of state and federal legislatures and administrators are subject to review by the courts.

5. Public utility firms provide service to various classes of customers and receive payment.

6. Consumers—industrial, commercial, and residential users—render service complaints and suggestions for rate level and structure changes.

7. Potential competition is largely limited, though specific types of competition are allowed in some areas by the regulators.

These institutional relationships may be compared and contrasted with the economic circular flow diagram presented in Figure 1.2. As with any economic circular flow, firms provide services in exchange for revenues and incur costs by purchasing resources, thereby providing income to resource suppliers. Since competition does not work well in many utility markets, the balance between revenues and costs and between utility services and resources is distorted. The public therefore regulates the rates and

9

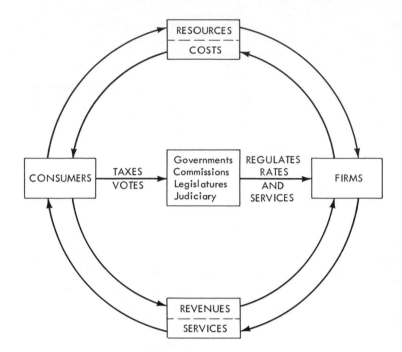

FIGURE 1.2   Economic Circular Flow

services of public utilities and attempts to restore the imbalance by eliminating monopoly profits and the underproduction of services. Tax revenues, raised from general revenues or from excise taxes on utility services,
finance regulatory commissions and other governmental bodies. The administration of the regulatory commission will also affect each regulatory
jurisdiction via public employment and governmental budget policies.

Caution must be exercised when relying upon economic concepts of
utility regulation. Our understanding to date of government regulation
has focused upon a negative rather than a positive concept of government.
Government regulation, in the negative laissez-faire concept, corrects the
market failures of capitalism, the market failures affecting public utility
rates and services. Often this view is condensed to the statement that
"regulation is a substitute for competition." Economics has not yet arrived
at a positive or purposive view of government regulation of public utilities.
The actions of government suggest purposes other than the mimicking of
competition,[20] such as serving the public interest.

Regulation may control the utility's exercise of arbitrary power and

---

[20] Joseph A. Schumpeter, *Capitalism, Socialism and Democracy*, 3rd ed. (New York: Harper & Row, 1962), p. 106.

the costs resulting from the exercise of monopoly power. Potential excess profits encourage the use of resources to secure a monopoly. Once secured, the actual excess profits may finance efforts to retain the monopoly power. Certainly, the history of public utilities is full of instances of monopolization. An early example is provided by Henry C. Adams, who in 1887 noted that certain grain elevators of Buffalo, New York, though unnecessary and unused for grain storage and whose very existence created excess capacity, received a share of the profits of the active grain elevators.[21] Other examples suggesting the costs of monopolization practices include the political and financial competition for electric and gas franchises; the telephone patent fight between the Bell Company and Western Union; the telephone war as the Bell patents expired at the turn of the century and independent telephone companies competed for customers and toll line interconnection; the utility holding company movements; and economic and political rivalry among private and public utilities.

Public utilities are ultimately public only by law. For example, oil refineries, though in many ways a public utility,[22] cannot be said to be a public utility without legislation establishing regulation. Fundamentally, a public utility is a creature of law, a creation of property rights more *limited* than those permitted businesses and consumers in general. Economists have for many decades studied public utilities, identified the economic behavior of public utilities both without regulation and with regulation, and analyzed the economic results of limiting the property rights of the public utilities. These economic studies form the basis of the following chapters.

OVERVIEW AND ORIENTATION
OF THE BOOK

The remainder of the book is organized into seven chapters that reflect seven important areas in public utility economics. Though these chapters concentrate on general economic and regulatory principles, numerous examples and applications, both current and historical, are also presented for illustration and to promote understanding. Current issues in utility regulation, such as inflation, nuclear power, and energy conservation, are discussed in appropriate sections throughout the text.

Chapters 2 and 3 set forth the relevant economic and legal concepts of public utilities. The economic characteristics, detailed in Chapter 2, relate

---

[21] Henry C. Adams, "Relation of the State to Industrial Action," *Publications of the American Economic Association*, I, 6 (January 1887), 18–19.

[22] Douglas N. Jones, "Making Refineries Public Utilities: An Incision into Vertical Integration in the Oil Industry," *The Annals of Regional Science*, 10 (March 1976), 1–15.

to the supply and demand analysis of utility services. An understanding of the relevant economic environment is essential to further study of public utilities. Utility management and regulation will fall short of the mark by not taking into account the important economic features of utilities. In sharp contrast, Chapter 3 presents the background needed to understand the public utility as a legal entity. The historical perspective given in this chapter is a prerequisite to a proper view of modern regulation. The statutory and case law relating to regulation of public utilities is summarized. The dynamic interaction of the economic and regulatory aspects of utilities has resulted in many of the traditional questions taken up in Chapter 4.

The basic issues that have arisen in the regulation of public utilities are considered in Chapter 4. These questions are concerned primarily with rate level, rate structure, and quality of service. Chapter 5 deals with the history and essence of the independent regulatory commission. The important criticisms of public utility regulation that have surfaced over the years are discussed in Chapter 6. Among other things, these attacks have focused upon the nature and effectiveness of regulation, the appropriateness of incentives, and resource allocation in utility industries. In response to these assaults, several alternatives to the present form of utility regulation have been advanced. A brief discussion of these alternatives, including the extremes of government ownership and abandonment of regulation, concludes Chapter 6.

The remaining two chapters, 7 and 8, consider several important activities of public utilities—pricing, capital budgeting, and financing—and how regulation affects each. In Chapter 7, pricing problems ranging from marginal cost pricing to price discrimination are introduced. Also, common pricing practices in each major utility industry are presented to illustrate how pragmatic and imperfect solutions are found to meet competing objectives in the pricing area. The final chapter is concerned with capital budgeting and the financing of public utilities. These two functions of utility management and regulation, which are reflected on the left side (assets) and the right side (liabilities and owners' equity) of the balance sheet, represent two of the most important, yet difficult, areas of utility analysis today. Capital budgeting, involving analysis of capital expenditures on extremely long-lived projects (perhaps 25 years or more) where future costs and benefits are uncertain, is tenuous at best. Still, careful analysis using a variety of techniques and sound judgment will improve utility performance. The method of financing the capital investments of utilities will typically have an impact on the profitability and risk of stockholders. Therefore, the effect of different financing alternatives is considered, along with a look at financing patterns.

The arrangement of these eight chapters reflects what the authors regard as an appropriate balance of the theoretical and institutional, the historical and current, and the insider and outsider views of utility matters. Theory is stressed and is usually presented first, and then public utility behavior and the reactions of regulators. Without claiming to have designed the optimal structure for a utility text, only a workable one, we turn now to our primary objective—obtaining a working knowledge of public utility economics and finance.

Study Questions

1. How is a public utility to be identified? Is this identification process infallible? Think of a nonutility enterprise that might be identified as a public utility.
2. The nature of the public utility enterprise as essential to modern living is stressed in most public utility texts. Aren't the clothing, food, and housing industries equally important? Can we conclude that the essential nature of public utility services is a distinguishing characteristic or a justification for regulation?
3. It is often claimed that public utilities are capital-intensive. What does this mean? Gather statistics to support this contention.
4. List the important groups that relate to public utilities and briefly describe the interaction which takes place between these groups and the public utility.
5. List at least three major differences between utilities and nonutilities found in Table 1.1. What do these differences tell us about the public utility?

Student Readings

ADAMS, HENRY CARTER.   "Relation of the State to Industrial Action." *Publications of The American Economic Association*, vol. I, no. 6. Baltimore: Guggenkeimer and Weil, 1887.

BONBRIGHT, JAMES C.   *Principles of Public Utility Rates*. New York: Columbia University Press, 1961, chap. 1.

BROOKS, JOHN NIXON.   *Telephone: The First Hundred Years*. New York: Harper & Row, 1976.

FARRIS, MARTIN T., and ROY J. SAMPSON.   *Public Utilities: Regulation, Management, and Ownership*. Boston: Houghton Mifflin, 1973, chap. 1.

GLAESER, MARTIN G.   *Outlines of Public Utility Economics*. New York: Macmillan, 1927, chap. 1.

McDONALD, FORREST. *Insull*. Chicago: University of Chicago Press, 1962.

PHILLIPS, CHARLES F. *The Economics of Regulation*, 2nd ed. Homewood, Ill.: Irwin, 1969, chap. 1.

PRIMEAUX, WALTER J. "Some Problems with Natural Monopoly." *The Antitrust Bulletin*, 24 (spring 1979), 63–85.

2

Economic Characteristics
of Public Utilities

Chapter Two analyzes the important economic characteristics of public utilities. They are economies of scale, elasticity of demand, short- versus long-run demand, and diversity of demand. These topics provide the foundation for the economic analysis of pricing, output, and investment. How these characteristics affect the regulation of these industries will be discussed in subsequent chapters.

Other topics considered in this chapter also relate to the cost and demand characteristics of utilities. First, technological features underlie the cost and demand relationships and help establish their status as utilities. Second, social overhead capital is a primary requirement for the direct production of goods and services. Finally, there is a body of empirical evidence drawn from numerous studies on economies of scale and demand for various utility industries. The bulk of this evidence is consistent with the theoretical notions set forth in the first part of the chapter.

ECONOMIES OF SCALE

In analyzing the supply and demand for utility services, economists rely upon various concepts, some supply-related and others demand-related. The principal concepts follow from a fundamental economic justification for granting an exclusive franchise to the utility—namely, decreasing unit costs throughout the relevant range of production. Henry C. Adams cited this reason as early as 1887.[1] Although economies of scale means the cost per unit of output declines as output increases, it is important to distinguish among various types of decreasing cost situations.[2] Essentially, there are three kinds of decreasing cost situations: short-run and long-run economies, and technological progress.

PRODUCTION RELATIONSHIPS

The production function describes the process by which inputs or resources such as labor and capital are transformed into output. The production function gives the maximum quantity of output or product that may be obtained by employing various combinations of inputs. It presupposes a given level of technical knowledge concerning the production process. The short run is defined as a period of time sufficiently short such that some of the inputs are fixed in amount. In the long run, all inputs are variable.

An important assertion by economists and engineers regarding the production relationship is called the *law of diminishing returns* or the *law of diminishing marginal productivity*. The idea is that as the amount of a variable input is increased, given the level of fixed inputs, eventually a point will be reached after which the *marginal product* (the additional total product resulting from an additional unit of variable input) decreases. As usually presented, the *average product* (total output divided by the amount of input used in the production of that output) rises over initial levels of output, reaches a maximum, and then falls. Therefore, the marginal product, by mathematical necessity, must rise, reaching its maximum before the maximum of the average product, and then fall, intersecting the average product curve at its maximum point. These relationships are depicted in Figure 2.1. Initially, as the variable input is increased, increasing returns (increasing average product) typically occur as the result of specialization, division of labor, and better use of facilities. But after these initial economies are exhausted, further increases in the variable resource result in smaller and smaller additions to output (declining marginal product and eventually average product). This production relationship is associated with one type of short-run decreasing cost, as we will see below.

The next question we ask is what happens to production when all inputs are permitted to vary. The term *returns to scale* refers to the output response to proportionate changes in all inputs. Returns to scale may be

[1] Henry C. Adams, "Relation of the State to Industrial Action," *Publications of the American Economic Association*, I, 6 (January 1887), 60.

[2] Often the term "economies of scale" is associated solely with long-run decreasing costs. We will use the term in a more general sense to mean any decreasing cost situation. Economists usually use the term "scale" as in "economies of scale" or "returns to scale" to refer to situations where adjustment of all inputs (and thus, scale of plant) is possible.

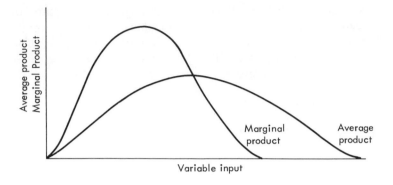

FIGURE 2.1 Production Relationships: Average and Marginal Products

of three types: increasing, constant, and decreasing. With *constant* returns to scale, a doubling of all inputs doubles production. With *decreasing* returns, a doubling of resource use will less than double production. With increasing returns, a doubling of resource use will more than double production. Thus, for example, if one worker produces 1 unit of production a day, under increasing returns to scale, two persons might produce 3 units. Under constant returns, the two workers would produce 2 units, and under decreasing returns, perhaps only 1.5 units would be produced. The type of returns to scale is extremely important in determining the nature of long-run costs.

SHORT-RUN DECREASING COSTS

There are three types of short-run decreasing cost situations. In one, short-run decreasing costs can occur when increasing returns dominate production. If the utility market produces output of less than M in Figure 2.2, the utility produces under conditions of increasing returns and decreasing cost. If these conditions prevail in an industry over the whole range of production levels, the cost-minimizing size of the utility will not be achieved. One firm will realize lower costs than will many competing firms, each of which is producing only a fraction of the output.

A second type of decreasing costs should be distinguished from the production relationship of increasing returns. A single firm may dominate the resource market; it may have monopsony power and receive concessions and quantity discounts from vendors. Such financial circumstances give rise to decreasing costs even with constant returns to scale or limited decreasing returns to scale.

In the short run, the firm does not change its technology, plant size, or capacity; in addition, certain elements of the firm's costs are fixed and do not vary as output changes. As a result, the fixed cost per unit of output declines as output increases, and a third type of decreasing cost results. In this instance, the firm spreads its fixed costs over a larger output, and therefore fixed costs per unit fall. Recall from microeconomics that variable costs are costs that increase as output increases. Total costs equal fixed costs plus variable costs. Fixed costs, as part of total costs, may dominate average total costs (total cost divided by quantity of output) such that average total costs fall over the initial range of output. This type of decreasing cost does not result from increasing returns but from the large size of the fixed resource. This form of short-run decreasing costs, like all other forms, is depicted in Figure 2.2 by the declining average total cost (*ATC*) curve to the left of point *M*, the minimum point on *ATC*.

LONG-RUN ECONOMIES OF SCALE

The long run, which varies from firm to firm, considers all the firm's costs to be variable. For a given technology and level of output, the firm is able to adjust the size of its operation (all inputs) so that total costs are minimized. If the minimum of the average short-run costs falls as output increases, given sufficient adjustment of all inputs, the firm is subject to economies of scale in the long run. Assuming input prices are held constant, long-run decreasing costs occur as a result of increasing returns to scale. Similarly, long-run increasing costs occur with decreasing returns to scale. Long-run economies of scale are thought to occur because of specialization, division of labor, and technological factors. Financial circumstances may also result in economies of scale. Examples include quantity discounts and advertising.

Long-run decreasing costs are shown in the graph in Figure 2.3. If the output is Q_1, costs are minimized by adjusting capacity to that associated with plant 1. Here the short-run average total costs (*SRAC*) of producing that output are minimized. At an output level of Q_2, however, a

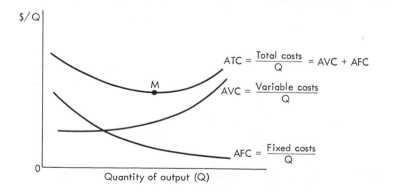

FIGURE 2.2   Average Total, Variable, and Fixed Costs

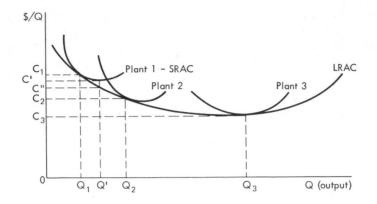

FIGURE 2.3 Long-run Average Cost Curve

larger plant (plant 2) is required to minimize costs and, as drawn, the average cost per unit of output (C_2) is lower at this point—i.e., the firm is subject to long-run economies of scale. Long-run economies of scale are present up to an output level of Q_3, after which diseconomies prevail. Suppose the firm's current capacity is that associated with plant 1 and Q' units of output are to be produced. In the short run the firm's unit costs would be C', but in the long run the firm will adjust its capacity, adopting a plant size somewhere between plant 1 and plant 2, and achieve lower average costs, specifically C''.

DYNAMIC ECONOMIES OF SCALE

The short- and long-run economies of scale discussed above are static phenomena indicating opportunities available with a given technology at a *particular point in time*. Economies of scale occurring *over time* as a result of technological progress will lower average total costs, but are usually not considered to be economies of scale. This is because, without inflation, the unit costs of a utility, or any other firm, will often decline over time; new plants and techniques are more efficient than older ones because they embody increased knowledge. For example, high-voltage transmission lines will have lower power losses than low-voltage lines, and the use of computers and microwave transmission has brought cost advantages to the telephone industry. There is one case where technological advance may properly be associated with economies of scale. If the technological advance is put into practice as a result of an increase in demand (over time) and would not otherwise have been implemented, it makes sense to view the unit-cost reduction that results as a sort of economy of scale. Because the increased demand led to the use of a technological advance and thus lowered costs, a situation which otherwise would not have been experienced, we can identify this particular situation as one involving

18

economies of scale.[3] Conventionally, however, economies of scale are viewed as a static concept.

THE NATURAL MONOPOLY CONCEPT

That public utilities are natural monopolies is a chief economic justification for extensive regulation of these industries. The chief prerequisite of a natural monopoly is that decreasing unit costs or economies of scale prevail over the entire output range of the market. These economies of scale also must be internal to the firm; economies of scale must accrue to the firm itself, as opposed to the industry as a whole, as it expands. Although an important source of these economies is the heavy fixed investment giving rise to short-run decreasing costs, long-run economies must be present for a natural monopoly setting to exist. A single supplier in this setting is able to achieve lower unit costs than if several firms served the market. Using the graph in Figure 2.3 depicting long-run economies, in a market requiring an output of Q_2, two firms could provide this quantity by each supplying Q_1 units at a minimum unit cost of C_1, while a single supplier with a larger plant (plant 2) would incur a lower unit cost of only C_2.

ELASTICITY OF DEMAND

Price elasticity and income elasticity of demand are two static concepts used by economists to indicate consumers' sensitivity or responsiveness in terms of the quantity of a particular item demanded to changes in its price and consumers' income, respectively.

PRICE ELASTICITY OF DEMAND

The concept of price elasticity centers on movements along a given demand curve. It is measured as the percentage change in quantity demanded divided by the percentage change in price, or $e_p = (\%\Delta Q_d)/(\%\Delta P)$. If the absolute value of e_p is greater than 1, demand is described as elastic in this region; if it is less than 1, it is inelastic; and if it equals 1, it is said to be unitary.

If demand is elastic, the firm's total revenue decreases as price increases; if demand is inelastic, total revenue increases as price increases; and if demand is of unitary elasticity, total revenue is constant as price changes. All other things being equal, the elasticity of a commodity will be less elastic the fewer and the poorer the substitutes for it and the more

---

[3] Alfred E. Kahn, *The Economics of Regulation*, vol. 1 (New York: Wiley, 1970), p. 127. For a different view, see Joseph A. Schumpeter, *Capitalism, Socialism and Democracy*, 2nd ed. (New York: Harper and Row, 1962), pp. 102–103.

indispensable the commodity. Empirical studies indicate that price elasticity of demand for utility services is relatively inelastic. This means that, as price increases, consumers will not substantially reduce consumption. More important, price elasticity of demand is often considered to be a measure of the extent to which monopoly profits can be extracted from an industry. The more inelastic the demand—whether the demand of customers in general, of classes of customers, or of individuals—the greater the income that can be diverted from consumer to producer by price discrimination.

An unregulated monopoly would not operate in the inelastic area of the demand curve unless selective price discrimination could be practiced. A profit-maximizing unregulated utility monopoly maximizes profit at an output where marginal revenue equals marginal cost. But marginal revenue is positive only in the elastic portion of the demand curve. Thus, profits are maximized only for sales within the elastic portion of the demand curve. In practice, unregulated utilities frequently did not announce a single price for all utility service. Rather, selective price discrimination was practiced. Different cities, different industries, different individuals received different utility rates, with some even receiving free service. When an unregulated monopoly must charge a uniform rate to all customers, *monopoly pricing* exists.

Departures from this uniform rate without cost justification are called *price discrimination*. There are three types, ranging from perfect discrimination, where the monopolist garners all the consumer surplus, to cruder, less precise forms.[4] In all cases, price discrimination by an unregulated monopolist results in a larger profit than charging a uniform price. When each individual pays different rates and retains no consumer surplus, first-degree or perfect discrimination exists. When a class or group of customers pays a uniform rate different from the rate applied to other groups in the same market, second-degree discrimination exists. Third-degree price discrimination, however, results from intergroup differences in demand curves rather than from the differences in quantities demanded for a given demand curve. Price differences between groups still result because of intergroup differences in price elasticities. Third-degree price discrimination will be discussed in more detail later in the chapter.

INCOME ELASTICITY OF DEMAND

This concept is measured as the percentage change in quantity demanded divided by the percentage change in income, or $(\%\Delta Q_d)/(\%\Delta Y)$. Here we are considering movement along an *Engel's curve*, the curve relating the

---

[4] F. M. Scherer, *Industrial Market Structure and Economic Performance*, (Chicago: Rand McNally 1970), pp. 254–255.

quantity demanded of a product and the income level of consumers, *ceteris paribus*. The smaller the income elasticity of demand, the less the percentage change in quantity in relation to percentage change in income. Since empirical studies show a relatively inelastic income elasticity of demand for utility services, one would expect a relatively small change in quantity demanded and in expenditures on utility services as income changes over the business cycle. An extreme example of the income elasticity effect appeared during the 1930s in the telephone industry when many customers discontinued telephone service because of the Great Depression.

CROSS ELASTICITY OF DEMAND

The demand for a product depends not only on its own price, but also on the prices of other goods. The consumption of electricity will depend upon the price of electric heaters and appliances (complements) and the price of gas (substitutes). A measure of this dependency is the *cross-elasticity of demand*, defined as the percentage change in quantity demanded of a product divided by the percentage price change of a related product. If the cross-elasticity is positive, the two products are called substitutes; if it is negative, the products are called complements.

For public utilities, cross-elasticity of demand can be an important consideration. It is commonly believed, for example, that gas and electricity are substitutes, especially in the long run and in certain uses. Moreover, for a multiproduct firm such as the telephone company, the degree of substitutability and complementarity of its products have been considered by AT&T and the Bell System in decisions regarding their products. An increase in the price of a product will increase the demand for substitute products and decrease the demand for complementary products.

INTERGROUP DIFFERENCES IN DEMAND

Different groupings or classifications of consumers generally have different price elasticities of demand. Empirical studies indicate, for example, that the residential demand for electricity is less elastic than industrial demand. One reason for this is that industry has more alternatives available to it, such as self-generation of power. Studies also indicate that business telephone use is less elastic than residential telephone use. It may be that rapid, reliable communication is relatively indispensable for business firms.

When markets can be segmented so that resale of the commodity or service is limited and different price elasticities exist at the same price, price discrimination is profitable for the firm. Price discrimination here means simply charging different prices for essentially the same product. Let us look more closely now at third-degree discrimination.

A hypothetical example of price discrimination is given in Figure 2.4. This construction uses two sets of positive axes, one inverted, and assumes a constant average cost, among other things. Suppose the relatively inelastic demand curve, D_1, is for residential electricity service, while D_2 is the demand curve for industrial service. The price in each market, P_1 and P_2, is set where marginal costs equal marginal revenue. Note that the inelastic group, in this case residential electricity, is charged the higher price. Relaxing the assumption of a constant average cost equal to marginal cost requires that the diagram be reformulated as in Figure 2.5. Third-degree discrimination at the monopolist's optimum requires equal marginal revenue of each customer class, a marginal revenue which in turn equals marginal cost. The nondiscriminating monopolist would charge a rate P' for sales of Q', the sum of sales to both customer classes ($Q_1 + Q_2$). This optimum occurs where marginal cost (MC) equals the horizontal summation of the marginal revenue in each class (ΣMR). By not discriminating, the monopolist that charges P' sells amounts Q_1' and Q_2' to each customer class, respectively. Then marginal cost is above the marginal revenue from class 1, but below marginal revenue from class 2. Revenue equals the area enclosed by $P'DQ'0$.

The monopolist can increase profits by charging a higher price to class 1 and a lower price to class 2 customers. By selling more to class 2, the increased revenue exceeds the added costs. Further, by reducing sales to class 1, revenues are diminished but by less than the reduction in costs.

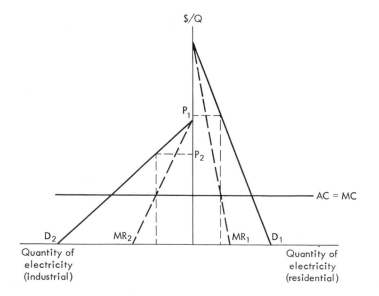

FIGURE 2.4 Price Discrimination with Constant Average Costs

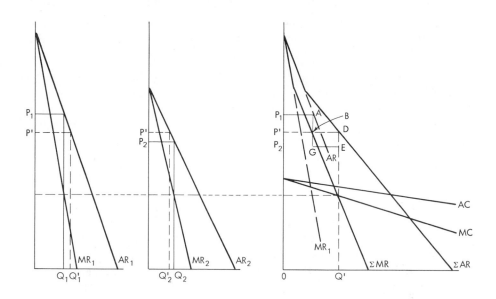

FIGURE 2.5 Price Discrimination with Decreasing Costs

Profits are increased from both classes. Since the overall gain in revenues (the area P_1ABP') exceeds the loss in revenues (the area $BDEG$), discrimination increases revenues to the utility. And since average cost has not changed, profits must have increased by the increase in revenue. In the process, the unregulated monopolist has ceased the use of a common price or rate, and instead achieved an equal marginal revenue from each customer class.

In general, the user with the more inelastic demand will pay a higher price. Recall that the marginal revenue of each group or class is set equal to marginal cost so that profits are maximized. Also, each group's price, P, is then related to its marginal revenue MR and demand elasticity e by the following formula: $MR = P - P/e$. To maximize profits, marginal revenue equals marginal cost; after rearranging the above formula, we have

$$P = MC + \frac{MC}{e - 1}$$

Thus, if the demand elasticity is close to 1, say, 1.25, the rate paid is five times marginal cost, whereas if the demand elasticity is substantially greater than 1, say, 2, the rate paid is only double the marginal cost. (The reader should note that an elasticity of 8 suggests the rate paid is 14 percent greater than marginal cost.)

In this section, we found that the unregulated utility has a profit incentive to discriminate with respect to price, provided that the market can be segmented and user groups have different demand elasticities. Moreover, the relatively inelastic group generally will be charged the higher price.

An Application of Price Discrimination.   A regulated utility may be required to operate at some particular point on the demand curve and to forego maximum profits. With decreasing costs, marginal costs are less than average cost. If the overall price is set equal to marginal cost as many economists suggest, revenue deficits will result. These losses must be funded if adequate service is to be continued. A type of third-degree discrimination mechanism has been suggested for designing utility rates to cover such deficits; it is called the *inverse elasticity rule*.

The basic concept of the inverse elasticity rule is that by raising the price in the inelastic utility market, revenue is increased while sales are relatively little affected. If the elastic market experienced substantial price increases, both revenues and sales would decline substantially more. In the case of two services, the inverse elasticity rule is explained by the following formula:[5]

$$\frac{\dfrac{P_1 - MC_1}{P_1}}{\dfrac{P_2 - MC_2}{P_2}} = \frac{e_2 - e_{21}(P_2Q_2/P_1Q_1)}{e_1 - e_{12}(P_1Q_1/P_2Q_2)}$$

when

P_i = price of service i

MC_i = marginal cost of service i

e_i = the price elasticity of demand

e_{ij} = the cross-elasticity of demand for i of a change in the price of j

Q_i = the output of service, i = 1 or 2

This form of third-degree price discrimination has been attributed to Ramsey's 1927 article[6] and to Baumol's more recent work.[7] The inverse elasticity rule produces a criterion which states that the relative retail markup of price to marginal cost is inversely related to the product's own

---

[5] Chester G. Fenton and Robert F. Stone, "Cost Allocations and Rate Structure: Concepts and Misconceptions," *Public Utilities Fortnightly*, July 3, 1980, p. 20.

[6] Frank P. Ramsey, "A Contribution to the Theory of Taxation," *Economic Journal*, March 1927, pp. 47–61.

[7] William J. Baumol and David F. Bradford, "Optimal Departures from Marginal Cost Pricing," *American Economic Review*, 60 (June 1970), 265–283.

price elasticity and directly related to the product's cross-elasticities. If the cross-elasticities are zero, then the term inverse-elasticity rule is fully descriptive. For example, let us assume cross-elasticities are effectively zero, and residential and industrial customers' own price elasticities are approximately 0.15 and 0.25, respectively. According to the inverse elasticity rule, the retail markup for residential prices is 1.67 times the markup for industrial rates. With long-run price elasticities of 1.15 and 1.25 for customer group 1 and customer group 2, respectively, the residential class's relative retail markup over marginal cost as a percent of price is 1.09 times greater than the industrial markup.

Use of the inverse elasticity rule to establish utility prices is sensitive to the analyst's perspective, since estimates of demand elasticities do vary. The inverse elasticity rule suggests relatively higher rates for the inelastic utility customer—not a pleasing prospect for the inelastic user when necessities are involved.

SHORT-RUN VERSUS LONG-RUN DEMAND

Short-run demand in general should be distinguished from long-run demand. This is especially true for electricity and gas, since demand for them is a derived demand, and the existing stock of durables equipped to use these inputs will greatly affect the demand estimate in the short run. The greater the length of the run, the greater the ability of the consumer and firm to adjust their stocks of durables in response to relative price changes. As the stock of durables responds, so does the quantity demanded. Thus, price elasticity is greater in the long run than in the short run, and empirical studies must take this into account.

DIVERSITY OF DEMAND

The variability in demand imposes the requirement of excess capacity on the utility. This additional capacity requires fixed costs that are reduced on a per unit of sales basis, the greater the number of customers and regions served. That is, capacity is better utilized and average costs are lower because the peak usage period of one group is likely to fall at an off-peak period of another, and this is more likely the greater the number and diversity of groups. This diversification effect makes it more efficient for a single supplier or interconnected group of suppliers to serve several classes and regions of consumers, *ceteris paribus*, unless their peak demands should happen to coincide (a most unlikely prospect). A *diversity factor* is sometimes measured in the electric and gas utility industry (and is illustrated in this section under capacity utilization). Thus, diversity of demand results in a potential source of economies of scale.

Peak and Off-Peak Demand

Utility consumers generally have diurnal, periodic, and seasonal activities. Often, these are reflected in personal, social, and business habits such as the eight-hour workday. As a result, it is unlikely that demand over time could be equalized and peak demand eliminated. A common measure of utilization is the *load factor*, the ratio of actual sales to the total sales that could occur if the peak load prevailed over time. It is not uncommon to have load factors from 50 to 60 percent in the electric utility industry.

Capacity Utilization

Another measure of peak usage is the *capacity utilization* measure. Rather than relating annual sales to peak demand, as the load factor does, the capacity utilization measure divides annual sales by total capacity of the plant in service. In the utility industry, capacity is measured as the physical capacity. In order to insure continuing service, the utility's capacity will include a margin of capacity to provide reliability. For example, even if a major power plant is out of service at the period of peak demand, the load can still be met by using this margin of supply or purchasing excess capacity from other utilities.

The diversity factor, the load factor, and the capacity utilization are calculated in the following example. Assuming an electric utility has a capacity of 1000 MW (megawatts), the diversity factor is 1.5 (1200 MW ÷ 800 MW); the load factor is 50 percent (3,504,000 MWH ÷ (800 MW × 8760 hours)); and capacity utilization is 40 percent (3,504,000 MWH ÷ (1000 MW × 8760 hours)).

Customer Class	Coincident Peak Load	Noncoincident Peak Loads	Sales (Megawatt hours)
A	500 MW	800 MW	1,752,000
B	200	300	948,000
C	100	100	804,000
Total	800 MW	1200 MW	3,504,000 MWH

Generally, utility measures of capacity utilization and load factor cannot be compared to manufacturing capacity utilization. The utility measure is of capacity as the physical capability of the existing system as if it were continuously operating. The manufacturing measure relies upon maximum practical capacity, which is based upon a normal operating schedule.[8]

---

[8] Marie P. Hertzberg, Alfred I. Jacobs, and Jan E. Trevathan, *Survey of Current Business*, U.S. Department of Commerce, 54, 7 (July 1974), 47–57.

For example, a manufacturing plant operating an eight-hour shift might indicate a capacity utilization of 90 percent, but when measured relative to physical capacity, the capacity utilization would indicate 30 percent utilization.

TECHNOLOGICAL FEATURES
——————————— OF PUBLIC UTILITIES ———————————

It is clear that other industries have many of the characteristics mentioned above. For example, a store in a small town may have economies of scale over the entire market and its customers may have few convenient alternative sources of supply, thus making demand somewhat inelastic. The technological determinants of public utility costs, however, do help differentiate the public utility.

PHYSICAL CONNECTION OF PRODUCER AND CONSUMER

This characteristic provides the utility a greater opportunity to discriminate effectively because the utility is able to prevent resale or leakages from one group of consumers to another. It also makes it more difficult and costly for users to shift from one supplier to another. Finally, this feature contributes to the heavy fixed cost requirement of the utility.

SIMULTANEITY OF PRODUCTION AND CONSUMPTION

This is a property of the electricity and telephone industries, but to a lesser degree a property of gas or water industries that use storage. For industries that have this characteristic, production must vary through time with consumption, and thus the producer must have excess capacity at times. This is another contributing factor to the heavy investment requirement of utilities.

LOW MARGINAL RATE OF TECHNICAL
SUBSTITUTION OF CAPITAL FOR LABOR

This is a technical term used in microeconomic theory and means the rate at which capital can be substituted for labor, holding output constant. It is the negative of the slope of a production isoquant or equal-output curve. A graph will help illustrate the point. In Figure 2.6, two isoquants are drawn, one for a utility, the other for a nonutility firm.

If we change the units of capital employed from C_1 to C_2, the reduction in labor required to produce the same amount as previously is L_1 less L_2 for the nonutility, but it is a greater amount, L_1 less L_3, for the utility. At given labor rates, it is thus more efficient for the utility to substitute capital

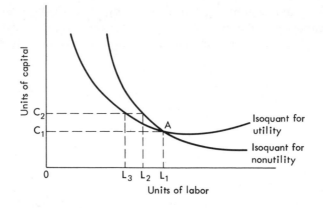

FIGURE 2.6 Production Isoquants for Utility and Nonutility Firms

for labor. For this reason, the utility adopts a large amount of capital relative to other inputs and is thus relatively capital-intensive.

A look at the capital turnover ratios of various industries helps to substantiate this point. Capital turnover ratio = Annual operating revenues/capital investment. Estimates of this ratio for various industries are given in Table 2.1. It is apparent from these figures that the capital turnover ratio for utilities is substantially lower than for nonutilities. This means, for example, that the average manufacturing firm needs only $0.43 invested

TABLE 2.1 Capital Turnover Ratios of U.S. Industries
1975

	Fixed Asset Turnover
Electric, gas and sanitation services	0.38 times
Communications	0.44
Transportation	1.00
Primary metals manufacturing	1.26
Paper and allied products manufacturing	1.42
Agriculture, forestry, and fishing	1.58
Total mining and energy	1.59
Chemicals and allied products manufacturing	1.69
Total services	1.93
All industries	2.14
Petroleum and coal manufacturing	2.25
Total manufacturing	2.31
Machinery, except electrical, manufacturing	2.36
Food and kindred products manufacturing	4.07
Total construction	4.45
Wholesale and retail trade	8.91

SOURCE: Internal Revenue Service, *Statistics of Income—1975, Corporation Income Tax Returns* (Washington, D.C.: U.S. Government Printing Office, 1979).

capital to generate $1 in revenue, while the typical utility requires about $2.50 of investment to generate $1 in revenue.

THE DEMAND FOR
SOCIAL OVERHEAD CAPITAL

Many of the ideas of decreasing costs and demand have been integrated into a coherent package by economists interested in economic development. This package has been used to analyze the role of public utilities as social overhead capital. Public utility services are necessities, have economies of scale, and require large units of capital, as we have seen. Two additional concepts in economics are necessary to understand social overhead capital: (1) derived demand and (2) joint demand.

DERIVED DEMAND

Utility services are often intermediate products rather than final consumer goods. For example, electricity and gas are used as energy sources but are not directly consumed. Even most water is used for production rather than for direct consumption by drinking. The demand for these intermediate products is derived from the demand of the final good.

Figure 2.7 illustrates derived demand. Consider the demand for a product D_q, which is supplied by combining two inputs, utility services Q_u and other inputs Q_o. The latter has a supply curve S_o. It is assumed utility services and other inputs are used in fixed proportions to output. The derived demand curve for utility service becomes the distance between the overall demand curve D_q and the supply of other factors S_o—i.e., the

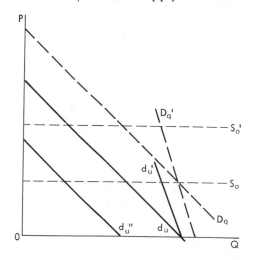

FIGURE 2.7   Derived Demand

demand curve d_u. If the overall demand curve were more inelastic, as in D_q', the derived demand curve would be more inelastic, as in d_u'. Because the demand for utility services is a derived demand, its relative price elasticity can be expected to be more inelastic the more of a necessity is the final product. If the supply of other inputs is more costly, as in S_o', then with the lower price of utility service, the demand curve d_u'' has a lower price elasticity. Utility customers whose utility costs are relatively small would tend to have more inelastic demands. Recall that the ratio, P_u/Q_u, multiplied by $\Delta Q_u/\Delta P_u$ is equal to the demand elasticity. The derived demands are more inelastic in either of these cases, a more inelastic final product or the other inputs being more expensive. In the first case, $\Delta Q_u/\Delta P_u$ declines in value and in the second P_u declines relative to Q_u.

The reader should determine the effect if the supply of other inputs is inelastic. For example, suppose the capital stock used by a manufacturer is, in the short run, in relatively fixed supply and requires utility service in its use. Is the derived demand for utility service more or less elastic? Why?

JOINT DEMAND

Utility plant and equipment are long-lived and consist of large investment units. The demand of many consumers can be met for several years with a given investment. The provision of utility service over time is nonexclusionary. The same capacity can provide services to meet demand now as well as to meet demand in the future. As a result, rather than adding the quantity demanded by different customers at a given price, joint demand adds the prices customers are willing to pay at a given quantity. The demand curves are added vertically. Several customers spread over time thus are willing to pay for a given capacity. This circumstance is of importance in utility regulation because peak capacity is also available off-peak during any year. Also, capacity built to meet today's load is also available next year.

THE DEMAND FOR SOCIAL OVERHEAD CAPITAL

Combining the derived joint demand for years 1 and 2, for example, with the economies of scale, the effects of social overhead capital can be seen. Not only are the external benefits of the economies of scale present, but also the external benefits of joint demand. Further, under such circumstances, the price mechanism is not likely to create a stable equilibrium. Rather, a proper response by government is to require a supply to meet demand at the existing price. Such a supply mechanism can lead to an equilibrium.

Given the joint demand D, made up of this year's demand d_1 and next year's demand d_2 and the supply curve S, the equilibrium price and quantity given in Figure 2.8 are P and Q_u. The price is the sum of the

amount paid today, P_1, and paid tomorrow, P_2. Thus the costs of production reflected in the supply curve S are covered over the two-year
period. If the demand next year rises from d_2 to d_2', then aggregate demand
rises from D to D'. *Two* external effects result: (1) economies of scale and
(2) the benefits of joint demand. Because of economies of scale, the supply
price drops from P to P', an external benefit to users in year 1. Also, for
users in year 1, the price drops from P_1 to P_1', which in the illustration
happens to be zero. As an exercise, the reader should show that the external benefits to users in year 1 arise even when an upward-sloping supply
curve is assumed.

In the short run, the price rises to P'' after demand rises initially. At
this price, additional supply is not necessarily forthcoming. But the monopoly, in its effort to maximize profits, will expand output, bringing about
price stability without government regulation. Price instability exists where
there is no automatic economic force that brings price back into equilibrium
(where supply equals demand) after a disturbance in supply or demand.
Economists have long held that price instability may result where the
absolute value of the slope of the supply curve is less than the slope of the
demand curve (*cobweb analysis of stability* in economics jargon). Since demand for utility service tends to be inelastic and increasing returns to scale
exist over portions of the production process, the price mechanism may
be unreliable in utility markets. But this is an empirical question. Still,
economies of scale, joint demand for capacity, and potential price instability combine to create a demand for governmental intervention. In many
countries of the world, government ownership and investment in social

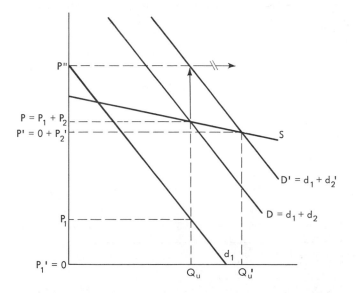

FIGURE 2.8　Demand and Supply of Social Overhead Capital

overhead capital have been the preferred approach. In the United States, government regulation has enforced the existing price and an obligation to serve. As a result, price P is maintained and the quantity supplied is the economic control mechanism. That is, the utility must be ready to meet the demand. As shown in Figure 2.8, such a supply mechanism can create expectations that lead to the new equilibrium point at Q_u'.

An Example: Suburban Water Systems.   Perhaps a clear example of social overhead capital exists when private developers install water systems for suburban developments, a problem area for regulators in recent years. The value of the lots is minimal unless water and other services are available. The wise developer should construct a water system sufficient to serve all potential lots that are to be developed. In the early years, water will be provided frequently as a loss leader, a practice that reflects the joint demand for water system capacity, since to do otherwise jeopardizes the sale price of the lot. As the sales grow, economies of scale are realized and external benefits of joint demand accrue to certain customers. But it is not uncommon for water systems, once having stopped growing, to become economically unstable. Developers then may raise price, defer maintenance, and reduce the quality of service in order to provide a cash flow and increase the return to investors.

——————— **SUMMARY OF THE EMPIRICAL EVIDENCE** ———————

Empirical studies have been performed on many of these economic characteristics of the public utility industry, notably in the area of economies of scale and demand elasticities. These empirical studies tend to support the economic assumptions that underlie public utility regulation. That is, economies of scale and inelastic demands exist for at least major segments of the utility market.

ECONOMIES OF SCALE

The Electric Power Industry

There have been numerous econometric studies[9] that analyze economies of scale in electric power generation. There is a consensus that substantial economies of scale exist in steam generation for small and intermediate generating units. For instance, Christensen and Greene found insignificant scale economies beyond 19 billion KWH per year, which cor-

_____

[9] A summary of the early literature is found in Franklin M. Fisher, "The Existence of Aggregate Production Functions," *Econometrica*, 37 (October 1969), 553–557. An outstanding survey of more recent work is provided by T. G. Cowing and V. K. Smith, "The Estimation of a Production Technology: A Survey of Econometric Analysis of Steam-Electric Generation," *Land Economics*, 54, 2 (May 1978).

responds with 4000 MW of capacity.[10] Still, at what point these economies become insignificant is a matter of controversy. The principal source of these economies of scale is the improved heat rates of larger units.

Researchers in the area of scale economies must be aware that the dimension along which they measure output (or scale) will greatly influence their results. Typically, the output of a utility is not one dimensional. Stewart developed a model that recognizes two important dimensions of output: KW capacity and plant utilization factor.[11] He found that at the plant level the utilization factor is a much more important source of cost reduction than are scale economies (in terms of KWs of capacity).

Very few studies have addressed the question of economies of scale in electric power transmission and distribution. However, using engineering data, Charles E. Olson found that average transmission costs are lower the larger the line capacity and the higher the load factor, all else being the same. Engineering requirements also suggest that a doubling of voltage levels in high-voltage transmission lines reduces the number of lines needed by approximately fivefold. Although we await an adequate study of distribution costs, we suspect them to vary inversely with customer density. The existence of small rural electric cooperatives and other small distribution utilities suggests that the absolute number of customers alone does not cause economies of scale.

The Telephone Industry

Numerous studies of economies of scale have appeared in recent years in the economics literature (see those listed under Advanced Readings, Chapter 2). These studies support the belief that substantial short- and long-run economies exist in the telephone industry, though the extent and range of these economies appear quite variable across studies. Moreover, the studies indicate the difficulty in statistically sorting out the scale effect from the effect of technological change.[12]

Natural Gas Transmission

The technological principle is that the cost of a pipeline is approximately proportional to its diameter, but its capacity is proportionate to the square of its diameter. Paul MacAvoy's study showed average total cost

---

[10] L. R. Christensen and W. H. Greene, "Economies of Scale in U.S. Electric Power Generation," *Journal of Political Economy*, 84, 4 (August 1976).

[11] John F. Stewart, "Plant Size, Plant Factor, and the Shape of the Average Cost Function in Electric Power Generation: A Nonhomogeneous Capital Approach," *The Bell Journal of Economics*, 10, 2 (autumn 1979), 549–565.

[12] For specific examples, see Alfred Kahn, *The Economics of Regulation*, vol. 1 (New York: Wiley, 1970), chap. 5, and S. C. Littlechild, "Peak-load Pricing of Telephone Calls," *The Bell Journal*, 1, 2 (1970), 191–210.

estimates for a thousand-mile haul declining from 10.1 cents per mcf for a 16-inch to 6.0 cents per mcf for a 36-inch line.[13] Studies show similar economies for oil pipelines.[14]

Water Utilities

Both in the short run, with capacity constraints, and in the long run, with capacity expansion, water utilities are apt to have economies of scale. In the short run, increased utilization creates efficiencies in operating and customer costs. In the long run, lower capacity costs are likely.[15]

DEMAND STUDIES

The Electric Power Industry

An excellent survey and critique of demand studies of the electrical industry was written by L. D. Taylor.[16] Several salient points regarding price and income elasticity emerge from a comparison of these studies.

a. All of the studies indicate that in the short run the demand for electricity is *inelastic*, though of course elasticity estimates vary considerably.
b. For all classes of consumers—residential, commercial, and industrial— the price elasticity of demand is substantially larger in the long run than in the short run.
c. The income elasticity estimates are also greater in the long run than in the short run.
d. The price elasticity estimates for industrial demand are greater than for residential demand.
e. The absolute values of long-run price elasticity estimates, with the exception of one early study, are all greater than 1 and less than 2; long-run demand is *elastic*.

A study of electric demand for Virginia Electric Power Company using econometric procedures demonstrates an analytic use for such information:

If the system KW peak income elasticity is larger than the system KWH demand income elasticity, as we find, then growth in income will bring about a large increase in required KW capacity relative to the actual KWH demand,

---

[13] Paul W. MacAvoy, *Price Formation in Natural Gas Fields* (New Haven, Conn.: Yale University Press, 1962).

[14] Leslie Cookenboo, Jr., *Crude Oil Pipelines and Competition in the Oil Industry* (Cambridge, Mass.: Harvard University Press, 1955).

[15] Patrick C. Mann, "Water Rates—An Evaluation of Options," *Journal of American Water Works Association*, 69, 2 (February 1977), 85.

[16] L. D. Taylor, "The Demand for Electricity: A Survey," *The Bell Journal*, 6, 1 (spring 1975), 74–110.

and the load factor will decline. Similarly, if system peak price elasticity is smaller in magnitude than the system KWH demand price elasticity, as we find, then increased real electricity prices will lead to a load factor decline.[17]

This same study also found demand elasticities demonstrated geographic differences, differences that would vary revenue and demand responses between regions.[18]

Consumer responsiveness to price changes was considered by commissions several decades ago. In 1935, the Public Service Commission of Wisconsin stated:

> For some time this Commission has been considering a plan for bringing additional electricity at relatively low cost within the reach of more users in the State. The experience of this Commission and of utilities in this State over many years, and the reported experience of other governmental agencies and utilities in other parts of the country and Canada, tend to show that average residential usage of 1,200 to 2,400 kilowatt-hours a year (100 to 200 a month) is not only possible but probable with low enough rates and the more general installation and use of so-called "heavy duty" appliances, such as refrigerators, ranges, and water heaters. In this and other states certain utilities have recently experimented with so-called "objective" or "bargain" rates.[19]

Though commissions have considered for many years the effects of changes in income and price in subjective and informal ways, the use of quantitative measures such as income and price elasticities are still not common in regulatory proceedings.

The Telephone Industry

Studies of price and income elasticities conducted principally by researchers employed by the Bell System[20] indicate very low price elasticity for local calls, ranging from − .1 to − .23. Long distance price elasticity estimates appear somewhat higher, but are often inelastic. Price elasticities for business users appear to be marginally less than those for residential

---

[17] Michael P. Murray, Robert Spann, Lawrence Pulley, and Edward Beauvais, "The Demand for Electricity in Virginia," *The Review of Economics and Statistics*, 60, 4 (November 1978), 589.

[18] Ibid., p. 593.

[19] "In the Matter of an Investigation, on Motion of the Commission, of a "Low-Cost" Rate Plan for Electric Service to Residential and Small Commercial Lighting Users," Docket 2-U-810, *Public Service Commission of Wisconsin Reports*, p. 195.

[20] See, for example, B. E. Davis et al., "An Econometric Planning Model for American Telephone and Telegraph Company," *The Bell Journal*, 4, 1 (1973), 29–56; A. R. Dobell et al., "Telephone Communications in Canada: Demand, Production, and Investment Decisions," *The Bell Journal*, 3, 1 (1972), 175–219; and S. C. Littlechild, "Peak-load Pricing of Telephone Calls," *The Bell Journal*, 1, 2 (1970), 191–210.

users. The demand elasticity with respect to income is inelastic in the short run and elastic in the long run. Cross-elasticities between various types of long distance service also appear to be inelastic.

Natural Gas

Price elasticities estimates for natural gas are variable, though it is likely that the domestic demand for natural gas is inelastic. Taylor's second survey looked at natural gas demand as well.[21] This survey found that: (a) price elasticities are quite inelastic in the short-run but rise in the long-run, and (b) gas and electricity are cross-elastic for residential and commercial use; gas and other fuels are cross-elastic for residential and commercial use; gas and other fuels are cross-elastic for industrial use. For wholesale sales it is probable that demand is inelastic in the short run and elastic in the long run.[22]

Water

The short-run and long-run price elasticities for water have been found to be inelastic and to have short-run and long-run income elasticities of an inferior good—i.e., less than 1.[23]

––––––––––––––––––––––––––––– **SUMMARY** –––––––––––––––––––––––––––––

The fundamental economic characteristic supporting the natural monopoly concept, and consequently the regulation of economies of scale, is economies of scale. Three types of economies of scale are present: short-run, long-run, and technological. A primary source of these economies is the production relation called increasing returns, wherein increases in inputs are accompanied by greater than proportional increases in production. These may occur with some factors fixed, in which case increasing marginal and average product (or returns) are present, or with all inputs variable, in which case increasing returns to scale are present. Other sources of decreasing costs relate to utilities' heavy fixed investment and to financial matters, such as obtaining quantity discounts. The existence of long-run decreasing costs is the chief prerequisite for public utility status.

Price and income elasticity of demand are concepts that indicate how

––

[21] Lester D. Taylor, "The Demand for Energy: A Survey of Price and Income Elasticities," in *International Studies of Energy Demand*, ed. W. D. Nordhaus (Amsterdam: North Holland, 1978), p. 20.

[22] Paul W. MacAvoy, "Relative Prices on Regulated Transactions of the Natural Gas Pipelines," *The Bell Journal*, 4, 1 (1973), 212–234.

[23] H. S. Houthakker and Lester D. Taylor, *Consumer Demand in the United States: Analyses and Projections*, 2nd ed. (Cambridge, Mass.: Harvard University Press, 1970), p. 89.

responsive the quantity demanded is to changes in price and income, respectively. The more inelastic the demand, the greater the profits that can be diverted from consumers to producers. Moreover, the price elasticity of demand is likely to be significantly greater in the long run than in the short run because consumers have more time to adjust to changes in relative prices. The cross-elasticity of demand relates the responsiveness in demand for a product not to its own price, but to the price of a related good. With substitute products (such as electricity and gas), the measured cross-elasticity will be positive; with complementary products (such as telephones and long-distance telephone service), cross-elasticity will be negative. Cross-elasticity, by showing the effect of related products on demand, is an important consideration for both regulators and managers. Another characteristic, price discrimination, is well established in the public utility area. Additional revenues may be obtained by discriminating among groups or customer classes, provided that these groups can be segmented to prevent resale of the product and that they have different price elasticities. Generally, the class with the more inelastic demand will be charged the higher price. The inverse elasticity rule of pricing is based on this price discrimination concept.

With diversity of demand comes decreases in capacity costs on a per unit basis, all else being the same. With greater diversity of customer groups, capacity is better utilized and average costs are lower. The idea is that one group's peak usage may fall at another's off-peak period, so better utilization results. Three ratios, the diversity factor, the load factor, and the capacity utilization factor, are employed to measure the extent of utilization or diversity.

Three technological features underlie the production function of most public utilities. The first is that the producer is connected physically to the consumer. This affords the utility a better opportunity to discriminate effectively by preventing or restricting resale of service. Second, for the electric and telephone industries, and to a lesser extent for gas and water, consumption and production of the utility service take place at essentially the same time. This property necessitates that the utility have excess capacity to meet consumption needs. Both factors contribute to the heavy investment requirement of utilities. The third feature is the low marginal rate of technical substitution of capital for labor. This normally implies that the utility will adopt a large capital input relative to other inputs. This notion is supported by the high relative capital turnover ratios for public utility industries.

The concept of social overhead capital also finds application in the public utility setting. External benefits to economies of scale and joint demand and the potential instability of the price mechanism are evident in public utility industries. Therefore, the government has deemed it appropriate to intervene to ensure a supply adequate to meet demand at a lower than monopoly price.

Finally, the available empirical evidence supports many of the usual economic assumptions concerning public utilities. Significant economies of scale, both in the short and long run, are indicated in the major public utility industries. For the electric power industry, price and income elasticity of demand are substantially greater in the long run than the short run. Most estimates indicate that demand for electricity is inelastic in the short run and elastic in the long run. Also, the price elasticity of demand for industrial users is greater than for residential customers. Regarding telephone service, local calls appear to have a lower price elasticity than long distance calls, though both are inelastic. Demand for natural gas and water is also inelastic. Finally, gas and electricity are cross-elastic in residential and commercial use.

Study Questions

1. Distinguish between the various types of decreasing cost.

2. Comment on the following statement: "Even if long-run decreasing costs do not exist in an industry, it is still correct to argue for a single regulated supplier in a market rather than for multiple suppliers, which would result in costly duplication of facilities."

3. What important economic characteristics are believed to exist in public utilities? What are the implications of these characteristics for the regulation of these industries?

4. Why do public utilities tend to be more capital-intensive than non-utility firms? (It may help to illustrate using constant-output curves (isoquants) and an isocost (constant-expenditure) line.)

5. What does it mean to say that the demand for electricity is inelastic? Will a monopolist supplier choose to operate on the inelastic portion of its demand curve?

6. Are the price elasticities of demand for the various categories of electric and telephone service the same? Of what consequence is this?

7. What is meant by the term *derived demand*? Does the fact that the demand for electricity is derived have any impact on the distinction between short- and long-run demand?

8. State whether the following statement is true or false and why: The diversity of demand found in the utility industry is really a source of economies of scale.

9. Give three prominent technological features of public utilities and indicate how each affects the economics (supply and demand) of public utilities.

10. Define the capital turnover ratio. Since it takes a substantially larger investment in plant and equipment per dollar of sales for utilities than for other firms, how are utilities able to earn a rate of return comparable to that in other industries?

11. What do the econometric studies of the telephone and electric industries indicate with respect to economies of scale and demand?

12. Give two reasons why studies of cross-elasticity of demand are important for public utilities. Illustrate each with an example.

13. If utilities have rates which in effect grant quantity discounts so that average price exceeds marginal price, what is the effect of measuring demand elasticity relative to average price? Relative to marginal price? Recall that $e = (p/q) (\Delta q/\Delta p)$.

14. The monopolist is operating at a point where its demand elasticity is 1.5 and selling price is $4. What is the firm's marginal cost at this output? What percentage above marginal cost is its price?

15. Suppose that a utility supplies two manufacturing firms with electricity service. In one firm the supply of other inputs (besides electricity) used in production is fairly elastic, while in the other firm the supply of other inputs is relatively fixed. In which firm is the derived demand for electricity service greater in the short run? Explain.

Student Readings

FARRIS, MARTIN T., AND R. SAMPSON. *Public Utilities.* Boston: Houghton Mifflin, 1973, pp. 18–21.

GARFIELD, PAUL J., AND W. LOVEJOY. *Public Utility Economics.* Englewood Cliffs, N.J.: Prentice-Hall, 1964, chap. 2.

PHILLIPS, CHARLES F. *The Economics of Regulation,* 2nd ed. Homewood, Ill.: Irwin, 1969, chap. 2.

YOUNGSON, A. J. *Overhead Capital.* Edinburgh: Edinburgh University Press, 1967.

Advanced Readings

Economies of Scale

BARZEL, Y. "Productivity in the Electric Power Industry." *Review of Economics and Statistics,* 45 (November 1963), 401–403.

COOKENBOO, LESLIE, JR. *Crude Oil Pipelines and Competition in the Oil Industry.* Cambridge, Mass.: Harvard University Press, 1955.

COURVILLE, LEON. "Regulation and Efficiency in the Electric Utility Industry." *The Bell Journal*, 5, 1 (1974), 53–74.

COWING, T. G., AND V. K. SMITH. "The Estimation of a Production Technology: A Survey of Econometric Analyses of Steam-Electric Generation." *Land Economics*, 54, 2 (May 1978).

DAVIS, B. E., ET AL. "An Econometric Planning Model for American Telephone and Telegraph Company." *The Bell Journal*, 4, 1 (1973), 29–56.

DHRYMES, PHOEBUS, J., AND M. KURZ. "Technology and Scale in Electricity Generation." *Econometrica*, 32 (June 1964), 287–315.

DOBELL, A. R., ET AL. "Telephone Communications in Canada: Demand, Production, and Investment Decisions." *The Bell Journal*, 3, 1 (1972), 175–219.

FISHER, FRANKLIN M. "The Existence of Aggregate Production Functions." *Econometrica*, 37 (October 1969), 553–557.

JOHNSTON, J. *Statistical Cost Analysis.* New York: McGraw-Hill, 1960.

KAHN, ALFRED E. *The Economics of Regulation*, vol. 1. New York: Wiley, 1970, chap. 5.

KOMIYA, RYUTANO. "Technical Process and the Production Function." *Review of Economics and Statistics*, 44 (May 1962), 156–166.

LITTLECHILD, S. C. "Peak-load Pricing of Telephone Calls." *The Bell Journal*, 1, 2 (1970), 191–210.

MACAVOY, PAUL W. *Price Formation in Natural Gas Fields.* New Haven, Conn.: Yale University Press, 1962.

NERLOVE, MARC. "Returns to Scale in Electricity." *Measurement in Economics*, ed. Carl Christ et al. Stanford, Calif.: Stanford University Press, 1963, pp. 167–198.

OLSON, CHARLES E. *Cost Considerations for Efficient Electric Supply.* M.S.U. Public Utility Studies. East Lansing: Michigan State University, 1970.

STEWART, J. F. "Plant Size, Plant Factor, and the Shape of the Average Cost Function in Electric Power Generation: A Nonhomogeneous Capital Approach." *The Bell Journal of Economics*, 10, 2, (1979), 549–565.

SUDIT, E. F. "Additive Nonhomogeneous Production Functions in Telecommunications." *The Bell Journal*, 4, 2 (1973), 499–515.

Demand

DAVIS, B. E., ET AL. "An Econometric Planning Model for American Telephone and Telegraph Company." *The Bell Journal*, 4, 1 (1973), 29–56.

DOBELL, A. R., ET AL.   "Telephone Communications in Canada: Demand, Production and Investment Decisions." *The Bell Journal*, 3, 1 (1972), 175–219.

HOUTHAKKER, H. S., AND L. D. TAYLOR.   *Consumer Demand in the United States: Analyses and Projections*, 2nd ed. Cambridge, Mass.: Harvard University Press, 1970.

LITTLECHILD, S. C.   "Peak-load Pricing of Telephone Calls." *The Bell Journal*, 1, 2 (1970), 191–210.

MACAVOY, PAUL W., AND R. NOLL.   "Relative Prices on Regulated Transactions of the Natural Gas Pipelines." *The Bell Journal*, 4, 1 (1973), 212–234.

TAYLOR, L. D.   "The Demand for Electricity: A Survey." *The Bell Journal*, 6, 1 (1975), 74–110. See also studies listed in bibliography.

TAYLOR, LESTER D.   "The Demand for Energy: A Survey of Price and Income Elasticities." In *International Studies of Energy Demand*, ed. W. D. Nordhaus. Amsterdam: North Holland, 1978.

TAYLOR, LESTER D.   *Telecommunications Demand: A Survey and Critique*. Cambridge, Mass.: Ballinger, 1980.

3

Legal Concepts
of Public Utilities

The legal concept of public utilities originated in early English business practice and was given substance in English court decisions. Out of early English judicial decisions, or *common law*, came many of our views, court decisions, and statutes relating to public utilities. The U.S. Constitution has been interpreted to give power to the federal government to regulate interstate commerce. Also, the Constitution reserves to the states the right to regulate certain intrastate business activities. In this regard, the U.S. Supreme Court first faced the question of the constitutionality of government regulation of private business in *Munn* v. *Illinois* (1877).[1] Based on common law, the Court found that certain industries "affected with a public interest" were subject to regulation. But because the criteria governing where regulation could be instituted were left vague, the Court was forced to wrestle often over the years with the issue of what could and could not be regulated.

Presumably, this issue was settled in *Nebbia* v. *New York* (1934)[2] by permitting state legislatures to regulate almost any economic activity so long as the public interest is served and the state's actions are not obviously arbitrary or discriminatory. Thus, the legal definition of a public utility is rather blurred; essentially, whatever the legislature deems to be a public utility is a public utility. As a practical matter, a relatively small number of industries are generally regarded as public utilities. These industries,

---

[1] 94 U.S. 113 (1877).
[2] 291 U.S. 502 (1934).

enumerated in Chapter 1, provide communications, electric, gas, and water (and sometimes certain transportation and sewage) services.

In this chapter, we will examine the legal concept of regulation and the limits to this regulation. We will review the relevant provisions of the U.S. Constitution and federal and state laws pertaining to utility regulation and the chief limitations to government regulation. These include the requirements of procedural and substantive due process of law, as well as judicial review. In essence, *procedural due process* requires that fair and reasonable procedures be followed in administering utility regulation. *Substantive due process* requires that commission decisions be nonconfiscatory, as prescribed in the Constitution and in numerous court cases. The right of *judicial review* permits the appeal of regulatory decisions under specified conditions. Next, we will trace the legal concept of the public utility through landmark court cases, beginning with *Munn* (1877). Finally, we will describe the rights and duties of public utilities and the rights of consumers.

THE LEGAL BASIS
OF GOVERNMENT REGULATION

THE U.S. CONSTITUTION

Federal Regulation

The power of the federal government to regulate business originates in Article I, Section 8 of the Constitution. Here the most important clause, known as the interstate commerce clause, gives Congress the power "to regulate Commerce . . . among the several States." The term "Commerce" has been broadly interpreted by the courts to mean that the federal government can regulate nearly any business engaged in interstate activity, but intrastate commerce only to the extent of eliminating undue discrimination. Also in Article I, "implied powers" are given to Congress "to make all laws which shall be necessary and proper for carrying into Execution the foregoing powers, and all other Powers vested by this Constitution in the Government of the United States." The "implied powers" clause has been interpreted to mean that the federal government not only has those powers which are enumerated explicitly in the Constitution, but also those which have not been denied by and are "consistent with the letter and spirit of the Constitution."

State Regulation

The Tenth Amendment to the Constitution reserves for the several states those powers not delegated to the federal government and not expressly prohibited to them. The broad powers of the states to protect the health, safety, morals, and general welfare of their citizenry, long recognized by the courts, are called the *police powers* of the states. These powers, along with those over intrastate commerce, have been used to justify state regulation of numerous business activities, as we will see in the Court's interpretation in *Nebbia* v. *New York* (1934).

Major Legislation

A number of national and state statutes control public utility regulation. Here we will review the major federal acts and present a short history of significant state laws and the included provisions.

Federal Acts

The Interstate Commerce Act of 1887 was a first step toward effective regulation in the railroad industry and a model for other regulatory endeavors. The Mann-Elkins Act of 1910 generally dealt with railroad regulation, but also granted the Interstate Commerce Commission authority over telephone, telegraph, and cable companies in interstate or foreign commerce. The ICC could establish rates and regulations, but only a few proceedings were carried out.

The Federal Water Power Act of 1920 established the Federal Power Commission with regulatory authority over water power and resources. The secretaries of agriculture, interior, and war, who made up the commission, issued licenses to develop water resources and supervise the construction and operation of projects in navigable waters in the United States. After 50 years, the licenses expired. At that time, the commission could renew the license of the U.S. government or another designated licensee could take over the project. If the project were taken over, the original licensee was to receive compensation set at the original cost of investment less accumulated depreciation, but not to exceed the fair value. Rate regulation for power in interstate or foreign commerce was permitted in states where rate regulation was absent. In 1930, the commission was reorganized as an independent commission made up of five full-time commissioners.

In the 1930s, regulatory reform occurred at the federal level. The Federal Power Commission's authority was expanded by the Federal Power Act of 1935, the Public Utility Holding Company Act of 1935, and the Natural Gas Act of 1938. In addition, the Federal Communications Act of 1934, and as amended in 1937, established the Federal Communictions Commission, with jurisdiction over telephone, telegraph, and radio companies. These federal acts closed the jurisdictional gaps in the regulation by the various states.

The Federal Power Act of 1935 dealt with the regulation of transmission and sale at wholesale of electric energy in interstate commerce. The Federal Power Commission was authorized to divide the country into regional areas for voluntary interconnection and coordination of facilities for generation, transmission, and sale of electric energy, and to require, under limited conditions, the physical connection of transmission systems. In addition, the commission had authority to approve the sale, lease, or disposition of facilities; the merger or consolidation of facilities; and the purchase, acquisition, or taking of securities in any other public utility. Security issuance of public utilities was also regulated. Conflicts of interest by officers or directors of public utilities were forbidden, as were interlocking directorates between utilities and those financial institutions marketing utility securities or suppliers of electrical equipment.

The most important powers conferred on the Federal Power Commission were these:

1. The power to find rates unjust, unreasonable, or unduly discriminatory or preferential and, if so found, to establish just and reasonable rates for the transmission of power and for wholesale sales in interstate commerce.
2. The requirement that public utilities keep a prescribed set of accounts and records.
3. The authority to set depreciation rates.
4. The authority to require that rates and charges of the public utility be made public, and that utilities make annual reports.

The Public Utility Holding Company Act of 1935 affected electric and gas utilities. This act was concerned with the information made available to investors; the lack of efficiency in raising capital; the excessive charges and the absence of bargaining because these utilities fell between the cracks of state regulatory commissions' limited jurisdiction; the complication and obstruction of state regulation; and the lack of economy in management, efficiency and adequacy of services, operation, integration, and coordination. The act sought to eliminate the evils connected with public utility holding companies, and to simplify the public utility holding company systems and eliminate their detrimental characteristics. Registration of public utility holding companies with the Securities and Exchange Commission was required. Issuance or sale of securities by holding companies was to be permitted by the Securities and Exchange Commission only under strict conditions. Security sales by subsidiaries were permitted to finance subsidiary operations. Holding companies could not borrow from or lend to utilities or subsidiaries to pay dividends or purchase or sell securities that would violate SEC rules and regulations.

The Securities and Exchange Commission was empowered to simplify the holding company systems by reducing excessive fixed charges or obligations, ensuring a fair and equitable distribution of voting power, and enforcing the so-called death-sentence clause. This clause limited holding companies to a single integrated public utility, restricted other nonutility business involvement, and abolished any holding company more than twice removed from its operating subsidiaries. The SEC eliminated write-ups above cost from asset and capital accounts, and replaced debt and preferred stock with common stock.

The holding company problem of that era was effectively dealt with by the Public Utility Holding Company Act. But the omissions in the act are equally important. The vertical and horizontal diversification by the telephone holding company was not treated. Nor was the establishment of a nonjurisdiction holding company. Beginning with a single gas or electric utility, a nonjurisdiction holding company undertakes conglomerate diversification and then horizontal and vertical diversification in non-utility activities. Manley R. Irwin and Kenneth B. Stanley have called for application of the principles of the Public Utility Holding Company Act to all regulated utilities.[3]

The Natural Gas Act of 1938 closed the gap in interstate regulation of the electric power and gas utility industry, a gap the states formerly could not regulate. The act provided for the regulation of transportation of natural gas in interstate commerce and the sale in interstate commerce of natural gas for resale for ultimate public consumption in domestic, commercial, industrial, or any other use. The U.S. Supreme Court interpreted this act to encompass sales by producers to interstate pipelines.[4] The court distinguished wellhead sales from the exclusion in the act for the production or gathering of natural gas.

The Natural Gas Act permitted the Federal Power Commission to fix lower just and reasonable rates where a utility's rates were found to be unjust, unduly discriminatory, or preferential. The FPC was to determine a system of accounts and the actual legitimate cost of the utility's property, set the depreciation rates, and establish the fair value of such property. The commission could also order certain construction or extensions and approve abandonments. A holder of a certificate of convenience and necessity issued by the commission could exercise the right of eminent domain. In 1977, many of the powers of the Federal Power Commission were transferred to the Federal Energy Regulatory Commission in the new federal Department of Energy.

The Natural Gas Policy Act of 1978 provided for the escalation of natural gas wellhead prices. Beginning from a legislated price per thousand cubic feet of natural gas in April 1977, the act raises the price on par with the quarterly implicit gross national product deflator. In the cases of new natural gas, rollover contracts, and stripper well gas, additional wellhead

---

[3] Manley R. Irwin and Kenneth B. Stanley, "Regulatory Circumvention and the Holding Company," *Journal of Economic Issues*, 7, 2 (June 1974), 408.

[4] *Phillips Petroleum Co.* v. *Wisconsin*, 347 U.S. 67 (1954).

price adjustments are made. Contract prices for existing interstate contracts were preserved. In 1985, many wellhead prices are to be fully deregulated, with the exception of high-cost natural gas, which was deregulated earlier. The Federal Energy Regulatory Commission has retained authority to set rates for certain gas at a just and reasonable rate only if in excess of the prices established by the act. The intermediate effect of this act is a return to an older form of price regulation—direct price setting by legislative statute—and a turning away from regulation by independent commission.

Title II of the Natural Gas Policy Act of 1978 provides that surcharges on the price of natural gas sold to certain fuel facilities be incrementally priced. These surcharges equal the difference between the price of natural gas and the cost of some alternative fuel determined by the Federal Energy Regulatory Commission (FERC). The surcharges are to cover, in part, the higher costs of new natural sources. The FERC has established rules for incremental pricing of gas for nonexempt users. Fuel oil prices have been used to set the alternative fuel price. Exempt users receive a reduced interstate purchased gas adjustment rate charge from the monies raised by the surcharge. State commissions responded by raising the retail rates of nonexempt users to the cost of the alternative fuel, and reduced their interstate purchased gas adjustment rate charge for exempt users.

The Public Utility Regulatory Policies Act (PURPA) of 1978 has three purposes: To encourage

1. Conservation of energy supplied by electric utilities.
2. The optimization of the efficiency of use of facilities and resources by electric utilities.
3. Equitable rates to electric consumers.[5]

Departing from the traditional noninvolvement in the regulation of intrastate electric retail sales, Congress established various rate design standards which each state regulatory commission and each unregulated electric utility are to consider and to determine whether or not the standards should or should not be implemented. A state regulatory commission or unregulated electric utility may determine that any such standard need not be implemented. The federal standards include these:

1. The design of rates for a class of customers shall be based on the class's cost of service.
2. The energy component of a rate may not decrease with kilowatt consumption unless energy costs decline as consumption increases.
3. Rates shall be on a time-of-day basis reflecting the cost to service different periods of time unless such time-of-day rates are not cost justified.

---

[5] Public Utility Regulatory Policies Act, 95th Cong., 2nd Sess., *Conference Report to Accompany H.R. 4018*, p. 5.

4. Rates shall be on a seasonal basis that reflects the seasonal cost of service.
5. Electric utilities shall offer interruptible service.
6. Utilities shall offer practicable, reliable, and cost-effective load management to customers.[6]

Other standards to be considered include prohibitions and restrictions on master metering, conditions that permit or restrict automatic adjustment clauses, the transmission to electric consumers of information regarding rate schedules, procedures regarding termination of electric service for disputed bills or for nonpayment of bills, especially when dangerous to health, and the exclusion from utility rates of costs for promotional or political advertising. The act does restrict the effect of any adoption of these standards so that

> Nothing in this title shall authorize or require the recovery by an electric utility of revenues, or of a rate of return, in excess of, or less than, the amount of revenues of the rate of return determined to be lawful under any other provision of law.[7]

Thus, determinations of a rate of return and overall revenue requirements are exclusively a matter of state law. PURPA is concerned with the structure of rates in the rate schedules of different classes of consumers.

The Federal Energy Regulatory Commission is also empowered to collect cost of service information that will permit separation of electric costs into customer cost, demand cost, and energy cost components; the costs of serving each customer class; the kilowatt load curves for each class; and disaggregated annual costs of providing service. The Federal Energy Regulatory Commission is also permitted to require interconnection and wheeling of power as well as to exempt utilities, under certain conditions, from state laws that restrict pooling.

PURPA established certain retail policies for natural gas utilities which states or utilities must consider also. These standards were designed to limit the termination of gas service and prohibit the inclusion in rates of the costs of promotional or political advertising. The standards are like those for electric utilities.

For the telecommunications utilities, the major law is the Federal Communications Act of 1934 and amendments in 1937. It established the Federal Communications Commission, with jurisdiction over interstate and foreign wire and radio communications. The act prohibits unjust and unreasonable discrimination in charges and services and allows the commission to set reasonable charges. Just and reasonable rates are permitted to be classified by day or night and other categories. Charges are made

---

[6] Ibid., p. 7.

[7] Ibid., p. 13.

TABLE 3.1 Commission Rate Authority over Investor-Owned Utilities

(The United States including the District of Columbia)

Sales by Investor-Owned Utilities	Number of Commissions
To ultimate consumers:	
Electric[a]	50
Gas	50
Telephone	51
For resale:	
Electric[b]	27
Gas	30

Authority to	
Suspend proposed rates:[c]	
Electric[a]	46
Gas	46
Telephone	48
Initiate rate investigations:	
Electric[a]	50
Gas	50
Telephone	51

[a] The State of Nebraska has no privately owned electric utilities, and only telephone utilities are regulated.
[b] Primarily Federal Energy Regulatory Commission jurisdiction.
[c] Hawaii, Michigan, and Wisconsin do not permit rates to become effective at a certain date, and suspensions are not required.
SOURCE: National Association of Regulatory Utility Commissions, *1978 Annual Report on Utility Regulation* (Washington, D.C.: National Association of Regulatory Utility Commissioners, 1979), pp. 372, 373, 375.

public. The FCC establishes a set of accounts and accompanying records, sets depreciation charges, examines company transactions that affect charges, issues certificates of convenience and necessity, and approves consolidations.

State Law

State public utility regulation predates federal regulation. The Massachusetts Commission was granted limited powers in the late 1800s. In 1907, the Wisconsin Public Utility Law and the New York Public Service Commission Law were passed. In the following decade, well over half the states established utility commissions.[8] The Wisconsin law provided for

---

[8] Ben W. Lewis, "Public Utilities," Chapter XXI in Leverett S. Lyon and Victor Abramson (eds.), *Government and Economic Life*, vol. II (Washington, D.C.: The Brookings Institution, 1940), p. 637.

valuation of investment, determination of depreciation rates, establishment of a uniform system of accounts, and complete control of rates and services. If rates were unreasonable or discriminatory or inadequate service was provided, the commission could set reasonable rates and require that service standards be met. By 1978, all fifty states and the District of Columbia had exercised regulatory authority over public utilities by establishing regulatory commissions. Their jurisdiction is shown in Table 3.1.

LIMITATIONS ON THE RIGHT OF GOVERNMENT _____ TO REGULATE BUSINESS ACTIVITY _____

THE CONSTITUTIONAL REQUIREMENT OF DUE PROCESS

Federal Government

The Fifth Amendment states that "No person shall . . . be deprived of life, liberty, or property without due process of law; nor shall private property be taken for public use, without just compensation." Ever since, a business enterprise has been declared by the Supreme Court to be a person.[9] This amendment has guaranteed the right of due process to firms, which means that the "law shall not be unreasonable, arbitrary, or capricious, and that the means selected shall have a real and substantial relation to the object sought to be attained."[10]

State Government

A state's power over business activity is limited by the Fourteenth Amendment, which reads: "No state shall make or enforce any law which shall abridge the privileges or immunities of citizens of the United States; nor shall any State deprive any person of life, liberty, or property, without due process of law; nor deny to any person within its jurisdiction the equal protection of the laws."

JUDICIAL REVIEW

The acts of the state and federal legislatures and administrators are subject to judicial review. The courts view orders of a commission as final unless it has gone beyond its statutory or constitutional powers, or its decision is based on a mistake in law, or it acted capriciously and arbitrarily in the face of the evidence. Such a review will determine whether procedural

---

[9] *Santa Clara County* v. *Southern Pacific Railroad Company*, 118 U.S. 394 (1886).

[10] *Nebbia* v. *New York*, 291 U.S. 502 (1934).

due process of the law was complied with. The U.S. Supreme Court has stated

> That the responsibilities of a reviewing court are essentially three. First, it must determine whether the Commission's order, viewed in light of the relevant facts, and of the Commission's broad regulatory duties, abused or exceeded its authority. Second, the court must examine the manner in which the Commission has employed the methods or regulation which it has itself selected, and must decide whether each of the order's essential elements is supported by substantial evidence. Third, the court must determine whether the order may reasonably be expected to maintain financial integrity, attract necessary capital, and fairly compensate investors for the risks they have assumed, and yet provide appropriate protection to the relevant public interests, both existing and foreseeable. The court's responsibility is not to supplant the Commission's balance of these interests with one more nearly to its liking but instead to assure itself that the Commission has given reasoned consideration to each of the pertinent factors.[11]

This review of the procedures used by the commission in reaching the decision is a far distance from the Supreme Court's earlier review of substantive due process. Substantive due process amounted to an extralegislative review by the Court and, not infrequently, a substitution of the conclusions preferred by the Court for the commission's conclusions regarding the facts before it. The climax of the substantive due process review is found in the U.S. Supreme Court's *Ben Avon* decision (1920), which required an independent judgment of the law and facts by a reviewing court.[12]

LEGISLATIVE REVIEW

Congress or the state legislature, as the occasion arises, reviews the extent and exercise of regulatory statutes. Legislation which may increase or reduce regulatory jurisdiction is introduced and considered. Failures and dissatisfaction can be appealed to the legislative branches through the political processes. The final authority on utility regulation lies in statutory legislation so long as it complies with the federal and state constitutions.

ADMINISTRATIVE LAW

Administrative law encompasses constitutional law, statutes concerning regulatory powers and procedures, judicial review, and agency administrative rules. Substantive regulatory law, such as the determination of

---

[11] *Permian Basin Area Rate Cases*, 390 U.S. 747 (1968), 20 L. ed 2d 312, 88 S CT 1344 at 350.

[12] *Ohio Valley Water Co.* v. *Ben Avon Borough*, 253 U.S. 287.

utility rates, is a separate concern to be reviewed in Chapter 4. Administrative law is not exclusively the concern of utility regulation, but the concern of many governmental agencies generally. The federal government, for example, has an Administrative Procedures Act which spells out the procedures or requirements administrative agencies must follow.

Agency administrative rules frequently are codified and serve as law. For example, the federal government publishes the *Code of Federal Regulations*. The legislation adopted by governmental agencies, including regulatory commissions, is set forth in such administrative codes at both federal and state levels. By such publications, administrative procedures are made public.

────────────── **THE PUBLIC UTILITY CONCEPT** ──────────────

Under the common law of England, from which our public utility concept is derived, certain occupations, called "common callings," were subject to prescribed rights and obligations. Included among the common callings were bakers, brewers, cab drivers, ferrymen, innkeepers, millers, smiths, surgeons, tailors, and wharfingers. Those employed in these callings were obligated to provide adequate service at reasonable prices to all who desired it.

Adam Smith proposed that "if proper courts of inspection and account have not yet been established for controlling their [the trustees or commissioners of turnpikes] conduct, and for reducing the tolls to what is barely sufficient for executing the work to be done,"[13] Parliament accordingly may remedy the situation. This proposal by the father of laissez-faire competition contains the service, accounting, and price regulation principles subsequently applied to public utilities.

In the United States throughout the first half of the nineteenth century, economic and political liberalism prevailed. The second half of the nineteenth century, however, was marked by increasing industrialization, economic concentration, and monopoly power. The Granger movement began in the late 1860s and early 1870s in response to alleged abuses against farmers, particularly by railroad companies, in the form of unfair and discriminatory pricing. The Grangers (the Patrons of Husbandry) pushed for government regulation of railroads. To this end, state regulatory commissions were established in the Middle West and soon spread throughout the country.

---

[13] Adam Smith, *The Wealth of Nations,* ed. Edwin Cannon (New York: The Modern Library, 1937), pp. 684–685.

Munn v. Illinois (1877)

The Grangers, numbering as many as a half million, supported the passage of numerous laws to curb some of the abuses of economic power affecting them. One such law was passed by the Illinois state legislature in 1871. According to this statute, owners of grain elevators must obtain a license, file their rates for grain storage, and charge no more than some maximum prescribed rate. Arguing that theirs was a private business engaged in interstate commerce, Munn and Scott, who owned a grain elevator business, challenged this statute. The case went to the Supreme Court, resulting in its first landmark pronouncement on the public interest concept. In the words of Chief Justice Waite:

> This brings us to inquire as to the principles upon which this power of regulation rests, in order that we may determine what is within and without its operative effect. Looking, then, to the common law, from whence came the right which the Constitution protects, we find when private property is "affected with a public interest, it ceases to be juris privati only." This was said by Lord Chief Justice Hale more than two hundred years ago . . . and has been accepted without objection as an essential element in the law of property ever since. Property does become clothed with a public interest when used in a manner to make it of public consequence, and affect the community at large. When, therefore, one devotes his property to a use in which the public has an interest in that use, and must submit to be controlled by the public for the common good, to the extent of the interest he has thus created. He may withdraw his grant by discontinuing the use; but, so long as he maintains the use, he must submit to the control.[14]

> Although in 1874 there were in Chicago fourteen warehouses adapted to this particular business, and owned by about thirty persons, nine business firms controlled them, and . . . the prices charged and received for storage were such "as have been from year to year agreed upon and established by the different elevators and warehouses in the City of Chicago, and which rates have been annually published in one or more newspapers printed in the city, in the month of January in each year, as the established rates for the year then next ensuing such publication." Thus it is apparent that all the elevating facilities through which the vast productions "of seven or eight great States of the West" must pass on the way "to four or five of the States on the seashore" may be a "virtual" monopoly.

> Under such circumstances it is difficult to see why, if the common carrier, or the miller, or the ferryman, or the innkeeper, or the wharfinger, or the baker, or the cartman, or the hackney-coachmen, pursues a public employment and exercises "a sort of public office," these plaintiffs in error do not. They stand, to use again the language of their counsel, in the very "gateway of commerce," and take a toll from all who pass. Their business most certainly "tends to a common charge, and is become a thing of public

---

[14] *Munn v. Illinois*, 94 U.S. 113, 125–26 (1877).

interest and use." Every bushel of grain for its passage "pays at toll, which is a common charge," . . . if any business can be clothed "with a public interest, and cease to be *juris privati* only," this has been . . . it is by the facts.[15]

The right of the state to regulate private business is clearly affirmed in this case. Moreover, a legal model, though crude, was established on which further regulation of a private business "clothed with a public interest" was to be founded.

In the years to follow, regulation of transportation companies and other firms expanded at a rather steady rate, even though many of these firms lacked the monopoly power evident in the grain operations in Chicago. Among those regulated were small grain elevators in North Dakota, Kansas fire insurance companies, certain types of rentals in the District of Columbia, Oklahoma cotton gins, and the retail price of milk in New York. On the other hand, the courts denied state regulation over certain types of businesses, including meat packing operations in Kansas, theater ticket brokering in New York, employment agencies in New Jersey, gasoline prices in Tennessee, and ice manufacturing in Oklahoma.

OTHER CASES

Cases subsequent to the *Munn* decision attempted to refine the concept of "clothed or affected with the public interest." The 1914 *German Alliance Insurance Co.* v. *Kansas*[16] decision noted that over time, a private business can become affected with the public interest. When a business became affected with the public interest was a legislative and not a judicial matter. Later U.S. Supreme Court decisions retreated from this view. In *Wolff Packing Co.* v. *Court of Industrial Relations of Kansas* (1923),[17] Chief Justice Taft tried to define three classes in which business is clothed with a public interest:

1. Businesses receiving a public grant of privilege such as a franchise and undertaking a corresponding duty.
2. Certain historical occupations such as innkeepers, cabs, and gristmills.
3. Businesses which have come to be devoted to the public use because of an indispensable nature of the service or arbitrary control to which the public might be subject without regulations.

Justice Taft argued that a legislative determination is not conclusive in justifying regulation.

[15] *Munn* v. *Illinois*, 131–132 (1877).
[16] 233 U.S. 389, 58 L. ed. 1011.
[17] 262 U.S. 522, 67 L. ed. 1103.

A 1927 decision, *Tyson & Brother* v. *Banton*,[18] tried to distinguish businesses operated for private interest and unregulated, businesses affected with a public interest and rate regulated, and a new third class, quasi-public businesses. *Quasi-public* businesses were said to be subject to the police power of the state but not rate regulation. Dissenting opinions to the decision noted that the decision to regulate was properly within the powers of the state legislature. It was also stated that the concept of business affected with a public interest was too vague to lay down a universal rule. In *Ribnik* v. *McBride* (1928)[19] and *Williams* v. *Standard Oil Co. of Louisiana* (1929),[20] the regulation of price was said to depend upon the business being affected with a public interest, while other types of regulation depended upon a less strict test. Justice Stone, joined by Justices Holmes and Brandeis, denied that the majority's distinction between price regulation and other regulation of contracts or property was justified.

In *New State Ice Co.* v. *Liebmann* (1932), Taft's test for businesses clothed with a public interest was used and not found to apply to the sale and manufacture of ice. Brandeis's dissent stated that the decision when a private business comes to be affected with a public interest is a matter primarily for the determination by the legislature. The proper role for judicial review is the determination of arbitrary, capricious, and unreasonable actions of the legislature.

NEBBIA V. NEW YORK (1934)

In *Nebbia*, 57 years after the Munn case, the Court embraced essentially a new doctrine that any industry which the state believed appropriate to regulate could be regulated as long as the principle of due process was observed. There was no longer a particular category of industry which was "affected with the public interest" and therefore subject to regulation. This doctrine represents the current status of regulation in this area.

In 1933 the New York legislature passed a law that set up the Milk Control Board to regulate the wholesale and retail price of milk in the public interest. Mr. Nebbia, who owned a retail grocery store in Rochester, sold milk below the established price of 9 cents a quart and was sued and convicted for violation of the statute. On appeal, Nebbia's principal arguments, that the milk business was competitive, not a public utility with monopoly characteristics, and that his Fourteenth Amendment rights were being violated, were rejected by the U.S. Supreme Court in a 5 to 4 decision. In the words of Justice Roberts, representing the majority:

---

[18] 273 U.S. 418, 71 L. ed. 718.

[19] 277 U.S. 350, 72 L. ed. 913.

[20] 278 U.S. 235, 73 L. ed. 287.

We may as well say at once that the dairy industry is not, in the accepted sense of the phrase, a public utility. We think the appellant is also right in asserting that there is in this case no suggestion of any monopoly or monopolistic practice. It goes without saying that those engaged in the business are in no way dependent upon public grants or franchises for the privilege of conducting their activities. But if, as must be conceded, the industry is subject to regulation in the public interest, what constitutional principle bars the state from correcting existing maladjustments by legislation touching prices? We think there is no such principle. . . .

It is clear that there is no closed class or category of businesses affected with a public interest and the function of courts in the application of the Fifth and Fourteenth Amendments is to determine in each case whether circumstances vindicate the challenged regulation as a reasonable exertion of governmental authority or condemn it as arbitrary or discriminatory. The phrase "affected with a public interest" can, in the nature of things, mean no more than that an industry, for adequate reason, is subject to control for the public good. In several of the decisions of this court wherein the expressions "affected with a public interest" and "clothed with a public use" have been brought forward as the criteria of the validity of price control, it has been admitted that they are not susceptible of definition and form an unsatisfactory test of the constitutionality of legislation directed at business practices or prices. These decisions must rest, finally, upon the basis that the requirements of due process were not met because the laws were found arbitrary in their operation and effect. But there can be no doubt that upon proper occasion and by appropriate measures the state may regulate a business in any of its aspects, including the prices to be charged for the products or commodities it sells.

So far as the requirement of due process is concerned, and in the absence of other constitutional restriction, a state is free to adopt whatever economic policy may reasonably be deemed to promote public welfare, and to enforce that policy by legislation adapted to its purpose. The courts are without authority either to declare such policy, or, when it is declared by the legislature, to override it.[21]

The implication of this landmark case is that the state with sufficient cause can declare almost any industry to be "affected with the public interest" and thus subject to regulation. Moreover, the notion of "affected with the public interest" need not be linked to the public utility concept in its traditional sense; "affected with the public interest" is a broader concept. Following *Nebbia*, regulation has been extended to numerous industries. Yet the most pervasive regulation has been reserved for the traditional public utility category, where monopolistic characteristics play an important role.

---

[21] *Nebbia* v. *New York*, 291 U.S. 531–32, 536–37 (1934).

The obligations and rights of public utilities are specified in statutes and court decisions. They will only be briefly mentioned here.

RIGHTS

a. Public utilities may charge reasonable rates for their services which provide them at least the opportunity to cover all costs, including a reasonable rate of return to the capital provided by owners.
b. They have the right of exclusive franchise to offer the service in the franchise area.
c. The right of eminent domain to secure private property, justly compensated, necessary for public use is frequently given public utilities.
d. They have the right to operate under reasonable rules and regulations, such as reasonable office hours, and prompt payment and service deposits.

OBLIGATIONS

a. Utilities must serve all customers who are willing to pay the prescribed rate for the service.
b. They must provide safe and adequate service. Plant and equipment must be maintained and expanded as demand grows within the franchise area so that quality of service is above a certain minimum level.
c. Utilities must charge reasonable rates that are not unduly discriminatory to any class of consumer.
d. Extension, alteration, and abandonment of service must be approved by the regulating authority.

RIGHTS OF CONSUMERS

The quiescence of large numbers of consumers of utility services as compared with the activism of utility companies in commission proceedings is understandable.[22] A divergence of interests between the consumer and the utility certainly exists. The utility prefers higher rates and profits, while consumers in general have a direct interest in lower rates and profits. Yet consumers, except for certain large industrial customers, find it difficult to have the commission focus on their interests. No one consumer, in general, could hope to gain from active participation in a rate proceeding a savings adequate to justify the costs of participation. However, this

---

[22] Murray Edelman, "Symbols and Political Quiescence," *The American Political Science Review*, vol. LIX, No. 3, Sept. 1960, p. 703.

appears to be changing somewhat with the consumer movement of the 1970s. Consumer groups have been formed to make it easier to bring consumer issues before regulators.

The interests of the consuming public have taken up less time in the courts but have not been ignored. Justice Brandeis, in his famous concurrence in the Southwestern Bell Telephone case, noted that, "Upon the capital so invested the Federal Constitution guarantees to the utility the opportunity to earn a fair return."[23] But in the footnote thereto, he adds, "Except that rates may, in no event, be prohibitive, exorbitant, or unduly burdensome to the public."[24]

Justice Harlan, in the majority opinion in the Permian Basin Area Rate cases, observed that the criteria in the Hope case regarding the rate of return to the utility investor

> scarcely exhaust the relevant considerations. . . .
>
> The Commission cannot confine its inquiries either to the computation of costs of service or to conjectures about the prospective responses of the capital market; it is instead obliged at each step of its regulatory process to assess the requirements of the broad public interests entrusted to its protection by Congress.
>
> Accordingly, the "end result" of the Commission's orders must be measured as much by the success with which they protect those interests as by the effectiveness with which they "maintain credit . . . and . . . attract capital."[25]

The Nebraska Supreme Court in 1975 found that consumers have the very same right to protection against confiscation of property without due process as do utilities. That court wrote:

> The Commission can no more permit the utility to have confiscatory rates for the service it performs than it can compel a utility to provide service without just and equitable compensation. As a matter of elemental justice, consumers of utility services are entitled to the same protection as against confiscation of property or arbitrary action on the part of the utility as are the utilities.[26]

The consumers' interest must be before the commission in its decision making if the reviewing court permits the decision to stand. The court can

---

[23] *Missouri ex rel Southwestern Bell Telephone Co.* v. *Public Service Commission*, 67 U.S. L. ed. 986.

[24] Ibid.

[25] *Permian Basin Area Rate Cases*, 390 U.S. 747, 20 L. ed. 2d. 312, 88 S. CT 1344 at pp. 349–350.

[26] *Meyers* v. *Blair Telephone Company*, 230 NW 2d. 196.

only determine if reasonable people could reach the same decision as the commission based upon the record in the case if a full and complete record of the public's interest is before the commission. The appearance of consumer representatives before commissions has increased in recent years. The first consumer advocacy statute was probably passed in 1911 in Iowa, where the office of commerce counsel was established. Among that office's duties were these: "As attorney for any person, or persons, or for the public generally, in proceedings before the Commerce Commission."[27]

The National Association of Regulatory Utility Commissioners identifies approximately 200 staff members, other than commission staff, in 18 states, which represent consumer interests.[28] Commission staffs generally remain the primary source of expert testimony to counterbalance the utility company arguments to the commissions.

For the consumer advocate on the commission staff to be effective in presenting the public's interests, certain difficulties must be faced. The commission itself must be supportive of such a staff role and recognize that the utilities typically can and do present their own interests very well. Second, a sufficient, broadly trained professional staff is necessary. These staff members should be experienced, highly trained, and well paid; they should view themselves as career public servants. Finally, professional standards and the integrity of the commission's impartiality should not be seen as compromised by advocacy of the consuming public's interest. A well-trained and experienced professional staff member, after careful review and study of the issues, can formulate reasonable conclusions regarding regulatory issues and their resolution.[29]

SUMMARY

As permitted under the U.S. Constitution, numerous federal and state laws have been enacted to govern the regulation of public utilities. The rights of procedural and substantive due process and of judicial review are the primary limitations on government's power to regulate private business. The right of government to regulate private business activity was first tested in the Munn case (1877). Relying rather heavily on English common law, *Munn* affirmed that states have the authority to regulate

---

[27] Iowa State Commerce Commission, "Powers and Duties of the Iowa State Commerce Commission" (Des Moines: State of Iowa, 1938), p. 4.

[28] National Association of Regulatory Utility Commissions, *1978 Annual Report* (Washington, D.C.: National Association of Regulatory Utility Commissioners, 1978), pp. 761–762.

[29] A detailed discussion of the procedural shortcomings of the regulatory process is contained in Chapter 6.

certain private business activities—in particular, those business activities "affected with the public interest." Thus the legal concept of a public utility has evolved from a series of court cases, beginning with *Munn* (1877) and ending, at least for the present, with *Nebbia* (1934). Also specified in statutes and court decisions are the rights of public utilities, such as the rights of reasonable rates and exclusive franchise, and their obligations, such as the requirements to serve all and to charge nondiscriminatory rates (within certain broad limits).

Currently, almost any business may be regulated provided the state deems it appropriate to do so in the public interest. As a practical matter, however, only a small number of pervasively regulated industries are commonly regarded as public utilities.

It is well to note the sharp contrast between the economic concept of a public utility, which relies heavily on economies of scale and monopolistic elements, and the legal concept, which relies heavily on case law. Nonetheless, the distinction of what is and what is not a public utility in either case is not a sharp one. There is a certain vagueness in both definitions.

Study Questions

1. Is the legal right of the federal and state governments to regulate private business a constitutional right? If so, under what articles?

2. What limitations are placed on the right of the state to regulate business?

3. In a legal sense, how do we determine which industries are public utilities and therefore should be subject to regulation?

4. What is the importance of the Munn (1877) case? Of the Nebbia (1934) case?

5. Outline the rights and duties of a public utility. Which ones are also the rights or duties of a private business? Do you see any problems likely to occur in an administrative procedure attempting to implement and enforce their rights and duties? Discuss two or three in detail.

6. State whether the following statement is true or false and explain why. The Nebbia (1934) case restricted the possibilities for state regulation of private businesses.

7. State whether the following statement is true or false and briefly comment. The Court decided the principal legal issue of *Munn* v. *Illinois* (1877) in favor of Illinois by *requiring* that all businesses "affected with the public interest" be regulated.

Student Readings

FARRIS, M. T., AND R. J. SAMPSON. *Public Utilities.* Boston: Houghton Mifflin, 1973, chap. 3, pp. 22–30.

GARFIELD, PAUL J., AND WALLACE F. LOVEJOY. *Public Utility Economics.* Englewood Cliffs, N.J.: Prentice-Hall, 1964, chaps. 1, 3, 4.

MANUS, PETER C. "Competition in Regulated Industries: Economics." In *Essays on Economic Issues,* ed. J. Niss and M. Pledge. Macomb, Ill.: Center for Business and Economic Research, Western Illinois University, 1975, pp. 11–27.

MUNN v. ILLINOIS, 94 U.S. 113 (1877).

PHILLIPS, CHARLES F., JR. *The Economics of Regulation,* 2nd ed. Homewood, Ill.: Irwin, 1969, chap. 3.

WELCH, FRANCIS X. *Public Utility Regulation.* Washington, D.C.: Public Utilities Reports, Inc., 1961, chaps. 1–4.

4

Traditional Issues
in Regulation

A fundamental objective of public utility regulation is the establishment of just and reasonable utility rates. Procedures widely used by utility commissions in setting utility rates will be discussed in this chapter. The three component parts—the overall revenue requirements, the class of service revenue responsibility, and the rate design for individual services—will be examined. The primary method of determining revenue requirements is the cost of service approach. The necessary revenues are set by commissions to equal the costs reasonably incurred in providing service. Among the costs considered are operating expenses, depreciation, taxes, and return on investment. Return on investment is broken down further into the product of the allowed rate of return and the rate base. This chapter also includes a discussion of how regulation deals with the effects of inflation. Finally, a brief discussion of the importance of the quality of service to utility regulation concludes the chapter.

_____ **OVERVIEW OF THE REGULATORY PROCESS** _____

In the United States, an administrative process for the regulation of public utilities replaced competition among firms as a means of prescribing acceptable performance. The responsibility of public utility regulation is generally delegated to federal and state regulatory commissions. In general, their mandate is to ensure adequate service at minimum cost to consumers consistent with a reasonable return to creditors and owners. In furtherance of this objective, commissions typically exercise control over entry, quality and conditions of service, and prices. Each of these will be discussed in turn, but our emphasis will be on the price-fixing process and especially on rate level determination.

Generally, no entry into the market is permitted by any firm other than the original licensed utility. Although the franchise must be renewed from time to time, government agencies tend to continue franchising the original licensee. Early in the history of public utilities, this exclusivity was abandoned in several instances to force reduction of rates. Rates typically were lower, but so was the quality of service. After a short period, consolidation took place—thus the "naturalness" of a natural monopoly.

The bulk of the commission's effort is devoted to regulation of utility prices. There are two principal aspects of setting utility rates in a formal proceeding. First, based on the company's costs, the regulatory agency determines the total revenue to which the company is entitled for provision of service. Second, this total must be translated into a rate pattern or structure yielding individual prices on each segment of service. The exact procedure followed in establishing prices varies among commissions, but a typical rate case would include selection of a recent test year; calculation of operating expenses including taxes and depreciation in the test year modified for certain documented changes in costs; determination of the utility's rate base (the net investment in utility operations); estimation of the allowed rate of return to be permitted on the utility's rate base; comparison of test-year earnings after taxes with the allowed return (product of the allowed rate of return and the rate base determination) and adjustment of rate levels so that expected revenues after taxes equal the permitted revenues (usually made as if demand were completely inelastic); and finally, adjustment of prices on individual segments of service to generate revenue of the magnitude required. These rates would remain in effect until the commission deemed the rates too high or too low, based mainly on the magnitude of the rate of return realized. The rate case process in Iowa is a typical one:

> The essential elements in the process of a contested rate increase application constitute: (1) filing of the utility company proposal under Commission rules and regulations; (2) statutory suspension of the proposed effectiveness of the new rates under bond and subject to refund; (3) investigation of the filing by qualified members of the Commission's technical division under the general direction of an attorney assigned from the Office of Commerce Counsel; (4) the filing of prepared written testimony and exhibits by the proponent company under a procedural schedule set by Commission order; (5) the selection of expert witnesses by the Commerce Counsel's prosecuting attorney and the development and filing of prepared testimony in answer to the company's direct case; (6) the filing of other prepared testimony by intervenors, if any; (7) the submission of rebuttal testimony by the proponent company; (8) recorded trial-type hearings devoted to cross-examination of

the proffered evidence, with the Commission presiding; (9) written briefs by the parties prepared with citation to the hearing transcript and relevant economic and legal authority; (10) Commission decision and order, often followed by applications for rehearing; and (11) appeals, if any, to a district court and from there to the Iowa Supreme Court. . . . When it actually transpires, the Commerce Counsel represents the Commission before the courts. At that point in time, the record of the contested case will be formed by thousands of pages of transcript and hundreds of pages of exhibits and briefs.[1]

In other jurisdictions, the details of the process may vary but the fundamental steps—rate filings, suspension, review, testimony, hearings, briefs, commission decision and order, and *possible* appeals—remain.

In addition to the formal rate cases, an informal process of interaction between commissions and utilities necessarily proceeds on a day-to-day basis. Indeed, this is really the principal way the commission exercises its responsibility for continuous surveillance over the quality and adequacy of service to consumers and the efficiency of the utility's operations. Studies of this process are scarce, and therefore our discussion of this informal process is limited. The informal process, for example, may range from referring an individual customer's problem or complaint to the utility and monitering its resolution, to providing public documents such as tariffs affecting a customer, to the stipulation of the facts and resolution of a rate case through negotiations between the parties in a rate proceeding. All these actions ultimately can be presented to the commission for final decision, or to resolve disputes and disagreements. As a result, even informal procedures must always be focused on the legal rights of the customer or the utility. Another type of informal activity can best be described as lobbying by utilities, consumer groups, politicians and other interested persons. Even there, the participants must take care to avoid prohibited *ex parte* communications, such as one party's undisclosed attempts to influence the commission regarding a contested case, and to avoid the appearance of impropriety.

DETERMINATION OF THE
GENERAL RATE LEVEL

The total revenue to which the utility is entitled an opportunity to recover, called the *revenue requirement*, is most frequently set equal to the utility's cost of service. Thus, the public utility rate-making formula is given by the equation $RR = O + T + (V - D)R$, where RR denotes the revenue

---

[1] Don Charles Uthus and Diane McIntire, "Public Utility Rate Regulation and the Iowa Administrative Procedure Act—Extending Maximum Procedural Protection to Public Utilities at Public Expense," *Drake Law Review*, 26, 3 (1976–1977), 494–495.

requirement and the righthand side of the equation denotes the cost of service. The cost of service includes operating expenses and annual depreciation expense, O, annual taxes, T, the value of the utility plant, V, accumulated depreciation, D, and the allowed rate of return, R. The term $(V - D)$ is referred to as the rate base. Although the formula itself is rather simple, the calculations, estimations, and decisions involved in obtaining its components are complex, and the criteria guiding determination of each component have a long and rich history. Before discussing the individual components of the cost of service formula, let us look at the basic economic concepts and the practical principles of the formula.

CUTTING THE REGULATORY KNOT: THE ACCOUNTING RATE OF RETURN AND THE ECONOMIC COST OF CAPITAL

The cost of service method has ancient antecedents: The medieval, as well as the Roman, determination of the just price reflected the cost of service.

The modern cost of service standard applied to public service companies has been traced to the English railroad commissioners under the Railroad and Canal Act of 1854.[2] American courts also used the cost of service in railroad rate determination. Federal Judge Brewer, in connection with the Iowa Railroad Law of 1888, observed: "Compensation implies three things: payment of cost of service, interest on bonds, and then some dividends."[3] Mr. Dabney interprets these three things to be "1st, operating expenses; 2d, interest on bonds; and 3d, some dividends, however small,"[4] and points out:

> The true conclusion seems to be that the corporation (which is a person entirely distinct from either its creditors or its stockholders) is entitled to such a schedule of rates as will enable it to earn operating expenses, and, in addition thereto, a sum which shall be reasonable income on the just value of its property.[5]

In 1905, the Wisconsin Railroad Commission Law was enacted, "modeled after the Iowa statute regulating railroads, but it profited by the experience of other nations and the decisions of state and federal courts."[6] In 1907, the Wisconsin commission's powers were extended to include public utilities. Earlier in the same year, the New York Commission had

---

[2] W. D. Dabney, *The Public Regulation of Railways* (New York: Putnam's, 1889), p. 181.

[3] Ibid., p. 61.

[4] Ibid., p. 63.

[5] Ibid., p. 64.

[6] Fred L. Holmes, *Regulation of Railroads and Public Utilities in Wisconsin* (New York: Appleton, 1915), p. 2.

been established. Many states subsequently adopted public utility regulation modeled on the Wisconsin statute.[7]

In the 1910 *State Journal Printing Co.* v. *Madison Gas & Electric Co.*
decision, the Wisconsin commission adopted the cost of service formula,
and stated:

> Under the laws of Wisconsin, public utilities, under ordinary conditions, are
> entitled to earnings for their service that will yield enough to cover operating
> expenses, including depreciation and a reasonable return on the property
> actually used and useful for the convenience of the public.[8]

Much of the concern of the early regulatory commissions focused on
the valuation of the rate base. By adopting uniform accounting, current
revenues and expenses of a public utility could be relied upon as being
reasonably accurate. But in many cases the surviving balance sheets of a
utility, which were based on past data, could not be. Furthermore, the
market value of the utility property or the utility securities did not establish
a suitable value. These values are based upon circular reasoning; they rise
and fall with the level of regulated earnings. Also, the accounting for
securities was frequently overstated because franchise value and goodwill
had been capitalized and used to collaterize security issues. Frequently,
the records supporting the purchase price of utility property were missing
or written up for phantom transactions. Many public utilities had made
no provision for depreciation, but rather had allowed only for retirements.
As pragmatic policy makers, the early regulators had little choice but to
take an inventory of existing utility assets and evaluate this property. After
a time, the development of uniform accounting requirements made possible accurate determination of the *original cost* investment. This *investment
standard* later successfully challenged and generally supplanted property
appraisals, which were known as *reproduction* and *fair value* rate base
methods.

The basic accounting formats that support the cost of service formula
are the income statement and the balance sheet of the utility. The public
utility's balance sheet and income statement are presented in Figures 4.1
and 4.2. Because these accounting statements have somewhat unique characteristics, we will discuss them in some detail.

The income statement and balance sheet of the utility separate utility
operations from nonutility operations. In practice, nonutility income and
deductions, and nonutility property and other investments, are reported
"below-the-line." Conversely, the "above-the-line" financial data relate
to utility operations. Commissions, by enforcing proper accounting and

---

[7] Ben W. Lewis, "Public Utilities," in *Government and Economic Life*, vol. II, eds. Leverett
S. Lyon and Victor Abramson (Washington, D.C.: The Brookings Institution, 1940), p. 637.

[8] Holmes, *Regulation*, p. 50.

Operating revenues		XXXX
Less:		
Operating expenses	XXX	
Depreciation expense	XXX	
Taxes other than income taxes	XXX	
Income taxes	XXX	
Total operating deductions		XXXX
Utility operating income		XXXX
(above the line)		

(below the line)		
Other income and deductions:		
+ Other income	XXX	
− Miscellaneous income deductions	XXX	
		XXX
− Interest expense		XXX
Net income		XXXX

FIGURE 4.1 Income Statement

the requirement that certain categories of expenses and property or investments be recorded "below-the-line," control some costs of service items. Jurisdictional allocations of revenues, costs, and rate base are accomplished partly by each commission requiring segregated accounting for revenues, costs, and rate base. Certain common costs and rate base items are allocated to the different jurisdictions. Generally, uniform accounting facilitates, but does not control or govern, rate making and the determination of the revenue requirement. Recorded costs are adjusted in practice to reflect more accurately cost realities.

Certain other features of the utility's financial statements differ from those of nonregulated enterprises. Income taxes are an operating deduction rather than a charge against earnings. On the balance sheet, utility and nonutility property and long-term capitalization both appear before, rather than after, current assets and liabilities. Even though the accounting of utilities in general conforms to most generally accepted accounting principles, the accountant who deals with utility financial statements must have specialized knowledge of these and other unique features of utility accounting.

These accounts record the costs of the utility. The term *cost* means the amount of money actually paid for property or services, the usual accounting meaning for cost. Utility plant is recorded at original cost—i.e., the money cost of the property at the time when it was first dedicated to the public use, whether by the present utility or its predecessors. Where a nonutility would record plant at the firm's acquisition cost, a utility that acquires plant from another utility must record the money cost originally paid by the first utility using the property. Use of original cost accounting

	Assets:		
(*above*	Utility plant (at original cost)		XXXX
the	Less: Accumulated depreciation		XXX
line)	Net utility plant		XXXX

	Investments		
(*below*	Nonutility property		
the	less accumulated depreciation	XXX	
line)	Other investments	XXX	
	Total other property and investments		XXXX
	Current and accrued assets		
	Cash	XXX	
	Notes and accounts receivable	XXX	
	Materials and supplies	XXX	
	Prepayments	XXX	
	Other current assets	XXX	
	Total current assets		XXXX
	Deferred debits		XXX
	Total assets and other debits		XXXXX
	Liabilities and other credits:		
	Capitalization		
	Common stock issued	XXX	
	Preferred stock issued	XXX	
	Paid-in surplus	XXX	
	Retained earnings	XXX	
	Total proprietary capital	XXXX	
	Bonds	XXX	
	Other long-term debt	XXX	
	Total long-term debt	XXXX	
	Total capitalization		XXXXX
	Total current and accrued liabilities		XXXX
	Total deferred credits		XXX
	Total accumulated deferred income taxes		XXXX
	Total liabilities and other credits		XXXXX

FIGURE 4.2 Balance Sheet

for utility plant controls interutility transfers of property and the capitalization of excess earnings by writing up the acquisition price. Purchases at prices in excess of original cost give rise to below-the-line acquisitions adjustments, amounts that are not charged to consumers.

The U.S. Supreme Court in its famous Hope Natural Gas (1944) decision, following close on the heels of the Natural Gas Pipeline Co. (1942) case, ceased its attempts to prescribe a reproduction cost (the cost of duplicating existing plant and equipment at current prices) or the fair value valuation (value based on both original cost and reproduction cost) rate base. Following Justice Jackson's separate opinion and Justice Brandeis's opinion in the 1923 *Southwestern Bell* decision, the investment standard or the original cost method was adopted by most commissions.

Modern economic thought, needless to say, does not include the terms rate of return or rate base in its day-to-day vocabulary. Rather, the economist who studies public utility economics must learn the fundamentals of the rate-making formula. The tie between the rate of return on rate base formula, $R = [RR - (O + T)]/(V - D)$, and the economist's cost of capital is seldom clear, however. The economist often defines the rate of return as the internal rate of return rather than, as the accountant does, the rate of return on investment. An internal rate of return is a sort of average rate of return. For example, if Joe offers to pay Frank $257 at the end of each of the next five years in exchange for investing $1000 now, the economist would ask: What is the internal rate of return? The internal rate of return is that discount rate which makes the present value of the returns to the investor just equal to the initial investment—i.e., the net present value equals zero.

In Table 4.1, the economist's internal rate of return is 9 percent; 9 percent is that discount rate which just sets the present worth of the return equal to the initial investment. The accountant would measure the return differently, however, as Table 4.2 shows. In Table 4.2, the computation of rate of return is the net return divided by net investment (i.e., net of accumulated depreciation). As is quite apparent in this case, the accounting rate of return never equals the internal rate of return. A common alternative accounting rate of return measure is the average net return divided by the average investment. For the example in Table 4.2, this rate equals $57 ÷ ($\frac{1}{2}$ × $1000) or 11.4 percent.

By charging a rate of return equal to the cost of capital, say, 9 percent, on the net investment or, in other words, the rate base, the rate of return formula approximates the internal rate of return. The rate-making use of the revenue requirement/cost of service or rate of return formula is demonstrated in Table 4.3. The internal rate of return is 9 percent, as the net present value is zero. The accounting rate of return applied in rate making

TABLE 4.1   Internal Rate of Return

		PRESENT WORTH FOR DISCOUNT RATE OF		
Year	Return	8%	9%	10%
1	$257	$ 238	$ 236	$ 233
2	257	220	216	212
3	257	204	199	193
4	257	189	182	176
5	257	175	167	160
Present worth		$1026	$1000	$ 974
Initial investment		−1000	−1000	−1000
Net present value		$ 26	0	$−26

TABLE 4.2 Accounting Rate of Return

Year	Original Cost of Investment	Gross Return	Depreciation	Net Return	Rate of Return[a]	Accumulated Depreciation	Net Investment (year end)
1	$1000	$257	$200	$57	5.7%	$ 200	$800
2	1000	257	200	57	7.125	400	600
3	1000	257	200	57	9.5	600	400
4	1000	257	200	57	14.25	800	200
5	1000	257	200	57	28.5	1000	0

[a] Based on net return divided by net investment at beginning of year.

satisfies both the economist's and the accountant's definition of the average return on investment. The cost of capital becomes the rate of return included in the revenue requirement/cost of service formula.

THE PRINCIPLES OF REVENUE REQUIREMENT DETERMINATION

The determination of the revenue requirement using the cost of service formula relies upon several principles of rate making. These include the following concepts: the test period; actual cost; the matching principle; allowance of necessary, prudent, and efficient costs; *pro forma* adjustments; and used and useful property in the rate base.

The *test period* is a fundamental rate-making concept. A period of time is selected and that period's revenues, costs, and rate base are examined. The accounting records of the revenues and costs for the test period, generally a 12-month period, are audited to see that only reasonable and proper costs are included and to determine the nature of the transactions included. The nature of these transactions determines the proper manner in which to reflect these costs in the cost of service. A review of test-year data is important, for "wherever costs enter into financial accounts, non-objectively measured data are produced having their own sources and forms of errors."[9] This inherent error, coupled with the moral hazard that

TABLE 4.3 Rate Making Rate of Return

Year	Investment	Accumulated Depreciation	Net Investment	Net Return	Rate of Return	Depreciation	Gross Return
1	$1000	0	$1000	$90	9%	$200	$290
2	1000	$200	800	72	9	200	272
3	1000	400	600	54	9	200	254
4	1000	600	400	36	9	200	236
5	1000	800	200	18	9	200	218

[9] Oskar Morgenstern, *On the Accuracy of Economic Observations*, 2nd ed. (Princeton, N.J.: Princeton University Press, 1963), p. 79.

the utility will try to represent a high level of annual costs and the morale hazard that the utility may be indifferent to certain types of excessive costs such as "gold-plating" of rate base and non-arms-length bargains, makes the review of test-year financial data a critical task.

Two basic types of test years are used—historical test periods, which predominate, and forecast test periods, an approach recently used in some jurisdictions. Various combinations of historical and forecast test periods have also been used, such as six months historical and six months forecasted data. Justice Cardozo, writing in the 1935 *West Ohio Gas Co.* decision, stated well the distinction between a historical test period relying on actual operating data and a forecast test period employing estimates:

> There are times, to be sure, when resort to prophecy becomes inevitable in default of methods more precise. At such times, "an honest and intelligent forecast of probable future values made upon a view of all the relevant circumstances." . . . is the only organon at hand, and hence the only one to be employed in order to make the hearing fair. But prophecy, however honest, is generally a poor substitute for experience. "Estimates for tomorrow cannot ignore prices of today." . . . We have said of an attempt by a utility to give prophecy the first place and experience the second that "elaborate calculations which are at war with realities are to no avail." . . . We say the same of a like attempt by officers of government prescribing rates to be effective in years when experience has spoken. A forecast gives us one rate. A survey gives another. To prefer the forecast to the survey is an arbitrary judgment.[10]

In its 1977 *West Iowa Telephone Co.* decision rejecting a forecast test period, the Iowa State Commerce Commission stated:

> We have always rejected attempts at using projected data in lieu of known and measurable facts. Speculation is the anathema of regulation.[11]

Use of a historical test period dominates the use of forecast test periods. Notable exceptions such as the New York Public Service Commission exist. Future test periods are among the regulatory methods used to deal with inflation. With a future test period, the increased concern with inflation and rising costs exacts its toll, a reduced ability to control both the moral and the morale hazards in the rate case.

A second important concept is that of *actual costs*. Actual costs from a test period reflect the amount of money actually paid for property or services. The use of historical test periods permits the examination of the transactions that incurred these costs, the isolation of legitimate costs, and a high degree of protection against the moral and morale hazards. A con-

---

[10] 294 U.S. 79, 82.
[11] 18 PUR 4th 227.

tinuing exception to the actual cost principle began during the 1970s, as a result of the federal income tax laws. Accelerated depreciation for tax purposes and the investment tax credit—except in jurisdictions that flow through to the consumer the tax savings from accelerated depreciation and in California, which sends through the tax savings of the investment tax credit—results in hypothetical or deferred taxes charged consumers exceeding the actual taxes paid to the government.[12] This excess over the actual cost paid is a capital contribution to the utility, a contribution legally but involuntarily obtained from consumers. Generally, however, only actual costs serve as the basis for the test period revenue requirement.

The *matching principle* is another fundamental concept in rate making. Matching means identifying all revenues and expense items along with the associated rate base that should be included in the test period. Since the utility services and associated revenues and costs represented on an income statement for a utility occur *over time*, while the costs represented on the balance sheet occur *at a point in time*, it is necessary to match revenues, sales, and expenses with rate base and capital costs. For example, operating expenses for a full calendar year do not match the year-end rate base. A 1982 income statement matches an *average* 1982 balance sheet, not a December 31, 1982, balance sheet.

Investment in utility property *throughout* the test year provides service coincident with a full year's sales, revenues, and costs. Revenues, expenses, capital costs, and depreciation for the annual test period match or are appropriately associated with the average rate base of the test period. Use of a year-end rate base, on the other hand, requires the estimation of the matching year-end levels of sales, revenues, and costs. Such estimates require recognition that plant is added generally to meet a different, probably increasing, level of utility demand, and to take advantage of operating efficiencies. Since nowhere in the records of a utility are year-end levels of revenues and expenses recorded, use of a year-end rate base requires seasonally adjusted, annualized estimates of year-end levels of revenues and expenses.

Early in the history of utility accounting and rate making, depreciation expense was not matched with the accumulated depreciation on the balance sheet or deducted in the rate base. Straight-line depreciation expense was included in the cost of service, but the observed condition of the property determined the accumulated depreciation. High depreciation expenses were included as increased operating expenses, but the lower accumulated depreciation increased the rate base. Today, amounts charged to depreciation expense are also credited to accumulated depreciation. Upon subsequent retirement of items of property, both the utility plant

---

[12] This is discussed in detail later in this chapter under taxes.

and accumulated depreciation are reduced. Depreciation expense matches the accumulated depreciation in the rate base.

Jurisdiction matching is important as well. Utilities commonly have r.onutility unregulated operations such as merchandising, manufacturing, o. real estate investments. Also, jurisdictional utility costs must be matched with jurisdictional utility services; nonutility costs with nonutility sales and plant; nonjurisdictional utility revenues with nonjurisdictional utility cost and rate base. One utility may provide different kinds of utility service, such as gas and electricity, operate in several states, or be subject to various state and federal commission jurisdictions. For example, telephone utilities often operate in several states, have affiliated manufacturing and telephone directory publishing companies, and nonutility affiliates selling directly to the public.

Since the 1960s several utilities have established holding companies that own a single gas or electric utility, thereby conforming to the Public Utility Holding Company Act. Telephone and water utilities, not covered by the Public Utility Holding Company Act, continue to have controlling interests in several utilities and follow the older pattern of an integrated holding company. The single utility holding company today diversifies its investments into real estate, computer services, energy exploration and the like. With diversified interests, the matching of general corporate overhead expenses and capital charges becomes difficult. For example, the nonutility operations can trade on the lower risk of the utility. The high, stable dividend stream from the utility can be used to support nonutility financing. But the more risky financing and its costs cannot be readily traced to the nonutility investments. A direct cost of capital adjustment is required to match lower capital costs with the utility.

Having examined the concepts of the test period, actual cost, and matching, we can turn to more realistic, less general, principles of rate making—allowance of necessary, prudent and efficient cost, *pro forma* adjustments, and used and useful property in the rate base.

In 1936, the U.S. Supreme Court ruled in *Acker* v. *United States* that when a charge is for a public service, "regulation cannot be frustrated by a requirement that the rate be made to compensate extravagant or unnecessary costs."[13] If such expenditures do not result from arms-length bargaining, then "more proof is required than mere description of activities engaged in or their reasonableness"[14] to establish the level of expense chargeable in rates. Where an arms-length bargain has occurred, a commission may still disallow costs that result from an abuse of discretion on

---

[13] 298 U.S. 426.

[14] *Park View Utilities Co.* v. *Iowa State Commerce Commission*, 360/2-63163 (Iowa Court of Appeals, Slip Opinion, April 29, 1980), p. 6.

the part of management. The discretion of utility management to incur costs and have these costs reflected in rates does not extend to rates based on imprudent, extravagant, unnecessary, or inefficient costs. Costs associated with illegal activities are likewise not permitted in rates. The Federal Energy Regulatory Commission, in its general instructions for its system of accounts, states:

> All amounts included in the accounts prescribed herein for electric plant and operating expenses shall be just and reasonable and any payments or accruals by the utility in excess of just and reasonable charges shall be included in account 426.5, Other Deductions.[15]

Only prudent and efficient costs should be charged to the consumer. In other words, the consumer is responsible for the lowest cost of providing reasonable service, and no more. And the commission is responsible for seeing that the consumer does not pay more. However, hindsight is not sufficient to prove costs were unreasonable or imprudent. Rather, a commission should show that at the time of the questionable transactions, the utility's management, acting reasonably, should have known or did know that the cost was unreasonable. Costs frequently questioned include the costs of goodwill and institutional advertising, charitable contributions, social memberships, and political activities. These expenditures are generally unnecessary for a utility to maintain its market, as it has an exclusive franchise. Provision of a reasonable level and quality of service serves to enhance the utility's public image, in any case. The utility is not prohibited from making such unreasonable expenditures; it is only prevented from recovering from rates the costs of such activities.

The cost of service determined by a commission is to be representative of the conditions that will prevail when the rates will be effective; i.e., rate making is prospective. As a result, *pro forma* adjustments are made to the test year actual costs to represent more accurately prospective conditions. For example, during the test period, negotiation of a union contract will usually raise labor rates. An increase in postage will increase customer billing expense. Such increases are annualized, and the revenue requirement includes a full year of the higher expenses. Separating the known and measurable changes from changes that might cause unknown effects on costs and revenues is the difficult task. Various changes, particularly additions to plant in service, are associated with an unforeseeable level of sales, revenues, and costs. A new power plant is built usually to meet growing demand and to achieve operating efficiencies, for example. To annualize such new construction violates the principle that the rate base be matched with the corresponding level of sales, revenues, and costs. All

---

[15] Code of Federal Regulations, Title 18 (Washington, D.C.: U.S. Government Printing Office, 1979), p. 311.

concomitant annual levels of sales, revenues, and costs accompanying the change in rate base are probably not known.

Another type of *pro forma* adjustment includes adjustments for abnormal and extraordinary revenues or costs. Abnormal levels of revenues and costs may be changed to normal levels. For example, abnormally cold winters may increase sales of gas for heating. Adjustment of gas expense and revenues of heating and curtailed industrial customers are made in many jurisdictions. A strike at a large industrial customer of a utility during the test period may likewise reduce revenues and costs abnormally. To determine prospective rates, normal levels of sales, revenues, and costs would be included in the cost of service. Extraordinary costs are removed from the cost of service when costs are unlikely to be incurred prospectively. An example of an extraordinary expense is the cost of repairing a turbine generator damaged in an accident. To incorporate extraordinary costs would generate revenues unneeded in the future to cover actual costs incurred. A windfall profit would occur, a windfall profit not needed to cover costs.

A final important rate-making principle relates to rate base. The *rate base*, in original cost jurisdictions, reflects the investment in property used and useful in rendering utility services.[16] (In those few fair value jurisdictions, the requirement that the property be used and useful also holds, although the original cost standard does not.) The asset side of the utility balance sheet segregates the investment in property used in utility operations from other investments or property. Property that provides a different type of utility service, utility service for another regulatory jurisdiction, nonutility services, or property that has been retired from service is not "used and useful." Commissions may also find unnecessary plant, gold-plated or extravagant property, or excessive duplication of property and declare that such property is not "used and useful." Property that is not used and useful is then excluded from the rate base.

By developing the original cost rate base from the asset side of the balance sheet, the rate base can be limited to investments in utility property. The righthand or liabilities and owner's equity side of the balance sheet shows total capitalization, but utility capitalization alone cannot generally be segregated. Therefore, the righthand side of the balance sheet is used to determine the cost of capital and the lefthand or asset side is used to segregate the investment in "used and useful" utility property.

Table 4.4 shows a simplified example of the determination of general rate levels for a utility. The revenue requirement or cost of service formula is used, $RR = O + T + (V - D)R$. The $1.4 million cost of service results in a rate or cost to the ratepayer of $0.02 per unit of service. The public utility rates are set so that the firm has the opportunity to earn revenues

---

[16] *Davenport Water Co.* v. *Iowa State Commerce Commission*, 190 NW 2d 588.

TABLE 4.4 Simplified Example of Utility Rate Determination

	Test Period Amount per Book	Pro Forma Adjustments	Adjusted Test Period Cost
Operating expenses (O)	$ 600,000	$100,000	$ 700,000
plus: Annual depreciation (d)	230,000	(80,000)	150,000
plus: Taxes (T)	350,000	(50,000)	300,000
Subtotal	$1,180,000	$ (30,000)	$1,150,000
Rate base (V − D)	$3,000,000	$(500,000)	$2,500,000
Cost of capital/rate of return (R)			10%
Net operating income (R) (V − D)			$ 250,000
Cost of service = O + d + T + R (V − D)			$1,400,000

that cover the adjusted costs of service. Suppose the following figures have been established for the utility as shown in Table 4.4:

a. Operating expenses (O) = $700,000
b. Annual depreciation (d) = $150,000
c. Taxes (T) = $300,000
d. Rate base (V − D) = $2,500,000
e. Rate of return (R) = 10 percent

Then the cost of service equals: $O + d + T + (V − D)R = 700,000 + 150,000 + 300,000 + (.10) (2,500,000) = \$1,400,000$. The commission would next attempt to set rates so that the utility would earn $1.4 million in revenues. If the utility is expected to provide 70 million units of a single type of service, the price per unit would be $1.4 million divided by 70.0 million units, or $0.02 per unit. At a price of $0.02 per unit, the utility may earn more or less than the 10 percent return allowed, depending on a variety of conditions that may occur in the future.

Our review of the determination of the general rate level continues with a discussion of each part of the revenue requirement/cost of service formula: operating expenses, including depreciation expense; taxes, including tax depreciation; rate base; and rate of return.

OPERATING EXPENSES

Operating expenses include expenses related to the utility's operation, such as maintenance expenses, wages and labor benefits, administrative expenses, and the like. Depreciation is another important expense. These expenses range from 50 to 65 percent of electric and telephone revenues.

Operating expenses incurred by the utility are subject to challenge by the commission and the public, as the Acker decision pointed out.[17] The commission's authority to disallow improper categories or levels of expenses was determined early in the history of public utility regulation.[18] The utility carries the burden of showing that a challenged expense is proper. It must demonstrate that the expenditure was in fact made, reasonable in amount, and necessary to the provision of utility service. Commissions generally control expenses deemed improper by disallowing them for rate-making purposes—i.e., by excluding them from the cost of service used in setting rates and thereby forcing stockholders to absorb the expense, not consumers.

Table 4.5 sets forth the operating expense chart and selected accounts for class A and B electric utilities, class A and B gas utilities and class A telephone companies as adopted by the Federal Energy Regulatory Commission and the Federal Communications Commission. The expenses related to each of these activities will be charged to individual accounts. Fuel used in steam production is a major electric cost. Fuel is an inventory item. Therefore, fuel is first charged to inventory accounts for fuel stock and fuel handling. Subsequently, using inventory costing methods such as last-in, first-out (LIFO); first-in, first-out (FIFO); or average cost, fuel expense will be charged to Account 151—steam power generation, operation, fuel. This fuel expense includes salaries and wages as well as the costs of the fuel itself, transportation, operating supplies, associated excise taxes, and insurance.

The repair of central office equipment, for a telephone company, account 604, includes costs of salaries, supplies, and materials used in inspecting and reporting on conditions of the equipment; repairing central office equipment and batteries; routine work of operating equipment or disconnecting customers' lines in the central offices upon termination of service; employee training; supervision; and maintenance.

Not all salaries, materials and supplies, and supervisory and administrative costs are expensed. Parts of such expenditures are capitalized. For example, costs of construction of telephone plant include the cost of labor, materials and supplies, transportation, contract work, social security and property taxes, insurance, and overhead costs. These construction costs are included in the original cost of the plant and are to be depreciated. A common regulatory task is to ensure that such construction-related expenses are properly and fully capitalized and do not end up in current operating expense. By capitalizing such expenses, the future consumers receiving the service are responsible for and charged the costs of providing their service.

---

[17] *Acker* v. *U.S.*, 298 U.S. 426 (1936).

[18] *Chicago and Grand Trunk Railway* v. *Wellman*, 143 U.S. 339 (1892).

TABLE 4.5 Selected Operating and Maintenance Expense Accounts

CLASS A AND B Electric	CLASS A AND B Gas	CLASS A AND B Telephone

1. Power production expenses
  A. Steam power generation
    501 Fuel
    513 Maintenance of electric plant
  B. Nuclear power generation
    519 Coolants and water
    528 Maintenance supervision and
           engineering
  C. Hydraulic power generation
  D. Other power generation
  E. Purchased power expenses
    555 Purchased power
    556 System control and load dispatching
2. Transmission expense
    563 Overhead line expense
3. Distribution expenses
    586 Meter expenses
    595 Maintenance of line transformers
4. Customer accounts expenses
5. Customer service and informational expense
6. Sales expenses
7. Administrative and general expense
	1. Production expense
	  A. Manufactured gas production
	  B. Natural gas production expense
	    752 Gas wells expense
	    786 Maintenance of extraction and
	           refining equipment
	  C. Exploration and development expenses
	  D. Other gas supply expenses
	    800 Natural gas wellhead purchases
	    804 Natural gas city gate purchases
	2. Natural gas storage, terminaling and
	   processing expenses
	  A. Underground storage expenses
	  B. Other storage expenses
	  C. Liquified natural gas terminaling and
	     processing expenses
	3. Transmission expenses
	    852 Communication system expenses
	    864 Maintenance of compression station
	           equipment
	4. Distribution expenses
	    874 Mains and services expenses
	    892 Maintenance of services
	5. Customer accounts expenses
	6. Customer service and informational expenses
	7. Sales expense
	8. Administrative and general expense
	    924 Property insurance
	    928 Regulatory commission expense
		1. Maintenance expenses
		    602:1 Repair of pole lines
		    604 Repairs of central office equipment
		2. Traffic expenses
		    624 Operators' wages
		    632 Public telephone expenses
		3. Commercial expense
		    642 Advertising
		    649 Directory expenses
		4. General office salaries and expenses
		    662 Accounting department
		5. Other operating expenses
		    673 Telephone franchise requirements
		    674 General services and licenses

SOURCE: *Code of Federal Regulations* Title 47, October 1, 1978 (Washington, D.C.: U.S. Government Printing Office, 1978) pp. 240–241; Title 18, April 1, 1979 (Washington, D.C.: U.S. Government Printing Office, 1979) pp. 205–207, 388–389.

Annual depreciation expense is an important expense. Depreciation accounting in public utilities is a complex matter that received early attention in the courts. In the 1909 Knoxville Water Company v. Knoxville case,[19] the Supreme Court recognized depreciation as a legitimate expense item and as a measure of reduction in service value. The Court asserted that depreciation based on original cost is designed to keep the initial investment intact by recouping the expenditure over the service life. Among the causes of depreciation to be given consideration in establishing the amount of depreciation charge are wear and tear, deterioration, obsolescence, changes in demand, and requirements of public authorities.

Three general causes of depreciation are apparent—physical causes, functional causes, and contingent casualties. Physical causes include wear and tear resulting from use that cannot be repaired by maintenance, and nonuse-related deterioration from weather and time. Functional depreciation reflects such things as obsolescence, inadequacy, and requirements of public authorities. The physical state of the property may not have diminished, but its usefulness may have. Finally, contingent casualties not covered by insurance are a cause of depreciation. For example, traffic accidents involving telephone and electric poles and storm damage to lines may reduce the average life of these types of property.

Early attempts to use observed depreciation as an offset to reproduction cost reflected attempts to appraise the usefulness of utility plant. Depreciation resulting from functional causes and casualties was ignored. In order to be more comprehensive, depreciation based upon observed usefulness was replaced by depreciation based on time as measured by average useful life. Using time as a basis for depreciation allocates a *pro rata* share of investment to each time period in which the property can be expected to be used. In practice, the annual depreciation charge depends on the net or service value of the property (usually original cost minus estimated salvage value), the estimated property life (usually determined by engineering estimates), and the depreciation method employed to distribute the cost over the life of the property (typically the straight-line method).

In addition to the attempts to appraise usefulness, public service companies, particularly railroads, had adopted retirement cost rather than depreciation expense accounting. Under retirement cost accounting, replacements of property were expensed and only the cost of the original property remained on the balance sheet. The Interstate Commerce Commission rejected retirement cost in favor of depreciation expense early in the century. Retirement cost tended to make operating expense erratic and understated the balance sheet. The present use of depreciation expense, the recording at original costs of the replacements and additions and the

---

[19] 212 U.S. 13.

charging of retirements against plant in service and accumulated depreciation, stabilizes the income statement and keeps the balance sheet timely. Whether growth in services or inflation requires increased investment, the expense and rate base tracks such increases.

In 1930, the U.S. Supreme Court's *United Railways Electric Co.* v. *West* decision[20] calculated depreciation on reproduction cost. Justice Brandeis dissented and set forth what later came to be the standard concept of utility depreciation.[21] Justice Brandeis viewed the equitable allocation of the ascertainable original cost less salvage value over life as the proper measure of depreciation expense. In 1934, the U.S. Supreme Court's *Lindheimer* v. *Illinois Bell Telephone Co.* decision[22] restored depreciation based on costs and recognized the need to synchronize depreciation expense and accumulated depreciation. In the 1944 *Federal Power Commission* v. *Hope Natural Gas Co.* decision,[23] the U.S. Supreme Court accepted Justice Brandeis's and the Lindheimer view and overturned the majority opinion in the *United Railway* decision. The allocation of the original cost less salvage value over the expected period of use became the expected measure of depreciation expense. In 1943, the National Association of Railroad and Utilities Commissioners issued a report on depreciation that endorsed this measure of depreciation.

Uniform systems of accounts list retirement units. Retirement units are to be capitalized when installed. Their costs are depreciated over time and are retired at the end of their useful life. Expenditures for maintenance are directly expensed and are distinguished from retirement units.

Group depreciation instead of unit depreciation is generally used. Several units of property are recorded in a mass account, and the depreciation expense is determined for the account as a whole rather than for each individual unit within the account.

Application of straight-line depreciation by commissions uses this formula:

$$\text{Depreciation expense} = \frac{\text{Original cost} - \text{net salvage value}}{\text{Estimated service life}}$$

The numerator, the original cost less the net salvage value, is the service value. The net salvage value is the salvage value of the property less the cost of removal. The estimated service life is an average life. Not all property will last this long, but some will last longer. Historical data regarding the useful lives and the frequency of retirements are used to estimate average service life. For example, a unit of property that has a $5 million original

---

[20] 280 U.S. 234.

[21] 280 U.S. 255, 74 L. ed. 411.

[22] 320 U.S. 591.

[23] 51 PUR(NS) 202–3.

cost, a net salvage value of $200,000, and a 20-year estimated service life would have a $240,000 annual depreciation expense based on the straight-line method.

The depreciation expense is charged not only currently as an operating expense, but also accumulated as an offset to the original cost of the rate base. By the tenth year, the accumulated depreciation, in the above example, would be $2.4 million and rate base would be only $2.6 million. This treatment indicates that over the 10 years $2.4 million of the initial investment was restored to the investors.

Table 4.6 illustrates plant and depreciation accounting with a simple example. Initially the investment is recorded. Subsequently, depreciation is both expensed and accumulated. Upon retirement, the original cost is removed from the utility plant and accumulated depreciation accounts. Net salvage is also credited to accumulated depreciation to write off the entire original cost. Investors—who no longer have all their principal invested, it having been recovered—receive a return only on their remaining investment. The purpose of depreciation is to restore the loss of service value, not restored by currrent maintenance, incurred in connection with

TABLE 4.6 Accounting for Utility Plant

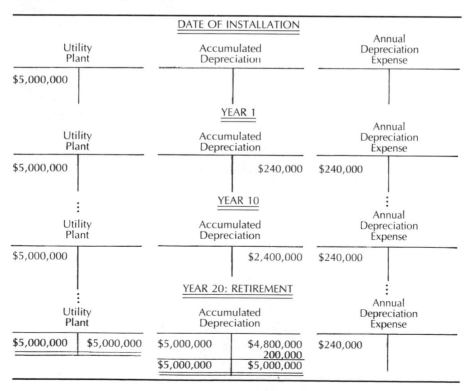

the use of utility plant to provide service, known to be caused by current operation, but not insured against. The service value restored through depreciation is the initial investment at its original cost, not the physical property itself.

TAXES, INCLUDING TAX DEPRECIATION

Public utilities, like other businesses, pay various taxes. These tax payments constitute the second element of the cost of service in the revenue requirement formula. The local, state, and federal taxes for which a utility is liable include income, property or *ad valorem*, gross receipts, franchise, capital stock, and unemployment and the employer's share of social security taxes. The various taxes included in the cost of service have different tax rates and tax bases for each kind of tax. In addition, the utility collects excise and sales taxes from customers and withholds the employees' income taxes and social security taxes. When accounting for the utility's own tax liabilities, *accrual* accounting is used. Under accrual accounting, tax expenses are recorded in the period when the tax liability is incurred, not when the tax is actually paid and the money expended. Utilities segregate income taxes from taxes other than income taxes and utility taxes from nonutility taxes. Taxes which the utility only collects are recorded as an account payable and are not expensed.

Public utilities are permitted to collect taxes through the rates they charge. In the 1922 *Galveston Electric Company* v. *Galveston* decision, the U.S. Supreme Court ruled:

> in calculating . . . a proper return, it is necessary to deduct from gross revenue the expenses and charges; and all taxes which would be payable if their return were earned are appropriate deductions. There is no difference in this respect between state and federal taxes, or between income taxes and others.[24]

Property taxes vary from state to state. Many states centrally administer utility property taxes. A central state board or department assesses utility property. The assessment is then allocated to the local taxing districts, or the state collects the property tax and the proceeds are distributed to the local authorities. Some states, however, permit local assessment of utility property. The result is that assessments differ or even overlap among local taxing authorities. Property-taxing authorities generally do not rely upon original cost as a tax base or property value. Also, such things as construction work in progress and inventories, which may be excluded from the rate base, may be valued in the property tax base.

Gross receipts taxes are taxes charged as a percentage of gross rev-

---

[24] 258 U.S. 399–400.

enues. No deductions are allowed for business expenses. The late Senator Metcalf of Montana proposed that a gross receipts tax be substituted for the federal income tax on utilities. A sales tax also would be charged as a percentage of gross revenues. Instead of the gross revenues of the utility, though, the sales revenues collected from each sale to a consumer serves as the tax base. The utility acts as a tax collector for sales tax, and the consumer incurs the sales tax liability rather than as the utility would under a gross receipts tax. Excise taxes are also levied on sales. A federal excise tax on telephone service was only being phased out in the early 1980s.

The social security tax rate for the calendar year 1980 was 6.13 percent for both employer and employee. The wage base limitation was $25,900 in 1980. The federal unemployment tax rate for 1979 was 3.4 percent on the first $6,000 of cash wages paid to each employee during the calendar year. The tax was imposed on the employer and could not be collected or deducted from the wages of the employee. A credit against the federal unemployment tax of up to 2.7 percent could be taken for payments for state unemployment taxes. Since a tax base ceiling applies to these wage taxes, increases in wages and salaries over the maximum do not cause increased tax expenses. *Pro forma* adjustments to annualize labor contracts will include both the increased wages and the increased employment taxes. Because of the maximum tax base, however, employment taxes adjustments may not be strictly proportional to wage increase.

Franchise taxes are taxes by local authorities for granting the utility the right to serve or to use public facilities and rights of way. Commissions frequently require such local franchise taxes to be charged only to the residents of the area levying the tax. To require all customers of a utility to pay the franchise tax is discriminatory. Some localities also have required free service as consideration for a franchise. Such free service has, for many years, also been considered a discriminatory utility rate. Many states impose a general franchise tax on a corporation's privilege to do business. This tax is often levied on the value of a corporation's capital stock.

State and federal corporate income taxes raise the most significant tax issues in rate cases. The corporate income tax uses business income as the tax base. But taxable business income usually differs from the book business income of the utility. These differences arise from the use of consolidated tax returns for affiliated utilities and other corporations, from timing differences between the use of the accelerated depreciation for tax calculation and straight-line depreciation for book purposes, from the current tax deductibility of capitalized expenses and interest paid during construction, and from nontaxable utility income in the form of the allowance for funds used during construction. The rate-making treatment of investment tax credits, which directly reduce taxes paid, is another important tax issue. The following discussion deals with the issues of consolidated income tax returns, the timing differences between accelerated depreciation and book depreciation, and the investment tax credit. The other tax issues cited are of smaller magnitude and are reducible to the question of what is the actual tax cost incurred by the utility.

The presumption is that a consolidated tax return is filed by affiliated corporations because tax savings result. If all affiliates participating in a consolidated return have a positive taxable income, the total income tax can be allocated on the basis of the taxable income of each of the affiliates. But when one or more of the affiliates has a loss, the question arises as to whether to allocate the actual taxes to affiliates in proportion to their taxable income, or whether to first allocate negative taxes to the loss companies and then allocate to the affiliates the total income taxes that would have been paid at the full statutory rate in the absence of the tax loss. The former alternative recovers only the actual taxes, while the latter method allocates to the profitable affiliates income taxes that exceed the actual tax cost.

A nonregulated holding company or nonutility affiliate may be one of the loss companies included in the consolidated tax return with a utility. Several pure holding companies, particularly in the independent telephone industry, are permanent loss companies. These holding companies have both tax deductible interest expense and general corporate costs, but generally tax-exempt dividends from subsidiaries are their major revenue source. These holding companies will regularly have a tax loss. The tax savings therefrom reduce the actual income tax cost and correspondingly lower the effective income tax rate of the subsidiaries. The effective income tax rate has been used to calculate subsidiary tax costs.

The U.S. Supreme Court in the 1967 *Federal Power Commission* v. *United Gas Pipe Line Co.* decision addressed the question of net losses from unregulated affiliates.[25] The court found that if losses of the unregulated companies exceed their net income so as to reduce the taxes of the regulated utilities, the actual consolidated taxes paid should be allocated among the regulated utilities in proportion to their taxable incomes. This tax saving serves to reduce the utility's taxes included in the cost of service.

Two principal areas of depreciation relate to the tax bill. The first has been the regulatory handling of accelerated depreciation, permissible under the Revenue Act of 1954, with the objective of encouraging capital investment. The other is Asset Depreciation Range (ADR) Guideline Lives, which permits tax lives less than the accounting lives for utility plants. Since public utilities, like other firms, are permitted to adopt accelerated depreciation and ADR Guideline Lives for tax purposes, the question arises of whether or not the resulting tax saving should be allowed as an operating expense.

Table 4.7 illustrates the difference between the accelerated tax depreciation expense for double-declining-balance and sum-of-years-digits

---

[25] 386 U.S. 237, 18 L. ed. 2d 18.

TABLE 4.7 A Comparison of Accelerated and Straight-Line Depreciation Expense

Year	DEPRECIATION EXPENSE		
	Straight Line	Double-Declining Balance	Sum-of-Years Digits
1	$ 100	$200	$ 182
2	100	160	164
3	100	128	145
4	100	102	127
5	100	82	109
6	100	66	91
7	100	52	73
8	100	42	55
9	100	34	36
10	100	27	18
Total depreciation	$1000	$893	$1000

depreciation methods and straight-line book depreciation expense. The example considers an asset with a cost of $1000, a ten-year life, and no salvage value. The double-declining-balance method differs from the straight-line method in that the depreciation rate is double the straight-line rate, 20 percent as opposed to 10 percent. However, the depreciation taken in each year is subtracted from the cost of the property before calculating the next year's depreciation. Thus, a larger depreciation deduction is taken for the first year and a gradually smaller deduction in each following year. The remaining undepreciated balance at the end of the 10-year period, $107, could be expensed in the last year or earlier by switching to straight-line depreciation of the remaining undepreciated cost. For example, in Table 4.7 the utility may switch to straight-line depreciation in year 7. Thereafter, the straight-line remaining life depreciation expense, $65.50, exceeds the double-declining-balance depreciation expense. The sum-of-years method is another form of accelerated depreciation permitted for tax purposes. Its rate is calculated by the ratio of the years remaining to the sum of all the year's digits. In Table 4.7, the first year has a depreciation rate of 10/55, the second year 9/55, the third year 8/55, and so on to the tenth year, 1/55. The depreciation rate is applied to the original cost minus the salvage value of the asset.

Since only the original cost can be charged off for income tax purposes, accelerated depreciation does not affect the total taxes paid over the life of an individual investment, but it does affect the timing of the annual tax payments. The adoption of accelerated depreciation means that the firm may write off a disproportionately large amount during the early years of the service and a correspondingly lower proportion in later years. Therefore, in early years taxable income and the annual tax payment will be lower, but in later years it will be higher. This amounts to a tax-free loan to the utility in the early years and benefits the utility because they have use of these funds for a time for capital investment purposes before they actually must be paid. But if the firm continues to reinvest or to grow, the tax deductions will continue to be greater under accelerated depreciation than under straight-line depreciation, resulting in a permanent tax saving to the utility.

The effect of accelerated depreciation on the public utility depends to a large extent on how commissions react to the utility's tax depreciation charge. Two methods have been used by commissions to deal with accelerated tax depreciation. Under the *normalization method*, commissions treat accelerated depreciation as a deferment of taxes, not a permanent tax saving. A reserve for deferred taxes is established and credited in each period with the difference between the annual tax bill under accelerated depreciation (actually paid) and the hypothetical amount paid had straight-line depreciation been employed. This hypothetical tax is treated as an allowable service cost, resulting in no change in operating costs from what would have been the case under straight-line depreciation. The question of whether utilities should be permitted a return on the cumulative reserve for deferred taxes is another matter. Most commissions deduct the tax reserve from the rate base or include it in the cost of capital calculation as zero cost capital. The public utility therefore obtains no return from the consumer-contributed capital represented by the deferred tax reserve.

Other commissions advocate and some require the *flow-through method*. With the view that only a current tax liability is a legitimate charge against a utility's customers, some commissions use flow-through accounting, treating the tax actually paid as the cost of service. If the general rate level is adjusted to reflect the lower tax payments, this procedure gives the full benefit of accelerated depreciation to current utility customers through lower initial rates. Future customers will have to bear higher tax payments if the utility investment should ever decline. However, a declining utility could switch to straight-line depreciation for tax purposes and further postpone the taxes. Also, when such utilities as street railways declined in the past, they had little income. It would be surprising if a declining utility would have taxable income in any case.

The second major tax issue involves the investment tax credit. Any firm can deduct from its current federal income tax bill a predetermined percentage of its new investment under the Revenue Act of 1962. For rate-making purposes, two questions arise: (1) Should this tax benefit accrue to company owners or to utility customers? (2) Should the tax saving be normalized and returned to the consumer over the life of the property or in the current year by the flow-through method? The Revenue Act of 1964 restricted the federal regulatory commissions' ability to flow through the tax savings from investment tax credits. While the 1962 act reduced the depreciation base by the amount of the investment tax credit, the 1964 act provided that the depreciation base not be reduced by the amount of the investment tax credit. The Tax Reform Act of 1969 ended the investment tax credit for a time. The U.S. Revenue Act of 1971 restored the investment tax credit as the Job Development Investment Credit. However, for a utility to be eligible for the Job Development Investment Credit, the tax savings realized were to be normalized and returned to the consumer over the life of the asset. The Tax Reduction Act of 1975 raised the investment tax credit rate from 4 percent to 10 percent, with an additional 1 percent tax credit permitted if the utility has an employee stock option plan.

By requiring normalization, the 1971 act generated capital for the utility. Taxes were collected that were not paid, in turn, to the U.S. Treasury. If the post-1971 investment tax credits had been treated as normalized tax savings from accelerated depreciation, the rate base would have been reduced by the amount of customer-contributed capital and the utility would derive no return on the customer-contributed capital. However, many utilities selected eligibility for the investment tax credit under option 2, which did not permit reduction of rate base. Under this option, customers receive the tax savings in lowered rates over the life of the assets. In the meantime, the growing utility collects even more investment tax credits paid by the consumer on which a return is earned.

The California Public Service Commission and state Supreme Court challenged the normalization requirement by continuing that state's long-standing policy of flowing through the tax savings from the investment tax credit. Whether the use of flow-through in California denies the investment tax credit to California utilities and leads to recapture of past investment tax credits taken by California utilities is not yet answered.

The U.S. Treasury and the utilities' advocacy of tax normalization of earning a return on a rate base financed by investment tax credits and general opposition to flow-through is understandable. The utility gains substantial cost-free financing that may be used at management's discretion. An excess return accruing to the stockholder is also earned by the failure to deduct the investment tax credit from the rate base. The U.S. Treasury's interests are also served, for taxable income and taxes paid are greater than under flow-through. A utility that normalizes the investment tax credit will include in the cost of service $2 of revenues for every $1 of investment tax credit charged by the utility. Likewise, requiring a return on the investment tax credit requires $2 of revenue for every $1 in earnings. Normalization of accelerated depreciation likewise requires $2 of revenues for each $1 of tax savings. The additional revenues raised by normalization and the investment tax credit increase the utility's corporate taxable income above the amount it would be if tax savings were flowed through.

Although unregulated corporations generally cannot shift all their taxes forward to the consumer, the tax decision in the Galveston case makes utilities an exception.[26] The Galveston decision effectively permits the utility to compute its income taxes after imputing cost of equity and to shift the taxes onto the consumer.

Local property and other taxes on utilities are likely to be exported outside the taxing authorities' jurisdiction. Other localities served by the utility or even the market areas of the utility's industrial and commercial customers incur part of the burden of the tax. Centralized state assessments and taxation of utilities should ameliorate this tendency of local authorities to export property taxes. State authorities, however, have opportunities to export the taxes of utilities that serve multistate territories.

Since the ratio of taxes to operating revenues in 1978 was 22, 9, and 17 percent for telephone, gas, and electric utilities, respectively, the taxation of utilities is a major rate case issue. The Galveston decision made the utility little more than the stakes holder. However, recent federal tax law has made utility companies net beneficiaries of the income tax statutes.

In order to minimize consumer rates, the utility commissions should require a utility to avail itself of all tax savings available to it. Should tax savings not be taken by the utility, the utility commission has an obligation to impute such savings to reduce the cost of service. During the rate case, the utility's claimed taxes ought to be reviewed closely. Tax overaccruals by utilities should not overstate actual taxes and increase the cost of service. The discrepancies between the tax base and book amounts must be recognized if claimed taxes are to be accurately reviewed. Likewise, both the tax rate and the tax base must be ascertainable for known and measurable changes to tax costs during the test period to be made accurately.

THE RATE BASE

The final element in the cost-of-service equation is the cost of securing and maintaining money capital for utility investment. This is the combined after-tax (corporate) return to all capital suppliers, including bondholders, preferred stockholders, and common stockholders. It is calculated as the product of the rate base $(V - D)$ and the allowed rate of return (R). We will consider each of these components in turn.

The rate base $(V - D)$ is composed primarily of the investment in utility plant in service. Lesser amounts of investment for working capital, certain plant held for future use, and sometimes intangible assets are included. Taken together, they approximate investor capital in the business. Consumers also at times provide limited amounts of capital. Generally, investors are not permitted a return on customer-contributed capital.

The question of "reasonableness" of a rate base determination was

---

[26] *Galveston Electric Co.* v. *Galveston*, 258 U.S. 388 (1922).

an early problem that plagued rate making. The original statement on standards of reasonableness was given in 1898 by the U.S. Supreme Court in *Smythe* v. *Ames*,[27] a decision which influenced rate decisions for nearly half a century. The Court held:

> The basis of all calculations as to the reasonableness of rates . . . must be the fair value of the property being used . . . for the convenience of the public. . . . The company is entitled to ask for a fair return upon the value of that which it employs for the public convenience . . . while the public is entitled to demand . . . that no more be extracted from it . . . than the services . . . are reasonably worth.[28]

The Court failed, however, to define fair return on fair value. According to *Smythe* v. *Ames*, a number of factors were to be considered in valuing property:

1. The original cost of construction
2. Expenditures for permanent improvements
3. The present as compared with the original cost of construction
4. The amount and market value of the stocks and bonds
5. The probable earning capacity
6. The amount of operating expenses

It was soon recognized the latter three factors were faulty. The market value of securities depended upon earnings which, in turn, depended upon the existing rate levels. Likewise, operating expenses affect capital values only by increasing or decreasing the earnings at given rate levels. These three methods failed to recognize that utility rates are determined by the rate-making proceeding and therefore cannot be used as the basis for setting the same rates. The other three factors then came to the forefront. The first two jointly became known as the *original cost* or *investment standard*. The third factor became known as the *reproduction cost standard*. Reproduction costs either relied upon an inventory and appraisal of existing plant or a trending of the original cost to current price levels to value the rate base. Offsetting the reproduction costs were observed depreciation estimates. The observed depreciation estimate attempted to ascertain the current usefulness of the utility plant relative to its usefulness when new. To further their interests, utilities invariably exaggerated reproduction costs and minimized observed depreciation.

Among the elements to be considered in ascertaining fair value, the Court included the original cost of the property and the present cost of construction (now known as reproduction cost). Each of these elements

---

[27] 169 U.S. 466.
[28] *Smyth* v. *Ames*, pp. 546–557.

was to be given an appropriate weight which was "just and right" in each case. Thus, the lines were drawn for the rate-base battles that followed. After the World War I price rises, commissions usually sought original-cost valuations, while utilities wanted reproduction cost valuations which were higher because of inflation. The Court decisions that followed invariably required commissions to give substantial weight to reproduction costs, typically computed by estimating the construction and equipment costs of utility property in terms of current prices and then deducting observed depreciation.

The bright spot in this period was Justice Brandeis's concurrence in the Southwestern Bell case in 1923.[29] Justice Brandeis, long experienced in utility regulation, pointed out the inaccuracy, unreliability, and time-consuming nature of reproduction cost estimates. Also, he pointed out that in periods of declining prices, reproduction cost could jeopardize the payment of interest and dividends. For example, if the rate base were valued at $1 million and had a capital cost of 10 percent, some $100,000 would be the required return. A 10 percent drop in the price level, reducing reproduction cost to $900,000, would allow only $90,000 toward interest and dividends though the fixed charges would not decline. Assuming a 60 percent debt ratio, a 2.5 percent reduction in equity rate of return would occur. Losses and bankruptcy would be likely. The result is that utility companies historically have advocated the higher of original cost or reproduction cost. A converse problem of excessive returns to equity exists when reproduction cost rises higher than original cost. All of a reproduction cost increase of 10 percent over original cost accrues to the common equity owner. Therefore, assuming a 60 percent debt ratio, the excess rate of return to equity is 2.5 percent.

During the 1930s, the Court's reliance on reproduction cost in rate-base determinations was diminished and finally in the 1944 landmark case, *FPC* v. *Hope Natural Gas Co.*,[30] the Court completely severed its long-standing ties with reproduction cost and set forth the "end-result doctrine." In upholding the FPC's use of an original cost rate base, Justice Douglas stated:

> Under the statutory standard of "just and reasonable" it is the result reached and not the method employed which is controlling. It is not the theory but the impact of the rate order which counts. If the total effect of the rate order cannot be said to be unjust and unreasonable, judicial inquiry . . . is at an end.[31]

---

[29] 262 U.S. 276.

[30] 320 U.S. 591.

[31] 320 U.S. 602.

Abandoning the fair value doctrine, the Hope decision ushered in commission discretion and judgment of widely increased scope. Although some commissions continued to use the reproduction rate-base standard, many commissions opted for historical cost methods. These historical cost methods include the original cost method, which allows only the cost of utility property when first devoted to public service less accrued depreciation in the rate base; the prudent investment method, in which the depreciated historical cost of utility property less any amount found to be "dishonest or obviously wasteful" is included; and the historical cost method, wherein the historical cost found in public utility records is used in the rate base. The use of historical cost methods works to simplify the administrative difficulties in rate-base determination and eliminates instability in the rate base.

It was Justice Jackson's separate opinion in *Hope* that set out the prudent or historical investment rate base. This opinion stated:

> The prudent investment theory has relative merits in fixing rates for a utility which creates its service merely by its investments. The amount and quality of service rendered by the usual utility will, at least roughly, be measured by the amount of capital it puts into the enterprise. But it has no rational application where there is no such relationship between investment and capacity to serve.[32]

Justice Brandeis, to whom Justice Jackson attributed the prudent investment concept, had in the Southwestern Bell case defined investment to be:

> The thing devoted by the investor to the public use is not specific property, tangible and intangible, but capital embarked in the enterprise.[33]

Most commissions opted for the historical or original cost rate base. The property illusion that so hampered reproduction cost was discarded and the investment standard was adopted. The discarded concept of capital as material objects emphasized the disparity between prices in the past and in the present. The investment or original cost standard, however, emphasized current transactions between the public utility and investors. An emphasis on the principal invested in the public utility replaced the emphasis on physical property.

Rate base includes a number of major components. Of greatest importance is plant in service. Except in the few states—such as Indiana, Missouri, North Carolina, and Illinois—which continue to rely upon re-

---

[32] 51 PUR(NS) 227.
[33] 262 U.S. 276.

production cost or fair value, the original cost is used. As pointed out above, the original cost is the money cost to the utility when first devoted to public service. Some small amount of this cost will be offset by contributions in aid of construction, nonrefundable amounts which utilities have charged consumers for installing abnormally costly or extensive facilities. The major offset to plant in service in the rate base is accumulated depreciation. Other offsets to the rate base include refundable customer advances for construction, certain deferred income taxes resulting from accelerated depreciation, and pre-1971 investment tax credits and customer deposits.

One of the more controversial rate-base issues has been whether or not to include construction work in progress in the rate base. Construction work in progress (or CWIP) is the investment in plant under construction. Its inclusion can lead to a mismatch of rate base with revenues and expenses and to the inclusion of property not used and useful in the rate base. Some jurisdictions have included CWIP in rate bases. Others follow more traditional rate making and do not include CWIP. The allowance for funds used during construction has been developed to permit the capital costs the utility has during the construction period to be compensated by the future consumer actually to be served by the plant under construction. The cost of capital used in financing the construction is capitalized; i.e., the original cost of the plant recorded on the utility's books includes capital changes and other overheads. The Federal Energy Regulatory Commission provides in its uniform system of accounts that the costs of short-term debt should be applied to construction first. If the short-term debt is not sufficient to cover the amount of construction work in progress, the weighted cost of long-term financing is then applied to the remaining amount of construction.

The use of an allowance for funds used during construction is less costly than is construction work in progress. An allowance for funds used during construction does not produce taxable income to the utility. Rather, the taxable income results in higher book depreciation charges and more earnings in later years when the plant is used and useful. Allowing a return on construction work in progress does create taxable income, on the other hand. As a result, $1 of equity return earned on construction work in progress increases the cost of service by $2. A tax deferral accompanies the allowance for funds used during construction, which makes this method of recovering capital costs during construction less costly than the inclusion of construction work in progress in the rate base.

A part of the rate base is not for investment in property but for investment in working capital. Working capital allowance in the rate base includes investor-contributed capital needed for cash balances to meet expenses as they come due, prepayments such as insurance premiums, materials and supplies inventories, and minimum or compensating bank balances. To ascertain the net investment by investors in working capital, the gross working capital requirement must be offset by customer-contributed working capital. Investors require a return only on their investment in working capital. Use of customer-contributed working capital does not incur a cost for the utility.

Cash working capital is the amount of money necessary to meet bills as they come due between the rendition of service and the receipt of revenues therefrom. One method of determining gross cash working capital has been to include 45 days of average daily cash expenses—i.e., operating expenses *less* depreciation—in working capital. However, since utilities billing monthly average 15 days between delivery of services and billing date, this rule of thumb assumes that 30 days elapse before the utility customer pays the bill. A shorter period is much more often found in fact.

The utility's vendors do not require payment at the time services are rendered and expenses are incurred. The utility will be billed by its supplier, and in due course the bills are paid. As a result, a lead-lag study can measure this cash working-capital requirement more accurately than a 45-day rule of thumb. Using lead-lag studies, cash balances need only amount to a few days or weeks. For example, the telephone industry, by billing local service in advance, needs little if any investor-contributed working capital.

Since utility accounting relies on an accrual rather than a cash basis, other offsets to working capital result. For example, utility rates include receipts to cover accrued taxes. But not until months later are the actual cash payments for taxes made. In the meantime, the cash is in the hands of the utility. Average accrued property taxes and state and federal income taxes, as well as accrued interest and preferred stock dividends, are therefore sources of customer-contributed capital that provide cost-free working capital to the utility.

Table 4.8 provides an example of the determination of a working capital allowance. This example displays a negative working capital. A negative working capital allowance indicates that the receipts from customers provide more than enough cash to meet the utility's bills as they come due and to finance the utility's inventories and prepayments.

From time to time, a utility will borrow from banks. A common practice of banks is to negotiate with the utility a requirement that the utility maintain bank balances equal to from 10 to 20 percent of the loan. This is called a *compensating* balance. The effective interest rate to the utility on the loan is inflated by this practice. The interest cost is calculated on 100 percent of the loan, while only 80 to 90 percent of the loan can be used by the utility. Utilities generally fail to bargain for fees in lieu of minimum or compensating bank balances. Banks negotiate such fees for a minority of the loans they make. Where the utility pays such fees, lower costs typically result because a tax deduction is created that is not available if

TABLE 4.8 Working Capital Allowance in Rate Base

		Amount
Material and supplies inventories		$10,000
Prepayments		300
Cash working capital		
Operation and maintenance expense		
Revenue lag	$ 4,000	
Expense lead	(1,300)	
Subtotal	2,700	
Accrued income taxes	(2,300)	
Accrued property taxes	(10,000)	
Accrued interest	(2,100)	
Preferred stock dividends	(200)	
Total		
Cash working capital		(11,900)
Total working capital		($1,600)

minimum or compensating bank balances are added to the rate base. Further, claimed minimum or compensating bank balances may be overstated. The bank balances on the bank ledgers should be covered partly or entirely by the utility's bank float. Speedy check clearing for utility receipts and cautious processing of the utility's own payments by checks, or the warrants used by the Bell System, would maximize bank float. Positive float results in greater balances on the bank ledger than are shown on the books of the utility. The effect of this larger bank balance owing to the utility's float is partially to offset the compensating balance requirement.

Certain items are also excluded from or not permitted in the rate base. We will look at a few of these. At one time, it was believed that an operating utility had a value greater than the sum of the values of the constituent property of the utility—i.e., the utility had a going concern value. Presently, going concern value is not included in the rate base. Acquisition adjustments, the amount paid for utility property in excess of original cost, are also excluded from the rate base. Extraordinary retirements of property are another exclusion. Property whose cost was improperly charged in earlier periods is already recovered and cannot be claimed again in the rate base.

Rate base determination remains a debated issue, though less controversial than when reproduction cost and fair value rate base were relied upon. Original cost has made rate base calculation much more precise and systematic. Since capital costs are the product of the rate of return and the rate base, much of the controversy has shifted to the determination of the rate of return. While a 10 percent deviation from the original cost rate base might stand out in a rate case, an increase in the rate of return of 10 percent, say, from 9 to 9.9 percent, is more easily concealed. With 40 percent equity in the capital structure, the 2.25 percentage point increase in return on equity in this example, a difference commonly found in rate cases, can be argued. Significant differences in the capital costs in the revenue requirement thus remain an issue as a result of the rate of return. Financing methods, such as holding companies, and varied approaches to determining equity costs became important areas of dispute. We now turn, in the following section as well as in Appendix B, to the determination of this rate of return component.

RATE OF RETURN

The allowed return to capital suppliers is neither the rate base alone nor solely the allowed rate of return; rather, it is the product of the two. Commissions heedful of one and mindless of the other are likely to produce poor judgments. Following the Smythe (1898) decision, little attention was given the fair rate of return the U.S. Supreme Court espoused; instead, a conventional 6 percent or so was considered proper. In the Bluefield Water Works case (1923), however, a first pass at standards for a reasonable rate of return was set forth. The Court stated:

> What annual rate will constitute just compensation depends upon many circumstances and must be determined by the exercise of a fair and enlightened judgement, having regard to all relevant facts. A public utility is entitled to such rates as will permit it to earn a return on the value of the property which it employs for the convenience of the public equal to that generally being made at the same time and in the same general part of the country on investments in other business undertakings which are attended by corresponding risks and uncertainties; but it has no constitutional right to profits such as are realized or anticipated in highly profitable enterprises or speculative ventures. The return should be reasonably sufficient to assure confidence in the financial soundness of the utility, and should be adequate, under efficient and economical management, to maintain and support its credit and enable it to raise the money necessary for the proper discharge of its public duties. A rate of return may be reasonable at one time, and become too high or too low by changes affecting opportunities for investment, the money market, and business conditions generally.[34]

The Court indicated that the terms and security prices investors bargain for in the financial markets when contracting for debt and preferred stock and when investing in common stock are principal factors in establishing rates of return. The Court stated:

> Investors take into account the result of past operations, especially in recent years, when determining the terms upon which they will invest in such an undertaking.

---

[34] 262 U.S. 67 L. ed. 1182–3.

Low, uncertain, or irregular income makes for low prices for the securities of the utility and higher rates of interest to be demanded by investors. The fact that the company may not insist as a matter of constitutional right that past losses be made up by rates to be applied in the present and future tends to weaken credit, and the fact that the utility is protected against being compelled to serve for confiscatory rates tends to support it.[35]

No reference is made to earned returns on book value of other businesses besides the Bluefield Water Works Company. However, the point of reference between the rate of return to utilities and to other enterprises is the financial markets, where the prices of the various securities balance the risk and the returns of investment in the utility against other businesses.

In subsequent years, the rates of return allowed by commissions were not confined to the conventional 6 percent rate of return. During the 1930s, the earnings-price ratio began to be used as a reference in determining the cost of common equity. The Hope case restated and emphasized two standards of reasonableness found in *Bluefield* which are often cited in rate-of-return regulation. In the words of the Court in *Hope*:

> The return to the equity owner should be commensurate with returns on investments in other enterprises having corresponding risks. That return, moreover, should be sufficient to assure confidence in the financial integrity of the enterprise, so as to maintain its credit and attract capital.[36]

The first statement, though reiterating the market investment in securities cited in *Bluefield*, gave rise to what is known by some as the "comparable earnings" standard; the second statement established the "capital attraction" standard.

In both the Federal Power Commission's and the U.S. Supreme Court's Hope decisions, there is in fact a marked lack of reliance upon comparable earnings on book value. Later readers claimed to have found the "comparable earnings" standard in the words of the Court.

One author has summarized well both interpretations that have accompanied the comparable earnings and capital attraction readings of the Hope decision:

> Those who advocate the traditional approach read the Hope decision in a particular way, namely:
>
> > The return to the equity owner should be commensurate with (*recent book*) returns on (*past*) investments (*made by*) other enterprises having corresponding risks.
>
> This approach rests on a special notion of opportunity cost—in this context,

---

[35] Ibid., p. 1183.

[36] *Federal Power Commission* v. *Hope Natural Gas Co.*, 320 U.S. 591, 603 (1944).

that a utility should be allowed to earn what it would have earned had its capital been invested in other firms of comparable risk.

The alternative suggested by finance theory is to define "commensurate" return as the rate of return investors anticipate when they purchase equity shares of comparable risks. This is a *market* rate of return, defined in terms of anticipated dividends and capital gains relative to stock prices.[37]

Not only is the alternative market cost of equity suggested by finance theory, the Bluefield decision made specific the link of commensurate returns to security prices, not book values.

In the 1968 Permian Basin Area Rate Cases decision, the U.S. Supreme Court expanded upon the Hope decision by stating:

> The Court in *Hope* found appropriate criteria by inquiring whether "the return to the equity owner (is) commensurate with returns on investments in other enterprises having corresponding risks," and whether the return was "sufficient to assure confidence in the financial integrity of the enterprise, so as to maintain its credit and to attract capital." . . . These criteria . . . remain pertinent, but they scarcely exhaust the relevant considerations.

> The Commission cannot confine its inquiries either to the computation of costs of service or to conjectures about prospective responses of the capital markets; it is instead obliged at each step of its regulatory process to assess the requirements of the broad public interests entrusted to its protection by Congress. Accordingly, the "end-result" of the Commission's orders must be measured as much by the success with which they protect those interests as by the effectiveness with which they "maintain credit . . . and . . . attract capital."[38]

The Court further extricated itself from the substantive issues of rate making while limiting its review to the procedural review of due process. Having freed itself from the substantive choice between a fair value or reproduction cost rate base and historical original cost rate base in the Hope case, in the Permian Basin Area Rate cases, the Court freed itself from attempting to make substantive decisions regarding the rate of return or the method used to establish the rate of return. Rather, a procedural standard was established. The Court specifically stated:

> The court must determine whether the order may reasonably be expected to maintain financial integrity, attract necessary capital, and fairly compensate investors for risks they have assumed, and yet provide appropriate protection to the relevant public interests, both existing and foreseeable. The court's responsibility is not to supplant the Commission's balance of these interests with one more nearly to its liking, but instead to assure itself that the Com-

---

[37] Stewart C. Meyers, "The Application of Finance Theory to Public Utility Rate Cases," *The Bell Journal of Economics and Management Science*, 3, 1 (spring 1972), 62.

[38] 390 U.S. 747, 20 L. ed. 349–350.

mission has given reasoned consideration to each of the pertinent factors. Judicial review of the Commission's orders will therefore function accurately and efficaciously only if the Commission indicates fully and carefully the methods by which, and the purposes for which, it has chosen to act, as well as its assessment of the consequences of its orders for the character and future development of the industry.[39]

No particular method or rate of return is required by the U.S. Supreme Court. Rather, the Court has given commissions wide latitude in the choice of a method by which to determine a rate of return. What is the standard set forth in the Bluefield, Hope, and Permian Basin decisions? The standard is that the end result—the net operating income—may be associated and be shown to be associated with the protection of the broad public interest entrusted to a commission by the legislature.

Various methods of implementing these standards have been sought. To utilize the comparable earnings standard, utilities have used rate-case testimony which shows the rate of return earned on the book value of common equity over some past time period by other regulated and unregulated firms or industries with similar, and not infrequently dissimilar, risk characteristics. The utilities consider this level of return as the reasonable rate of return on their capital. Problems exist in use of the comparable earnings standard in rate-case testimony. First, it is difficult to define comparable risk or to get agreement on firms or industries, particularly in the unregulated sector, that are comparable in risk to the utility whose rate of return is being considered. A second problem is related to comparing the rate of return of one utility with others because of circularity that results when one commission bases its decisions on those of other commissions whose methods and standards of regulation are different. Still another problem is that the data being compared are for a past time period, when economic conditions may have been different. Finally, accounting rates of return may be inaccurate in many cases. The accounting treatment used by nonutilities of many intangible assets, such as research and development, goodwill and promotional advertising, and the incentive to maximize expenses for tax purposes lead to understated capitalization and periodically overstated expenses. Also, firms that over time receive returns inferior to a normal return will quickly drop by the wayside, while firms receiving superior returns will continue to appear in financial statistics. As a result, the comparable earnings on book returns data are skewed to exceed a normal return on investment. Moreover, the economically relevant internal rate of return will only be approximated by the accounting rate of return in two cases: one, if the cost of capital is earned in each year; and two, if an average accounting rate of return is taken over a very long

[39] Ibid., p. 350.

period of time. Although these problems exist, many utilities and others continue to use the comparable earnings test in their rate-case testimony.

In view of the problems inherent in the comparable earnings test, many practitioners and academicians agree that the primary standard to be used is the capital attraction or market standard. Utilities are capital-intensive and have a continual need for new capital. As such, they need a rate of return that enables them to attract new capital on terms that are fair to both new and existing investors. Therefore, in rate proceedings commission staffs and, less frequently, utilities often have experts present testimony on their behalf based on the capital attraction standard.

Rate of return estimates found in rate proceedings are a weighted average of the cost of debt, the cost of preferred stock, and the required return on common equity capital. The costs of all outstanding debt and preferred stock for the utility are each weighted by the portion of that type of capital in the total capitalization. Book-valued weights are commonly used, not the market-valued weights.

Regulators and utilities are commonly in general agreement regarding the costs of debt and preferred stock. Disagreements regarding such related costs as amortization of issuance expense, net discount and premium, and the current portions of long-term debt do arise. But, in the estimation of the required return on equity capital, the harmony ends and the relative disagreement intensifies. In essence, the utility can attract equity capital from investors only if the utility offers them a fair and reasonable return on their investment, as measured by investors' standards. Identifying what return the equity investor requires is not a precise measurement. This contrasts sharply with return on debt capital and preferred stock, where an agreement is reached between the investor and the utility at the time of purchase. Therefore, determination of the return required on common equity capital is by far the most controversial aspect of the rate of return determination. The utility presents "in-house" and outside expert witnesses to make recommendations. Frequently, the commission hires a staff or an outside expert to testify. Intervenors, representing special consumer interests, also present expert witnesses.

Methods used to obtain equity return estimates vary from expert to expert and case to case. Included among these are the discounted cash flow technique, comparable earnings, risk premiums of the cost of equity over debt, earnings-price ratios, debt-equity ratios, simulations, regression analysis, and, more recently, analysis of the utility's Beta coefficient (see Appendix B to this chapter for a discussion of three of these techniques). There is no one universally accepted rule for calculating the return on equity capital, although several techniques have been used.

The discounted cash flow method, developed in the 1950s and first applied to utilities in the 1960s, has gained increasingly wide use in recent years. The Federal Energy Regulatory Commission, the best-known adherent of the comparable earnings method, also used the discounted cash flow method in 1978. In this case, the commission found that

> market oriented techniques, including the Discounted Cash Flow (DCF) approach, were useful in this regard. We observed that the DCF approach examines evidence regarding expectations of investors, which are critical in determining the attractiveness of a company's securities in accordance with *FPC* v. *Hope Natural Gas Co.*, 320 U.S. 591, 603 (1944); *Bluefield Water Works* v. *P.S.C.*, 262 U.S. 679, 692–693 (1923).[40]

Though no witness employed a DCF method, the data in the record enabled the commission to employ the method. This method, described in detail in Appendix B, indicates that current market cost of common equity equals

$$\frac{\text{Dividend per share}}{\text{Current market price per share}} + \text{Current growth rate}$$

Using an average market price of $17.53 per share and a dividend of $1.535 per share produced a current dividend yield of 8.76 percent. Estimates of geometric rates of growth in the utility's per share dividends, earnings, and book value over spans of time of 10 years and less, when added to the estimated dividend yield, resulted in a cost of equity estimate from 12.8 to 14.2 percent.

The allowed rate of return is computed as a weighted average of individual rates on debt, preferred stock, and common stock. This might be done as in the cost of capital in Table 4.9.

TABLE 4.9   Illustration of a Cost of Capital Calculation

SOURCE OF CAPITAL	PERCENTAGE OF TOTAL CAPITALIZATION	RATE OF RETURN	WEIGHTED RATE OF RETURN
Debt	45%	7.0%	3.15%
Preferred	5	8.0	0.40
Common stock	50	13.0	6.50
Total	100%		10.05%

Thus a 10.05 percent allowed rate of return is calculated.

A brief explanation is required about how these percentages are derived. The rate of return on common stock may have been calculated using the discounted cash flow method discussed above (and in more detail in Appendix B). The other rates are "embedded" costs; i.e., they represent total interest and preferred dividend costs divided by the book value, not

---

[40] Federal Energy Regulatory Commission, "Opinion and Order on Rate Increase," Minnesota Power and Light Company, Docket Nos. E-9499 and E-7502, Superior Water, Light and Power Company, Docket No. 76-20, Opinion No. 20, p. 10.

the market value, of debt and preferred stock, respectively. The current market rates for these instruments may be higher or lower than this rate. Likewise, the percentages of total capitalization are based upon book values at the time of the rate proceeding. For instance, the amount of debt on the books constitutes 45 percent of the total book capitalization of the firm. It is extremely unlikely that the market value of the utility's debt is 45 percent of the market value of the firm.

Two issues regarding the capital structure occasionally arise, particularly in the telephone industry. These are hypothetical capital structures and double-levered capital structures.

Hypothetical capital structures are used occasionally by commissions to determine a fair rate of return. A hypothetical capital structure may lower the computed cost of capital, which in turn can be passed on to consumers in the form of lower rates. By employing a higher than actual debt ratio (a lower equity ratio), a lower computed cost of capital is obtained because the cost of debt is generally lower than the cost of equity and also because the cost of debt is a tax-deductible expense.

Figure 4.3 illustrates the cost savings of a hypothetical capital structure. The cost of equity is 12.25 percent and the interest rate on debt is 8.33 percent. However, the income available for equity also gives rise to costs in the form of income taxes. Thus, Figure 4.3 shows that the before-

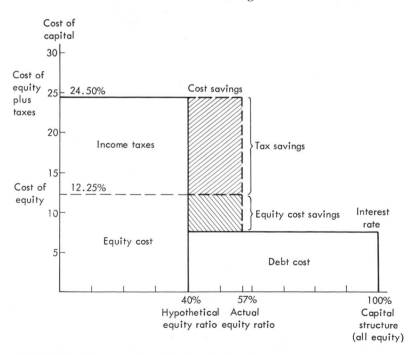

FIGURE 4.3 Demonstration of the Cost Savings from a Lower Equity Ratio

tax cost of equity is 24.5 percent, assuming a 50 percent income tax rate. If actual equity ratios include excess equity, these excess equity charges and income taxes are passed on to utility customers. Remedial action by commissions includes the imputation of hypothetical equity ratios. Figure 4.3 demonstrates that the equity cost savings and the tax savings equal the difference between the actual and hypothetical equity ratio times the sum of the cost of equity and the associated income tax cost less the interest rate on debt. For this example, the equity cost savings and the tax savings are 0.67 percent (i.e., (12.25% − 8.33%) × 17%) and 2.08% (i.e., (24.50% − 12.25%) × 17%), respectively.

All public utilities ought to avail themselves of all reasonable efficiencies in the conduct of their business. Efficient operation may improve service, but efficient operation will also reduce costs, and these cost reductions should be reflected in lower rates. Capital charges are a major component of costs. Capital should be efficient and reasonable, just as operating expenses must be efficient and reasonable. To the extent that these efficiencies are not employed, it is the responsibility of rate-making authorities to lower rates to what they would be after all such efficiencies are employed.

A firm's capitalization (invested capital) is divided between equity and debt. A nonregulated firm will be confronted with a ruthless free market setting the return on investment. Accordingly, equity investors and management of the firm can only profit by lowering costs as the free market overall sets the price. The firm is a price taker, and management must strive for cost savings to improve its return. Facing the given return on investment, the equity investors and its management are forced to cut capital costs by using debt as a source of financing. Such use of financial leverage allows the firm to trade on its equity and increase its return to equity. *Financial leverage*, a common financial term, refers to the use of debt (fixed financial claims) in a capital structure. The competitive firm and its management have, in fact, little discretion. The firm must strive to reduce costs, including capital costs, through the judicious use of leverage.

Some authors assume perfect capital markets in which leverage does not increase the firm's basic risk and rate of return, but transfers a greater proportion of risk to equity as leverage increases.[41] They argue that the higher required rate of return on equity resulting from the added risk of leverage is offset completely by the lower debt costs employed, with the result that the weighted average cost of capital remains unchanged with leverage. These authors admit, however, that such an argument ignores interest as an income tax deduction. Recognizing the income tax savings

---

[41] For a discussion of this phenomenon, known as the Miller and Modigliani hypothesis, see, for example, S. C. Meyers, "The Application of Finance Theory to Public Utility Rate Cases," *The Bell Journal*, 3, 1 (1972).

of interest, this argument implies a continued reduction in the cost of capital as the proportion of debt is increased. Therefore, the firm's minimum-cost capital structure is 99.999 percent debt.

Despite the obviously unrealistic conclusion of all debt, a fundamental proposition is set forth that can serve in determining a minimum cost of capital consistent with safety. The benefits of leverage—the lower interest rate and the income tax savings—must be offset by some "disadvantage" varying directly with leverage. If this were not so, every firm would tend to have a negligible amount of equity, a situation easily observed not to exist.

The offsetting disadvantage of leverage generally can be called "insolvency" costs. Debt contracts require that interest and other cash outflows be set in advance; debt cannot be renegotiated immediately to match the current yield. Given a firm's embedded costs of debt, the prospect of insolvency arises. Insolvency means that as the amount of debt utilized by a firm increases, the probability of default on the embedded costs of debt will increase with business downturns.

Figure 4.4 illustrates the insolvency risk accompanying leverage. Focusing on the income tax expense and assuming all other things equal, as leverage increases the fulfillment of debt service requirements become more sensitive to business conditions. As illustrated, the increased leverage in Figure 4.4b creates a savings equal to some 4 percent of revenues. Such a decrease in costs will be passed on to customers in the free market, albeit perhaps belatedly. This cost savings is accompanied by a greater chance of a failure to meet interest and sinking fund obligations of the debt. Where a 25 percent decline in revenues was necessary to cause default with the lesser leverage of Figure 4.4a, the greater leverage of Figure 4.4b suggests default occurs with only a 13 percent decline in revenues. The probability of insolvency thus depends upon the business conditions that may reduce revenues.

Accordingly, investors looking at the costs associated with insolvency find the decision regarding leverage definitive. The added cost savings from leverage at some debt level offsets the insolvency costs of debt. The optimal capital structure or the debt capacity for a firm just balances investors' and consumers' interests. While the investor is made less secure as the debt level rises, the consumer's gain more than offsets this disadvantage up to the debt capacity of the utility. Beyond this point, the advantage of added debt is more than offset by the prospect of insolvency. Required rates of both debt and equity suppliers rise rapidly in this range of high debt levels.

In a free market, the firm has no choice but to look to the consumer's interests. If the firm does not, a competitor will discover the profitable prospect of cutting costs by achieving a greater chance of insolvency within the limits of safety. For a well-regulated public utility, the benefits of

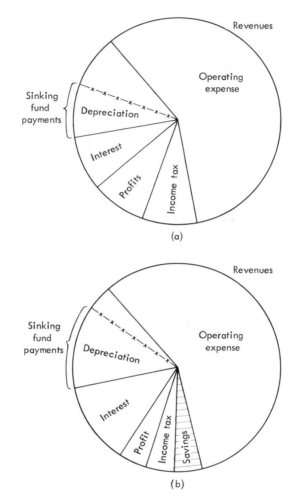

FIGURE 4.4 The Effects of Increased Leverage on Cost Reduction

income tax and interest savings are passed on to consumers by the regulatory commission, not by the forces of competition seeking lowest-cost capital structures. Management of a public utility, unless an efficient capital structure is enforced, may increase allowed returns while reducing risks by pursuing a high-equity capital structure. Because risk borne by investors is the reason for higher investor returns in financial markets, it is inconsistent in the utility industry to increase returns as risks decline with lower debt levels. Perhaps the primary incentive a utility management has to keep a low equity capital structure is regulatory lag in periods when rates of return exceed the cost of capital. If regulatory surveillance is lax, the utility firm can increase debt ratios and lever up the return on equity.

Lacking a strong motivation to minimize the overall before-tax cost of capital, utilities make capital structure decisions that may be based largely on raising the return on equity or reducing the risk borne by the common equity owner for the utility.

The actual capital structure of a public utility thus may not reflect a proper balance between the safety of capital, investors' interests, and the available cost savings, the consumers' interest. Accordingly, a public utility's capital structure ought to be reviewed by a regulatory commission to ascertain whether or not financial efficiencies consistent with safety are in fact practiced by the company. Where such financial efficiencies are not practiced, the revenue requirements using a before-tax cost of capital ought to be made consistent with the lower cost of a financially efficient, but relatively safe, capital structure.

Hypothetical capital structures have been widely used. One court decision cites 22 states and the District of Columbia as having used hypothetical capital structures, and only 2 states that have expressed some reservation regarding the imputation of a hypothetical capital structure.[42] The ability of the utility to carry a higher amount of debt consistent with safety for the capital investors and the capital structures of like utilities have been used as guides in the design of hypothetical capital structures.[43] During the 1950s, hypothetical capital structures were applied regularly to the Bell affiliates of AT&T. The Bell System carried as little as 25 percent debt in the early 1950s. For a company that did not have to lower its dividends even during the Great Depression, such a low debt ratio provided a great deal of safety for the common equity investor. Utilities that have not used the financial advantage of leverage, a fact of business life, have had debt imputed to their capital structure in order that a fair return might be calculated.

The use of a hypothetical capital structure does not imply that utility management is required to achieve such a capital structure. A hypothetical capital structure is a device used to calculate a fair rate of return in order that consumers are not burdened with excessive capital costs. On a rare occasion, a higher equity ratio has even been imputed. If management prefers to continue the safety of a low debt ratio while accepting the reduced rate of return based on a hypothetical capital structure, it may. Commissions may have powers of security regulation, although this authority is generally negative; it is the power to reject but not to require security issuance.

The use of double leverage is another controversial capital structure issue. Double leverage occurs when a holding company, with its own debt-

---

[42] United States Court of Appeals, The District of Columbia Circuit, *Communications Satellite Corp.* v. *Federal Communications Commission*, No. 75-2193, October 14, 1977, pp. 43–45.

[43] Ibid., p. 148.

levering equity, holds as an asset the common stock in a subsidiary which also has further debt levering the equity. The firm which has, let us say, a 9 percent return but can borrow 60 percent of its capital at 8 percent can increase or lever up its return on equity. Equity earns not only the 9 percent directly earned on the 40 percent equity capital, but on indirect additional return because of leverage. This additional 1 percent return on 60 percent of the invested capital provides an increment of 1.5 percent (or $(1\%)(.6/.4)$) to the 9 percent return to equity directly received. The resulting return to equity rises to 10.5 percent.

The equity in the subsidiary creates a corporate veil that must be removed to ascertain the effects of double leverage upon the costs of capital to the subsidiary. Figure 4.5 demonstrates the cost savings from a double-levered capital structure. The subsidiary itself is assumed to have an equity ratio of 57 percent. The holding or parent company, in turn, finances its holding of subsidiary equity through a levered capital structure. Suppose the parent capital structure is 70 percent equity. The resulting double-levered capital structure is 40 percent equity (i.e., 70% × .57), as shown in Figure 4.5. Resulting savings in the costs of capital come about in two ways: (1) savings in equity costs from the use of debt financing, and (2) tax savings from the tax deductibility of interest paid by the parent

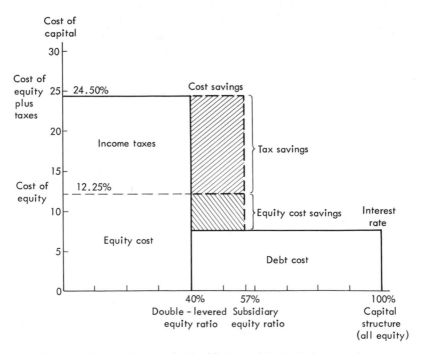

FIGURE 4.5 The Cost Savings of a Double-Levered Equity Ratio

company to finance its investment. The former savings is taken into account by calculating the double-levered capital structure. The latter savings is taken into account by using an effective income tax rate.

Let us assume the capital structures and costs shown in Figure 4.5 to demonstrate the calculation of a double-levered capital structure and the resulting cost of capital. The cost of debt is 8.33 percent, the cost of equity is 12.25 percent, and the income tax rate is 50 percent. A more realistic example would recognize different actual debt costs for parent and subsidiary debt as well as include preferred stock. The effect of the corporate veil that conceals the double leverage will also be identified in this example. Had a full equity return been provided on the subsidiary equity, that 17 percent of equity capital financed by parent debt costing but 8.33 percent would have received instead a full 12.25 percent return. The difference in weighted cost (12.25% − 8.33%)17%, or 0.67, would have accrued to the parent equity owner. Because of leverage, the return to the equity investor would have been increased 1.67 percent to 13.92 percent, an amount in excess of the 12.25 percent cost of capital assumed. Table 4.10 illustrates how the weighted cost of capital would be calculated after taking into account the effect of double leverage. The result is a 10 percent weighted cost of capital, which is significantly lower than the cost if the subsidiary's capital structure (57 percent equity) had been used.

The effective income tax rate is determined by allocating to the subsidiary the *pro rata* share of tax savings from interest deductions of the parent company. The return on the subsidiary equity, jointly made up of parent common equity and parent debt costs, has actual income taxes on only the parent's common equity portion. In our example, if taxes were permitted on the full 57 percent equity, a return of about 3.5 percent (12.25% × .57 × .5) would be paid in taxes by consumers, assuming a 50

TABLE 4.10 Double-Levered Capital Structure

| | RATIOS | | | |
	Individual Ratios	Double-Levered Ratios	Rates	Weighted Cost of Capital
Subsidiary equity ratio	57%			
Parent equity ratio	×70%			
Subtotal double-levered equity ratio		40%	12.25%	5.0%
Subsidiary equity ratio	57%			
Parent debt ratio	×30%			
Parent debt ratio	17%			
Subsidiary debt ratio	+43%			
Subtotal debt ratio		60%	8.33%	5.0%
Total		100%		10.0%

percent income tax rate. This percentage return is represented by the area labeled "income taxes" in Figure 4.5. However, the additional taxes on the 17 percent of equity capital financed by debt (labeled "tax savings" in Figure 4.5) would not be paid, but go toward providing an excess return to equity investors.

To remedy the overcharge of excess income tax expenses to consumers, an actual tax cost is determined by applying an effective income tax rate to the equity return of the subsidiary. The interest deductions of the parent, in addition to tax deductions for other general corporate expenses and occasionally tax losses of other subsidiaries, reduce the effective tax rate to be applied to the return on the subsidiary's equity. In our example, the subsidiary has weighted after-tax and before-tax costs of 6.3 percent and 11.2 percent, respectively. An effective income tax rate below the maximum statutory tax, when applied provides a mechanism by which the actual income taxes, but no more, are paid by the customer. This prevents an excessive return to the equity investor. In our example, an effective income tax rate of 43.6 percent, below the maximum 50 percent rate assumed, when applied to the before-tax return of the subsidiary, provides for the revenue requirement an amount just sufficient to cover actual income taxes.[44]

The need for double leverage became apparent in the telephone industry, especially after the early 1960s. Telephone holding companies were established and borrowed low-cost debt, some costing as little as 2 percent, from the Rural Electrification Administration and the Rural Telephone

---

[44] The calculations for weighted costs and the effective income tax rate follow.

Parent:
Cost of equity	12.25%	
Equity ratio	×.70	
Equity cost		8.575%
Interest rate	8.33%	
Debt ratio	×.30	
Debt cost		2.499
Parent cost of capital/subsidiary cost of equity		11.074%

Subsidiary:
Equity ratio		×.57
Equity cost (after income taxes)		6.312%
Parent equity cost	8.575%	
Subsidiary equity ratio	×.57	
Parent income tax cost @ 50% rate/ subsidiary income tax cost @ 43.6% rate		4.888
Subsidiary equity cost (before income tax)		11.200%
Subsidiary equity ratio		÷.57
Subsidiary cost of equity (before income taxes)		19.649%

Bank. These holding companies were highly leveraged with debt, which when coupled with a rate of return equal to that of the Bell System on the telephone rate base allocated to toll use, created very high returns on equity. These holding companies acquired large numbers of independent rural telephone companies. The Bell System companies are not permitted generally to acquire telephone operating companies. Other examples of double-levered holding companies exist in the investor-owned water industry.

The Bell System generally supports use of a consolidated capital structure rather than a double-levered capital structure. A consolidated capital structure eliminates any intercompany holdings of securities in a subsidiary from the balance sheet. The subsidiary investment of the parent, an asset, is offset by the claim against the subsidiary, the equity of the subsidiary. A consolidated capital structure will equal the double-levered capital structure when the subsidiaries all have equal amounts of leverage. The Bell System proposes a consolidated capital structure because its financing is based upon common, systemwide financing objectives, and differences are solely a matter of chance and timing. Western Electric, an AT&T subsidiary, does have a markedly higher equity ratio that is not eliminated in the consolidated capital structure. The result is a consolidated equity ratio higher than the average double-levered capital structure of the telephone operating companies.

In recent years, diversification in the utility industries, including gas and electric utilities, has been facilitated by the establishment of holding companies. These holding companies generally hold the equity investment in one utility, though perhaps in more in the telephone industry. The holding company then diversifies through the establishment of separate nonutility subsidiaries. By this device, gas and electric utilities have side-stepped the restrictions of the Public Utilities Holding Company Act. It is generally believed that higher operating risk will be offset in part by reduced leverage, and in part by higher capital costs. Many of the nonutility operations which are acquired have greater operating risk. Where the leverage of the nonutility operation is not fully adjusted to offset the higher nonutility operating risk, the parent company can trade upon the utility's equity, indirectly increasing the capital costs and reducing the leverage of the utility. Direct adjustment of the capital costs or the double-levered capital structure of the utility has been the only remedy to date.

It is evident that no simple formula exists to calculate the utility's cost of capital and its allowed rate of return. This does not mean that any formula will do, however. There is an inevitable element of decision involved which, presumably, is based on a variety of data and methods, as well as financial knowledge, judgment, and understanding of the public interest by the regulatory agency.

REGULATION OF THE RATE STRUCTURE

After the general rate level has been established, commissions must rule on the relative prices of each segment of service (the rate structure) that will generate this level of revenue. It is the commission's responsibility to ensure that these prices are reasonable and not unduly discriminatory to any class of service. However, beyond declaring personal discrimination—charging different rates to different customers for substantially the same service, provided under similar circumstances—to be illegal, the commission's mandate is less clear, and judgment and discretion are paramount. In the past, the commission has frequently ordered the utility to prepare proposed rate schedules that would yield an amount equal to the revenue requirements. These schedules were compared with prior schedules and were often approved perfunctorily with minimal supporting evidence and analysis. In this approach, the effort devoted to the regulation of rate structure tended to be but a small fraction of that involved in determining the general revenue level.

Over the past decade, however, this pattern of regulatory procedure has changed considerably. While the revenue requirement determination is more detailed than ever, rate structure and pricing issues now tend to be more prominent and controversial. This transition is undoubtedly a natural evolution, stimulated by inflation, with its resulting frequent rate cases, and extensive use of computer analysis techniques not previously available. And, predictably, the result today is a more extended rate case.

As suggested earlier, the issue of rate structure is especially complex for the telephone utility, where some thousands of tariff items may be involved. However, once these prices are approved, they remain in effect until the next rate hearing, which may be up to several years away. To lessen the adverse effects of inflation in the interim, electric utilities in most jurisdictions are allowed to increase rates automatically at monthly or quarterly intervals in response to changes in the cost of fuel. Gas distribution utilities, too, are usually allowed promptly to pass along increased costs for purchased gas.

The revenue requirement determination is only the first step in establishing the rates consumers pay for utility services. This revenue requirement must first be distributed among the various groups or classes of customers in a fair and reasonable manner. Each class's cost to serve must be transformed into a rate design, a price which when applied to the units of utility services billed will produce revenues sufficient to cover the class cost to serve and in turn the overall revenue requirement. Care must be taken to distinguish among: (1) the overall revenue requirements, (2) class cost to serve, and (3) rate design when utility rate making is considered.

COST TO SERVE

The different components of the revenue requirement—operating expenses including depreciation, taxes, and operating income—are distributed to the various customer classes. In gas and electric utilities, such customer classes include residential, commercial, and industrial customers; in telephone utilities such classes include residential and business local service, toll calls, and vertical or ancillary equipment leases and sales. A proportional amount of the various revenue requirements may be allocated to each class of service. Such a distribution is shown in Figure 4.6. Typically, residential customers of electric or gas utilities will be allocated proportionately more capital costs, such as return on investment (ROI) and taxes (T). Both of these are directly a function of investment, and typically a lower load factor exists for residential customers. On the other hand, proportionately less operating expense (O) is allocated to this group. These results are indicated in Figure 4.6. Of course, the depreciation component of expenses will follow the allocation of investment, as will return on investment and taxes.

RATE DESIGN

Once the overall revenue requirement is established and is distributed among the separate customer classes, a rate design is needed to establish actual rates used in the computation of individual customer bills. When

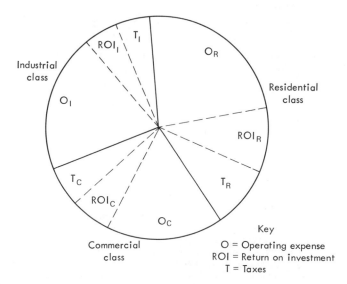

FIGURE 4.6   Cost to Serve Allocation

rate changes are not based upon a uniform percentage change, a uniform dollar-and-cents change per unit of sales such as KWHs, MCFs, and call minutes, or a flat or uniform amount per customer, usage data are necessary to establish the amount of revenues different rate designs will produce from each customer class.

A sample electric residential tariff is presented in Table 4.11. This type of rate design is called a *declining block rate* and is used commonly in electric and gas service to residential and smaller commercial customers.

A customer that used 600 kilowatt hours per month would be billed in accordance with Table 4.12. This sample bill is much like the bill a typical electric consumer would receive. The tariffs on which these billings are based are filed as public documents with utility commissions. Before these tariffs are accepted by commissions, they must be demonstrated to produce only the revenues permitted to be collected.

To ascertain the amount of revenue application of such a tariff to many utility customers will generate requires a bill frequency analysis. A *bill frequency analysis* determines the revenues a rate can produce. Actual experienced sales and the number of bills for various levels of usage per billing period make up the basic bill frequency. Each rate schedule in a utility will require a separate bill frequency. These rate schedules may vary among customer classes, among geographic areas served, among urban and rural areas, and because of other factors. According to the example in Table 4.13, revenue in the amount of $15,892,500 should be produced by the tariff. Note that the minimum bill pays for the first 50 KWH unless fewer KWH are used. In any case, at least a $3 charge is paid by all 500,000 customers. The remaining sales are charged on a per unit basis.

Though the measurement of units of sale may vary, the basic bill frequency concept as exemplified in Table 4.13 may be applied to other electric rates or to rates of other utilities. Other electric utilities may charge for kilowatt demand in addition to kilowatt hours of energy and customer charges. Telephone utilities may have per customer local rates and per minute long distance toll rates; gas utilities may have charges per MCF or therm; and water utilities may have charges per gallon or per fire hydrant.

TABLE 4.11 Sample Tariff

Customer charge (or minimum charge)	$3
Energy charge	
6¢ per KWH for the first 1000 KWH supplied in the month	
4.5¢ per KWH for all KWH in excess of 100 KWH in the month	
Energy adjustment clause (EAC)	
1¢ per KWH	
Late payment penalty charge	
5% of bill after 10 days	

TABLE 4.12 Sample Bill

Electric charge	$31.50
Energy adjustment clause (600 KWH @ 1¢)	6.00
Total due in 10 days	$37.50
Total due after 10 days	$39.38

The basic purpose, in all these cases, is to establish the amount of revenues a given set of rates and tariffs will produce for the utility. Only rates and tariffs that produce proper revenues, for each customer class and overall, are permitted. Later, in Chapter 7, further analysis of both cost to serve and rate design will be considered, especially in light of the economic concepts of marginal cost pricing and elasticities of demand, both of which have been much discussed in recent decades.

_____ INFLATION AND UTILITY RATES _____

Utility regulation began during a period of rising price levels and soon confronted rapid inflation during the World War I period. After somewhat stable price levels during the 1920s, deflation occurred during the Great Depression. Inflationary periods then followed during World War II, and the post-World War II and Korean war years. Low rates of inflation during the remaining years in the 1950s and into the 1960s were followed by increased rates of inflation until more rapid inflation began in 1973. Thus,

TABLE 4.13 Revenue Effect of Sample Tariff

Rate Block (KWH)	Number of Bills	Bill Frequency KWH	KWH BY RATE BLOCK 0–50	50–100	Over 100
0–50	10,000	250,000	250,000	—	—
50–100	100,000	3,000,000	500,000	2,500,000	—
Over 100	390,000	294,000,000	24,500,000	24,500,000	245,000,000
Total	500,000	297,250,000			
KWH's Billed in each Rate Block			25,250,000	27,000,000	245,000,000

Revenue Effect			
Electric charge	$1,500,000 @ $3 per customer	$1,620,000 @ 6¢ per KWH	$9,800,000 @ 4¢ per KWH
EAC @ 1¢ per KWH	252,500	270,000	2,450,000
Subtotal	$1,752,500	$1,890,000	$12,250,000
Grand total revenues			$15,892,500

regulation of utility rates has experienced inflation as well as deflation. Two important issues to consider are how regulation copes administratively with inflation and deflation, and whether traditional rate-making procedures deal well with the problems caused by inflation.

The commonly held view of rate regulation is that utility prices are set now to be fixed henceforth. This is a very static view of the rate-making procedures. A more dynamic perspective recognizes continuing rate filings and other regulatory mechanisms that ameliorate the effects of inflation. Finally, few unregulated segments of society have gained, or even remained constant, with the rapidly escalating inflation in recent years. Utilities have no special claim to preeminence in protection against inflation. A utility has a claim to make against administrative rate-making procedures that do not permit a reasonable opportunity to earn a fair return, but it has no claim to be protected against business hazards and economic forces such as inflation, which can be unfair to everyone.

INFLATION AND THE COST OF CAPITAL

Opinion regarding inflation and the utility cost of capital can best be described as confused. This confusion about inflation finds its way into proposals for reproduction, replacement, or current cost rate bases; replacement or current cost depreciation; and inflation premiums to be added to the cost of capital. In fact, use of these adjustments with an original cost rate base and cost of capital results in double compensation for inflation and provides an excess return to investors. The economic processes include inflation compensation in the nominal cost of capital, and it is this cost of capital that is applied to a utility rate base.

For example, consider the following simplified example of utility capital charges in Table 4.14. The example assumes a 4 percent real cost of capital and inflation, previously unexpected, rising to an expected level of 6 percent. The present value of both capital charge series in part (a) of Table 4.14 is $900 when discounted at 4 and 10 percent, respectively. An additional return of $108 spread over the three years provides the inflation compensation. Part (b) of Table 4.14 shows an inflation-adjusted rate base and depreciation expense. Only when the return applied to this inflation adjusted rate base is 4 percent, the real interest rate, is the present value of the capital charges, discounted at 10 percent, the appropriate amount, $900. The capital gains or noncash receipts in the early years defer cash receipts until later years under an inflation-adjusted depreciation and rate-base method.

Additional inflation compensation added to capital charges based on original cost rate base, original cost depreciation, and a nominal cost of capital lead to the double counting of inflation and excess returns. The addition of an inflation premium to the rate base is one form, which is

TABLE 4.14 Utility Capital Charges Under Inflation

Original Cost Method

| | | | | CAPITAL CHARGES | | | | | |
| | | | | NO INFLATION | | | 6% INFLATION | | |
Year	Investment	Accumulated Depreciation	Rate Base	Depreciation Expense	4% Return	Total	Depreciation Expense	10% Return	Total
0	$900	0	$900						
1	900	$300	600	$300	$36	$336	$300	$ 90	$ 390
2	900	600	300	300	24	324	300	60	360
3	900	900	0	300	12	312	300	30	330
Total				$900	$72	$972	$900	$180	$1080

Inflation-Adjusted Method

| | | | | CAPITAL CHARGES | | |
Year	Investment	Accumulated Depreciation	Rate Base	Depreciation Expense	4% Return	Total
0	$ 900	0	$900			
1	954	$ 318[a]	636	$ 318	$36	$ 354
2	1011	674[a]	337	338	25	363
3	1072	1072[a]	0	357	13	370
Total				$1013	$74	$1087

[a] Includes a 6% inflation of accumulated depreciation.

115

commonly called the *fair value rate base*. This inflation premium might be based on reproduction, replacement, or current cost valuations. To prevent an excessive return, only the lower real return on capital, not the nominal cost of capital, can be paid on this fair value rate base. Inflation premiums are also proposed to be added to depreciation expense. During the fair value era, the U.S. Supreme Court in the United Railway decision ruled that depreciation expense based on the fair value was appropriate. This was quickly reversed in the 1944 Hope decision, and depreciation expense was again based on original cost. Also, fair value depreciation reflected observed depreciation in physical plant, a very subjective, inexact, and time-consuming practice.

A third method would add a second inflation premium directly to the nominal rate of return. The inflation premium over and above the inflation compensation already included in the nominal rate of return results in double counting of inflation. An inflation premium is correctly added only to the real rate of return, not to the nominal rate of return. But even if the inflation premium is used as an addendum to the real rate of return or as a multiplicand of rate base and depreciation expense, severe computation problems exist in measuring the investor's expected real rate of return and the investor's expected inflation rate.

The nominal cost of capital payments to investors will compensate them for the real costs of refraining from consumption and for losses to inflation. Investors, of course, sometimes make mistakes, and their expected real return and expected inflation rates are not realized after the fact. To consider how the cost of capital considers the rate of inflation, consider a bank note that pays an interest amount of $1 per annum for each of three years. Assuming a 4 percent cost of capital with no inflation, the price of this note is $2.78, based on its discounted present value. Now should the investor become aware that inflation will be 6 percent for each of the next three years, the investor will convert the $1 per annum to real values per annum of 94 cents, 89 cents, and 84 cents, respectively. Then, discounting these real values at the 4 percent real cost of capital, the respective discounted present values of 91 cents, 82 cents, and 75 cents add up to a price of $2.48 for the note. Discounting the $1 per annum series at the 10 percent nominal cost of capital instead yields the same price, $2.48, for the note.

Two interesting economic questions are these: How do investors form inflation expectations? Does inflation cause the real cost of capital to decline? Both questions are not unique to public utility economics; they are also macroeconomic issues that affect the economy as a whole. Direct use of the nominal cost of capital ameliorates to some extent the problems inherent in such questions.

Poor stock market performance for public utility stock, including the view that stock price appreciation is less than the inflation rate or less than industrial stock prices, is a frequent complaint facing utility commissions. However, neither observation suggests that utility regulation affects utility stock market performance in a negative fashion. Lower earnings retention ratios and lower rates of return corresponding to lower risks of utilities permit less stock price appreciation for utilities than for industrials. The argument that investors require price growth equal to inflation also does not stand. Investors purchase debt and preferred stock expecting no inherent price appreciation. The variety of earnings retention rates and dividend yields among utilities of similar risk suggest that a variety of stock price appreciation rates are expected, rather than a singular expected appreciation rate equal to the expected inflation rate.

Inflation adjustments have been restricted to the common equity return. Preferred equity and debt holders do not expect or receive any lesser or greater inflation compensation, regardless of decreases or increases in the inflation rate. If increased inflation was reflected in an increase in the rate base of 10 percent over a period of time even though debtors' embedded inflation compensation was only 5 percent on half of total capitalization, the common equity return would outstrip inflation. Not only would the common equity holder receive 10 percent on the equity portion of capitalization, a remaining 5 percent appreciation on the debt-financed capital would accrue to the equity owner. The equity appreciation, 15 percent, would outstrip the inflation rate of 10 percent and hardly result in a fair return. The reader should calculate the return to equity if embedded debt costs contemplated a 10 percent inflation rate, but the current expected inflation rate drops to 6 percent. To 4 percent. Is the utility solvent?

Various inflation adjustments to capital charges as described above suffer from one preeminent flaw, a type of myopia. The increases in capital charges are observed, but the effect on noncash appreciation, a type of economic revenue, is often overlooked. In the immediately preceding example, the increase in the market interest rate on debt is offset by a capital gain as the real worth or present value of the amount of the liability declines with the increased inflation rates. An inflation-adjusted rate base likewise creates capital gains that must be recognized as noncash revenues to the utility. The incorporation of inflation adjustments in costs is not enough. Offsetting noncash gains and appreciation because of the diminished worth of liabilities and increased asset value must also be recorded.

Tables 4.15 and 4.16 show inflation-adjusted financial statements. The gains on debt caused by inflation and appreciation as noncash receipts are deferred until realized, though the charges based on so-called economic depreciation would substantially reduce the "cash operating income" from $31.50 to $5.50 per annum. Reversing the example to start with the $900

TABLE 4.15 Balance Sheet

		No Inflation	
ASSETS		LIABILITIES	
Rate base	$900	Common equity @ 4%	$450
		Long-term debt @ 3%	450
Total	$900	Total	$900

		6% Inflation Adjusted	
ASSETS		LIABILITIES	
Rate base	$954	Common equity @ 10%	$529
		Long-term debt @ 9%	425
Total	$954	Total	$954

rate base and 6 percent inflation embedded in debt costs is a worthwhile exercise; it shows that "cash operating income" would rise above the $31.50 amount if the utility is to continue to meet its fixed capital costs.

As indicated in Table 4.16, continuing inflation will cause the inflation-adjusted "cash operating income" to rise, while capital charges based on a depreciating rate base decline. The economic cost of $900, the discounted present value of the resources invested, is recovered from the sale of utility service at prices based on an original-cost rate base and depreciation coupled with a nominal cost of capital, or an inflation-adjusted rate base, economic depreciation, and a real cost of capital. The latter method—requiring determination of real, required rates of return, investors' expected inflation rates, appraisal of appreciation on assets and gains on liabilities—requires such a complex set of nonexistent, and inherently spec-

TABLE 4.16 Income Statement

No Inflation	
Equity cost @ 4%	$18.00
Long-term debt cost @ 3%	13.50
Cash operating income	$31.50

6% Inflation Adjusted		
Equity cost @ 10%	$45.00	
Long-term debt cost @ 9%	40.50	
Inflation-adjusted		
capital cost		$85.50
less: Noncash receipts		
appreciation on rate base		54.00
Real capital cost		30.50
Gain on long-term debt		25.00
Cash operating income		$ 5.50

ulative, inflation-adjusted balance sheets and income statements as to be impractical, in addition to being unnecessary. The original cost rate base, original cost depreciation, and nominal cost of capital developed from conventional accounting balance sheets and income statements have overwhelming practical advantages in developing capital charges during periods of inflation. The practical advantages include these: (1) readily and conventionally available data, (2) verifiable and auditable values, and (3) ascertainable nominal costs of capital.

ADJUSTMENT CLAUSES

By altering charges based on changes in specific costs, an adjustment clause in a tariff modifies consumer rates. Generally, the adjustments are for fuel costs of electric utilities and purchased gas costs of gas utilities. The former is called a *fuel adjustment clause* (*FAC*), while the latter is called a *purchased gas adjustment clause* (*PGA*). Those jurisictions which include purchased power costs in addition to fuel costs have *energy adjustment clauses* (*EAC*). Some jurisdictions permit inclusion of certain taxes. The Public Service Company of New Mexico, for example, had an adjustment clause which passed through all costs.

An example of an EAC is found in the bill frequency analysis of Table 4.13. In this example, an additional 1 cent per KWH was charged to the consumer. In most of the 51 utility regulatory commissions, adjustment clauses are permitted. These clauses have a twofold purpose:

1. Changes in the prices of purchased fuel and gas are largely not controlled by utilities, and an adjustment clause protects investors in the case of price rises and protects consumers in the case of price decreases.
2. Expensive and time-consuming rate-making proceedings are minimized.

Certain disadvantages attach to adjustment clauses:

1. The utility's incentives to conserve fuel and minimize costs are reduced where cost increases and savings are passed on to consumers.
2. Abuses may occur when prices are controlled indirectly or directly by the utility. Examples include captive coal mines or gas fields, scheduling of power plant or supplemental gas supplies that alter the mix of fuel or gas prices, or "padding" fuel and gas costs with inaccurate, improper, or excessive expenses, such as inflated prices or adding to fuel and gas costs other expenses like fuel handling and storage.
3. Excessive collections of revenues or of supplier refunds are refunded belatedly to the consumer.

The adjustment clauses essentially index the energy charge of the electric or gas tariff. As the cost rises and falls, the rate increment rises and falls accordingly. Many states use automatic adjustments. The commission reviews the rate adjustment factor based on a preexisting, approved automatic adjustment clause in the utility's tariff. Such an automatic adjustment clause does not require a hearing for changes in the adjustment factor to occur. Subsequent audits by the commission may review the propriety of the costs the utility passed through the automatic adjustment clause.

The calculation of the rate adjustment factor varies from jurisdiction to jurisdiction. Two types of formulas are used to determine the factor: a price formula and a value formula. The *price formula* determines the cost for fuel by applying the rates per BTU or MCF charged the utility by its supplier to weights, such as the heat rate, BTU per KWH, or historic purchases of natural gas. A weighted average cost is determined. The *value formula* finds average fuel cost per KWH or gas cost per MCF by dividing total cost by the units of sales. The average cost already included in the base rate is subtracted from the current average cost and the resulting difference, after adjustment for prior over- or undercollection of cost, is added to the base rate. A zero base adjustment clause includes no energy cost in the tariff; all the energy cost is included in the adjustment factor.

The price formula incorporates into the adjustment factor the changes in prices. The value formula reflects not only changes in prices, but also changes in the fuel or gas mix. For example, an outage of a base load generating unit or the increased injection of propane to increase the winter heating value of gas will affect the value formula but not the price formula. A sliding scale existed for a time, particularly early in the regulation of utility rates. Under this system, dividend or profit increases were accompanied by rate decreases. An incentive for the utility prevailed, since the profit or dividend increase was not fully passed through to the consumers.

Adjustment clauses are significant revenue producers for utilities. With the increases in fuel and gas costs beginning in the 1970s, significant increases in revenues have occurred. Fuel and gas costs are the electric and gas utilities' largest costs, representing some one-third and two-thirds of revenues, respectively. The indexing of the recovery of these large costs of fuel and gas protected utilities against some of the most rapid inflation during the 1970s, the inflation of energy costs.

REGULATORY LAG AND ATTRITION

A *lag* is the period of time between when action is initiated and when its effects are realized. Generally, economic lags are not uncommon. For example, the cobweb theorem, the monetarist basis for inflation, the investment accelerator, and long-run demand elasticity reflect economic lags. Administrative lags also occur. For example, prices are fixed or changed infrequently in retail catalogs as well as manufacturers' list prices, terms of contracts, real estate or equipment leases, and futures contracts. The occurrence of economic and administrative lags in utility regulation is not unique.

Regulatory lag is the period of time between the incurrence of costs and the implementation of rates that meet these costs. Some part of this time is occupied by the utility management itself. Rate case scenarios will be reviewed by managment on a continuing basis. These reviews will result in a decision to file or not to file a rate application before the regulatory commission. One response to inflation has been that a utility almost always has a rate case filed before the appropriate commission. A continuous series of rate-case filings has been the most pervasive response by utilities to inflation.

Another part of the time period we have called regulatory lag is taken up by the administrative proceedings before the utility commission. The proceeding starts with the rate filing by the utility and finally ends with lawful, just, and reasonable rates being implemented. Regulatory lag is part of the price paid for reasoned, thoughtful, and thorough consideration of proposed rates. The costs associated with regulatory lag can be less than the costs of a lack of reasoned, thoughtful, and thorough consideration. Regulatory lag itself is not unreasonable. Unreasonable regulatory lag occurs when too much time goes by without review. For example, in the 1960s regulatory lag prevented rate reductions. Utility commissions, through oversight or lack of initiative, failed to review the existing rates. During recent years, in some jurisdictions regulatory lag deferred implementation of rates. By deferment of rate increases, some commissions used regulatory lag to keep rates relatively low. Rather than directly trimming proposed rates, some commissions just waited until costs caught up with the proposed rates, and then approved the rates.

Other causes can lengthen the period of regulatory lag. The utility commission or intervenor may increase the decision time by raising complex issues that are in need of study. The question of what should be studied further and what should be postponed is a delicate issue. Also, commissions must weigh carefully some utilities' claims of prolonged regulatory lag as a rhetorical club in order to circumvent utilities' burden of proof.

Regulatory lag has had a number of effects attributed to it. The most common position is that utility earnings, or at least growth in earnings, are adversely affected. Such an effect has been called *attrition* or *erosion*. Countervailing opinion points out that regulatory lag is an incentive for the utility to be efficient and reduce costs. Also, posed against the adverse effect upon earnings is the effect upon the consumer of rapidly increasing utility rates. The value of consumer durables, purchased in periods of low rates, declines as utility rates increase. Moreover, one of the longest regulatory lags, the return to the customer of the income tax savings from the investment tax credit and normalization of accelerated depreciation, adversely affects the consumer. The return of these tax savings takes a period no shorter than the average life of the utility plant and equipment and, for a growing utility, an indefinitely long period. This regulatory lag results from the tax laws passed by the federal government.

A number of regulatory responses to regulatory lag have occurred. The most common has been the series of almost continuous rate proceedings. Use of automatic adjustment clauses has passed through to utility rates significant increases in costs. Interim rate collections, frequently subject to refund, have taken place before final rates are approved in a formal rate proceeding. Finally, test-period data or the test period itself have been adjusted. Future or forecasted test periods whose estimated data postdates the rate filing or even the effective date of the proposed rates has been the most extreme adjustment. Use of a year-end rate base or inclusion of construction work in progress in the rate has occurred in some jurisdictions. Other jurisdictions make no specific adjustment for attrition because an amount cannot be determined accurately and offsetting accretion occurs.

Attrition, strictly defined, occurs with the *replacement* of plant and equipment at a higher cost, even accounting for productivity increases, than the historic costs of the plant and equipment being replaced. The higher capital costs are not covered by the revenues produced because lower capital charges for return, depreciation, and taxes are included in existing rates. Regulatory commissions have gone beyond this strict definition of attrition to include *additions* to plant and equipment whose cost per unit of production has risen because of inflation. Also, rolling over or refinancing low-interest debt or issuing new debt or preferred stock at a cost in excess of the cost of capital has been considered attrition by some regulators. An example of attrition can be seen in Table 4.17, where plant and equipment costs as reflected in the rate base have outpaced operating income.

Erosion is a counterpart of attrition. *Erosion* is a result of the difference between average operating expense per unit of utility service and average operating expense per unit incorporated in utility rates. The incidence of erosion will depend, in part, upon the short-term rate of inflation. When replacing long-lived capital after many years, on the other hand, even low rates of inflation can accumulate to raise unit costs.

TABLE 4.17   Attrition

Year	Output	Rate Base	Operating Income	Rate of Return
1	100	$1000	$100	10.0%
2	100	1100	100	9.1

Significant offsets to attrition and erosion exist for utilities. Sales growth, increased operating efficiency, and economies of scale increase the productivity of a given level of capital on operating expenditure. Internal financing from cash flow such as depreciation does not raise the capital cost. A utility has access to tax savings that require no capital cost to be paid by the utility. On top of this, the income tax rate effectively halves the effect of any attrition or erosion on rate of return by increasing tax deductions and reducing income tax expense relatively. Thus, in Table 4.17, the operating income would be unlikely to stay at $100 but instead could rise.

Utility commissions differ in whether or not they believe the likely operating income increases will offset attrition. The New York Public Service Commission in a New York Telephone Company case stated:

> Given an historic test year, attrition and erosion are phenomena that must be taken into account in computing a proper revenue requirement for the first year of new rates. Growth is an offset of these items, but must itself be diminished on account of any restriction, or price elasticity response.[45]

The reader should consider the effect of rising rates on revenues if the utility service is price inelastic: Will revenues rise or fall?

We conclude this section with a second point of view on attrition. The West Virginia Public Service Commission, in a case regarding the Chesapeake and Potomac Telephone Company of West Virginia, found:

> Definitions abound describing attrition, but suffice it to say here, attrition is the decline in earnings during the period between rate case determinations, the reasons for which cannot be identified and measured with anything but speculation as to the future. One might look at one statistic of the cost of service and say attrition is due to an increase in investment per customer, ignoring and not examining operation and maintenance expenses. For example, new electronic switching equipment being installed in various central offices provides newer technology and additional services than equipment replaced. Depreciation expense increases, but in time, operation and maintenance expenses may be less. Also, less space may be required to house such equipment, an important factor in light of today's skyrocketing construction costs. To measure all related expense and revenues as to the future, is speculation.

> We do not guarantee a regulated utility it will earn the rate of return on rate base allowed by the commission in its rate making. However, we do determine a rate that will, in our judgment, allow the utility to earn a fair and just return upon its investment. The showing of the company that it is unable to earn the allowed return does not in itself justify an attrition allowance. Such an allowance will tend to stifle the utility's responsibility for

[45] 23 PUR 4th 585.

efficient management and shift the risk of the business enterprise from the investor, where it belongs, to the customer. The utility is subject to the same possibilities of slippage of earnings as is encountered in any other business, and this commission is not responsible to anticipate every unforeseen adverse development that may arise in utility operation.

The practical effect of granting CPWV's attrition allowance would be to base rates upon conjecture. Further, the expected continued growth into the foreseeable future of new services for the subscribers, as projected by the company, indicates that an attrition allowance is unacceptable to this commission.[46]

Thus, questions regarding the impact of attrition, its measurement, and its regulatory treatment are still open.

REGULATION OF THE QUALITY OF SERVICE

Why should the quality of service be regulated in the first place? If firms cannot compete on the basis of price, they can improve service to obtain customers, as the airlines did in the late 1960s and early 1970s. On the other hand, decreasing quality is analogous to increasing price. When a price is quoted, say $20 for a pair of shoes, the quality is understood; if the quality varies, the price means nothing. Price regulation would be rather ineffective if quality were left to the discretion of the regulated firm. Therefore, adequate quantity and quality of service are required by law, and commissions are empowered to specify and enforce standards to meet the law.

Regulatory commissions generally use a twofold approach to utility service standards. First, they determine, specify, and periodically update a detailed set of service quality and performance standards to be met by the utilities under their jurisdiction. To illustrate the detail of this regulation, the contents of the Illinois Commerce Commission's General Order 197 (dated November 6, 1970, and as periodically amended thereafter) are included here as Appendix A. This order specifies the current standards for telephone service in Illinois. For example, under dial service requirements, this order specifies that a dial tone must be received within three seconds on at least 95 percent of calls or the equivalent as measured by a traffic usage register. The second part of this approach attempts to recognize that service quality standards are difficult to specify and that, in the final analysis, service quality is in the eye of the beholder. Therefore, there is usually an extensive system for accepting and promptly resolving

---

[46] 26 PUR 4th 39.

quality complaints from customers. The presence of an effective avenue of appeal for complaints provides a strong incentive to the utility to supply high-quality service that will minimize the number of complaints.

Another concern of utility service is the accurate measurement of that service. Without accurate measurement, utility services cannot be accurately billed. Utility meters are required to be checked for accuracy on a scheduled basis. Meter reading is another source of measurement error. Meter readers are supervised, and computer billing programs generally will identify exceptionally low or high bills for a given customer. Utility usage is sometimes estimated when the meter reader does not have access to the meter. Local telephone service minimum bills or customer charges are flat rates and require accurate records of who is receiving services. Careful and accurate measurement of service is important, for without it no tariff can be used to assess utility bills.

SUMMARY

This chapter has examined the cost of service approach used in the determination of the overall revenue requirement. These costs include operating expenses, depreciation, taxes, and return on investment. Recent experiences with inflation have caused regulatory commissions to look closely at certain issues such as capital costs, adjustment clauses, attrition, and regulatory lag. The overall cost of service, when distributed to the various customer classes, determines the revenue responsibility of each class of utility customers. Finally, rates are designed for each class to produce revenues sufficient to cover the cost of service for the class alone and all classes together. Chapter 7, Pricing, will deal in depth with the latter two subjects and associated controversies. Standards for the quality of service are also determined by commissions. If quality of service decisions were left completely to the utility's discretion, rate regulation would be ineffective.

Appendix A

To help illustrate the detail of quality of service regulation, this appendix contains the Contents of Illinois General Order 197, dated November 6, 1970.

GENERAL ORDER 197

STANDARDS OF SERVICE FOR TELEPHONE COMPANIES IN THE STATE OF ILLINOIS

TABLE OF CONTENTS

100 GENERAL

600 STANDARDS OF QUALITY OF SERVICE

700 SAFETY

800 BOUNDARIES

APPENDICES

Appendix B

Three Methods of Estimating the Cost of Equity Capital

The DCF Approach

One method of estimating the cost of equity capital commonly found in rate testimony is the *discounted cash flow* or *DCF* approach. This valuation model is fairly general and may be adapted to suit a variety of growth situations. The central idea is that the present value of an asset may be represented by the stream of net benefits yielded by the asset discounted to the present by the market opportunity rate. For stock valuation, the market price may be considered the present value of the stream of expected dividends discounted at the cost of equity capital. This may be represented symbolically as:

$$P_0 = \sum_{t=1}^{\infty} \frac{DIV_t}{(1 + k)^t}$$

where P_0 is the current price per share, k is the cost of equity capital, and DIV_t is the dividend payment in period t or the stream of expected dividends.

The cost of equity capital is the discount rate at which the investor's discounted expected future stream of common stock dividends is equal to the market price of common equity. This concept is exactly the same as stating that the market interest rate is the discount rate for which the investor's discounted expected future stream of interest payments is equal to the market price of bonds, or that the market yield on preferred stock is that rate at which the investor's expected future stream of embedded preferred stock dividends is equal to the market price of preferred stock. For that matter, the cost of equity capital is not conceptually different from the rate computed on many assets purchased in expectation of future receipts, such as a savings account, real estate, or a home mortgage.

All market cost of capital rates have in common the same features:

1. A current market price
2. An expected future stream of cash receipts

The difference between the various financial and real assets is the pattern of cash flows expected. A bond pays a fixed interest periodically until the principal is returned. Preferred stock pays a fixed dividend periodically without the principal being repaid. Common stock owners receive a dividend periodically, but retained earnings also create, through profitable investment, higher future dividends. This is not a pattern unique to common stock. If an individual has a savings account with compound interest, the investor is paid an increasing interest amount by the bank. The amount of interest growth could be altered by the investor's periodic withdrawals from the account, just as the amount of dividends paid out alters the rate of growth in common stock dividends. Table 4.18 gives examples of various financial instruments with different patterns of cash flows. Annual payments for 10 years are used for pedagogical purposes. It is assumed the bond is due at the end of the 10 years, the preferred stock and common stock are sold in the stock market, and the savings account is cashed. The discount rate in each case equals the market cost of that security.

TABLE 4.18 Discount Rates for Various Financial Assets Are Computed in the Same Manner

Year		Bond	Preferred Stock	Savings Account ($\frac{1}{2}$ withdrawn, $\frac{1}{2}$ compounded annually)	Common Stock ($\frac{1}{2}$ paid out, $\frac{1}{2}$ retained annually)
	Current price	$1,000	$1,000	$1,000	$1,000
	Expected receipts				
1		$ 75.00	$ 85.00	$ 30.00	$ 60.00
2		75.00	85.00	30.90	63.60
3		75.00	85.00	31.83	67.42
4		75.00	85.00	32.78	71.46
5		75.00	85.00	33.77	75.75
6		75.00	85.00	34.78	80.29
7		75.00	85.00	35.82	85.11
8		75.00	85.00	36.90	90.22
9		75.00	85.00	38.00	95.63
10		$1,075.00	$1,085.00	$1,383.06	$1,892.22

	Interest Rate	Yield	Interest Rate	Cost of Equity
Yield	7.5%	8.5%	3.0%	6.0%
Growth rate	0	0	3.0	6.0
Discount rate which sets current price equal to expected receipts	7.5%	8.5%	6.0%	12.0%

The cost of equity computed using the discounting method is called the discounted cash flow formula. Stock prices are seen to depend ultimately on dividends, but capital gains are not ignored. Capital gains over a period may be viewed as reflecting increases in the expected value of discounted future dividends that might occur for any number of reasons. The preceding equation may be built up from a series of substitutions in the basic one-period valuation formula:

$$P_0 = \frac{DIV_1 + P_1}{1 + k}$$

Substituting $(DIV_2 + P_2)/(1 + k)$ for P_1 and $(DIV_3 + P_3)/(1 + k)$ for P_2, and so on for n periods, the general formula for P_0 is obtained as a limit as n approaches infinity. At the end of period 1, the stockholder receives the dividend payment and holds a stock that may have appreciated in price and may be sold for a capital gain. But that selling price is simply a claim to all future dividends from that point on. Thus, individual stockholders may obtain capital gains and losses, but all investors in the stock, taken as a group, receive only dividends from the firm.

To implement the DCF model, assumptions must be made about the future dividend stream. These assumptions can be tailored to the case at hand. The simplest assumption is that dividends are constant through time; this reduces to the dividend yield or earnings-price ratio. The currently most popular form assumes that the dividend and earnings stream are expected to grow indefinitely at some rate g because of future invest-ments which are financed through retained earnings. Under these assumptions,

$$P_0 = \frac{DIV_1}{(1 + k)} + \frac{DIV_1(1 + g)}{(1 + k)^2} + \ldots + \frac{DIV_1(1 + g)^{n-1}}{(1 + k)^n}$$

or

$$P_0 = \sum_{i=1}^{n} \frac{DIV_1(1 + g)^{i-1}}{(1 + k)^i}.$$

If we let n approach infinity and calculate the sum of the geometric pro-gression, assuming k is greater than g, we obtain $P = DIV_1/(k - g)$, which may be solved for k, yielding $k = [DIV_1/P] + g$. That is, the usual form of the DCF formula is given by:

Cost of equity capital = Dividend yield + Expected growth rate

Since earnings are collected frequently through the year, continuous com-pounding may be assumed and the current dividend substituted for D_1. The cost of equity capital is obtained by first computing the current divi-dend yield, which is observable. This dividend yield is added to the ex-pected growth rate in dividends, which is not directly observable and must be estimated with surrogate data, such as historical dividends, earnings, book value, retention ratios, rates of return on equity, and external growth data.

The earnings/price ratio is often proposed as a cost of equity measure. This measure is nothing more than a misspecification of the DCF method and, as such, incorrectly estimates the expected growth rate.

$$\text{Earnings/price ratio} = \frac{\text{Dividend}}{\text{Price}} + \frac{\text{Retained earnings}}{\text{Price}}$$

$$E/P = \frac{\text{Dividend}}{\text{Price}} + \frac{\text{Retained earnings}}{\text{Book value}} \times \frac{\text{Book value}}{\text{Price}}$$

$$E/P = D/P + g \text{ (misspecification error)}$$

The earnings/price ratio is thereby an accurate estimate of the cost of equity, k, only if the above assumptions are approximated and (1) all earnings are paid out as dividends, or (2) the market price to book value ratio equals 1. When the market-to-book ratio exceeds 1 or is less than 1, the earnings/price ratio understates and overstates the cost of equity, respectively.

The DCF cost of equity, k, takes into account a number of factors important in the determination of the fair rate of return:

1. Preferences of investors
2. Equity financing
3. Risk
4. Inflation

Each of these factors is discussed in turn.[47]

The discounted cash flow rate, k, is a combination of current and future investor preferences: (1) the rate at which equity investors expect current disposable income from an investment, D/P, plus (2) the rate of savings within the firm expected by equity investors, g. Accordingly, it can be seen that the DCF rate considers directly the time preferences of equity investors—i.e., their preferences for current disposable income and for savings. Since investors will pay a price for stock consistent with current and future dividends, the investor will be indifferent between adding another dollar to current personal income—dividends—and subtracting a dollar from savings—retained earnings. Accordingly, *ceteris paribus*, changes in the dividend payout ratio do not affect the cost of equity.[48]

Should the equity investor at some future date expect to sell his common stock, he would expect to receive a price equal to the discounted present value of the continuing dividend stream. Therefore, the DCF rate accurately reflects investor preferences whether the stock is held for income or traded speculatively.

Two types of equity financing are considered directly by the DCF rate:

1. Retained earnings
2. The sale of new common equity

Both types are considered in the expected growth rate, g. The expected growth rate in dividends equals the expected retained earnings rate—i.e., the ratio of retained earnings to book value. This rate provides growth by retained earnings, and further would allow sales of new common equity at approximately book value.

Where the cost of equity capital is expected to be earned on the book

---

[47] For a more thorough development of these issues, see Myron J. Gordon, *The Investment, Financing and Valuation of the Corporation* (Homewood, Ill.: Irwin, 1963). A more recent treatment is provided by James C. Van Horne in *Financial Management and Policy* (Englewood Cliffs, N.J.: Prentice-Hall, 1980).

[48] There is still some controversy about whether dividends matter in valuation. If dividends do matter, the effect is minimal. For a discussion, see Van Horne, *Financial Management and Policy*, chap. 11.

value of common equity, the common stock is traded at a price equal to the book value. When these conditions are approximated, new shares can be issued by the firm at roughly book value, as the securities are priced at near book value via market trading. Even when the firm's common stock sells below book value, common stock may be sold. Thus, with earnings below the cost of capital, common stock can often be sold below book value without a dividend and book value reduction. With new issues representing only a fraction of existing common equity, dilution—a reduction in book value—is minimal or unlikely until the rate of return is far below the DCF cost of equity capital. Dilution will result in an increase in dividend yield concomitant with the reduction in dividend growth.

Sale of new common equity at a market price substantially above book value could become a significant factor in expected dividend growth. Existing stockholders would thus expect an increment in book value investment at the expense of new investors paying a price for newly issued shares in excess of book value. Rates of return in excess of the cost of capital are required to generate a market price in excess of book value. In this situation, as was observed in the 1960s, retained earnings are usually plentiful, so external financing would be unlikely substantially to affect dividend growth. The DCF formula accordingly considers that increased equity can be obtained through retained earnings or new stock issues.

Risk is reflected directly in the DCF method through the stock price. Given the current dividend and the expected rate of growth in dividends, a more risky stock will have a correspondingly lower price and high cost of equity. Risk aversion by investors makes a more risky stock less valuable for the same expected dividend stream. For example, consider an investor viewing two expected dividend cash flows *equal in amount but of different risk*. The lower-risk stream of dividends would have the higher common stock price and lower yield. Using a numerical example, the dividend stream of a particular common stock is priced at $1000 a share with a 6 percent expected dividend growth rate and a 12 percent cost of capital. Suppose the other common stock with lower risk is priced at $2000 a share, resulting in a cost of capital of 9 percent. The first stock, as a result, receives a 3 percent risk premium over the second stock. Should investors' risk perceptions for a given expected dividend stream change, the market price would vary commensurately, and be accompanied by a changed cost of capital. Any discrepancy between the market risk premium and investors' perceptions of risk will lead to further changes until equilibrium is reached by equality between the market risk premium and investors' risk perceptions.

Where the market cost of equity is used with an original cost rate base reflecting straight-line original cost depreciation, investors receive both the real opportunity cost of capital and compensation for losses from expected inflation. An increase in the expected inflation rate will cause investors to require an equal increase in the market cost of capital, other conditions remaining the same. Investors, of course, sometimes make mistakes, and their expectations are not realized. The inflation expectations of investors may or may not equal historical realized inflation rates at each point in time. But it is not a regulatory commission's function to underwrite investor errors. Over a span of time, however, investors will form expectations by choosing an efficient method that will cause the long-term inflation compensation realized to equal the investor's expectations over the same span of time.

The nominal market cost of equity, directly calculated, is therefore the most appropriate measure of the sum of the real cost of capital and the inflation expectations of investors. To explain, consider hypothetical periods of no inflation and of inflation. Assume investors making an investment in a particular company in each period. The investors require a 6 percent real return on equity to purchase a share costing $100 with no inflation. The same investors will in another time expect 4 percent inflation and still require a 6 percent real return. Realizing that the $100 price from the noninflationary time will not provide this 10 percent return, investors will pay a lower price for the share and raise the cost of capital to receive the real 6 percent rate of return plus the extra 4 percent inflation compensation. This lower price raises the market cost of equity until the investor gets a return of 10 percent in nominal dollars, and maintains the real return of 6 percent.

Having derived the discounted cash flow method from the economic concept of discounted present value and explained that the discounted cash flow method applied to the cost of equity capital reflects investors' preferences, equity financing, risk, and inflation, we next consider empirical forms of the DCF function. As noted above, the cost of equity, k, can be solved to be equal to dividend yield (D/P) plus expected growth, g; i.e., $k = D/P + g$. This continuously compounded form uses D, the current dividend, for the firm continuously earns on monies slated for dividends even though they are paid only periodically. Just as a bank can accrue interest compounded continuously on savings accounts while paying the depositors only quarterly, so also the corporation can continuously earn on net income available for dividends throughout the quarter. The price, P, in the dividend yield requires some smoothing so that spot transactions are not overemphasized.

The expected growth rate, g, may be estimated by various procedures. Frequently, the precedure is to estimate the least square's growth rate for dividends per share, earnings per share, and book value per share. Another procedure recognizes that, fundamentally, dividend growth relies upon the retained earnings and sales of additional stock that accrues to current shareholders—$g = br + vs$

where

b = The expected earnings retention rate

r = The expected rate of return to equity

v = The fraction of funds raised from the sale of stock that accrues to current shareholders

s = Funds raised from the sale of stock as a fraction of existing common equity

The equality of the fundamental expected growth in dividends per share, earnings per share, and book value per share, ignoring statistical deviations, are all equal to g. Direct least squares computation of *a single firm's* actual growth in dividends per share, earnings per share, or book value per share is sensitive to:

1. The stair-step growth, rather than exact quarterly growth, in dividends which is represented by a seasonal variable
2. The deviations of observed dividends per share, earnings per share, and book value per share from the expected values, respectively
3. Outliers, when the rate of return or the retention ratios change dramatically for the firm

In growth models random observations are not independent; prior and current variations of the data from expected growth rates cause observed least squares growth rates to deviate from expected growth rates. Such variations occur for various reasons, such as delay or acceleration of dividend increases, realized returns that differ from the expected rate of return in some period, the random walk of earnings, or the target payout ratio not being met each and every period. Basically, once dividends grow more or less than expected, subsequent expected dividends grow from the new higher level and not from the expected level. Observed least squares growth rates deviate from the expected growth rate because of such dependence. Book value per share growth rates frequently are the least affected because the nonindependent error is a combination of several countervailing variations. Further, corporate policy can use variations from retention policies to offset transitory changes in rates of return and dividends, so that variations in growth in book value become relatively small and introduce less bias.

The alternative procedure begins with the fundamental definition of the Gordon DCF model, $k = D/P + br + vs$. The change in book value accruing to current stockholders from issuing stock at prices different from book value, vs, is difficult to estimate. It is difficult to estimate when, how much, and at what price stock will be issued. But when the utility is considering the issuance of common stock at a price selling much in excess of book value, the rate of return, r, is high and retained earnings are plentiful, so external financing is unlikely or small. Utilities are often reluctant to sell stock that dilutes earnings. The cost of capital then can be reasonably estimated as $k = D/P + br$.

Estimates of dividend yield can be derived as noted above, while estimates of expected retention rates, b, and expected rates of return, r, can be estimated from available and verifiable data. Average retention ratios and rates of return are reasonable methods of estimation to smooth out transitory variations about expected values. The random walk of a firm's earnings per share generally supports the use of statistical averages for b and r, though again outliers must be considered. Moving averages, over a limited span of years, of these variables b and r can account for the trends and the shifts in return and retention policy. This method is useful in applying the DCF method to a sample of firms, or a single firm, and permits checking the single firm's statistical bias in least squares estimates for dividend, earnings, and book value per share growth rates.

To give a hypothetical example, suppose the current annual dividend rate is $1.50 per share and the current price per share is $18.75. The dividend yield, D/P, is 8 percent. Next the growth rate, g, must be computed. This is usually done with a least squares estimate of the growth rate in dividends, earnings, or book value per share. If g is estimated to be 3.5 percent, then $k = 8\% + 3.5\% = 11.5\%$. This type of computation is usually done over several different time spans and under differing assumptions to check the plausibility of the cost-of-equity-capital estimate.

There are several difficulties in the application of the DCF approach. Assuming that one is satisfied with the dividend yield estimate, there is still the problem of estimating the growth component. Although this may be done by projecting the past growth rates of a data series, these growth rates are sensitive to the data series and the time frame selected.

The Risk-Premium Approach

The risk premium approach is a popular method of estimating the cost of equity capital for public utilities. The technique is based on the simple idea that since the returns on common stocks are inherently riskier than for bonds, investors will require a higher expected return to compensate them for the higher risk of the stocks. Therefore, the required rate of return on equity (k) can be viewed as the sum of two components: $k = \text{cost of debt} + \text{risk premium}$. This is consistent with modern finance concepts such as the capital asset pricing model (which is discussed briefly in the following subsection).

Several methods are used to implement this concept in rate proceedings. First, the current cost of debt must be established. This is typically done by taking a broad-based average of current market costs of debt for similar firms offering debt with similar characteristics to that of the firm in question. Second, the risk premium is calculated usually as the historical spread between the returns on debt and equity. This spread typically will be supported in a variety of ways. Several studies on the historical spread over different time frames have been performed by academicians and practitioners. In addition, the company itself may perform a study determining, for example, the average returns on utility bonds rated AAA over various time spans—perhaps 5-, 10-, 15-, and 20-year periods, and the returns to investors on its own common stock over these same time spans. The difference between the two, or *spread*, will vary somewhat depending on the time frame selected. Institutional investors may be surveyed to get their best estimate of the current spread between debt and equity returns for firms of this type. After the spread or risk premium is established, it is added to the current cost of debt to determine the estimate of the required rate of return on equity capital for the utility. A hypothetical example will illustrate the technique. Suppose 30-year utility bonds were issued last month at 8.75 percent. Utility ABC is a telephone utility. Moreover, assume the historical spread between utility bonds rated AAA and an average of cost on telephone utility equities over the last 20 years to be 4 percent. Based on these data, estimates of the required rate of return on equity for utility ABC would be 12.75 percent.

Obviously, the implementation of this technique requires substantial judgment and knowledge of capital market behavior. Several potential problems with the approach require attention. First, what is the appropriate time period to be used to determine the spread? This is especially important if the spread varies substantially as different time spans are considered. Second, if an average is used, what firms should be included in the average? If the risk of the common stocks included in the average is greater than the risk of the utility in question, the spread will be biased upward. Third, to what extent does the historical spread reflect what is expected in the future? The required rate of return on equity is a forward-looking concept and is influenced largely by current and future economic and political conditions, not past conditions. Fourth, it would be helpful to have a better understanding of the factors affecting the spread. For example, how does the spread change with the level and changes in interest rates, inflation, and other factors? Because of the forward-looking nature of the estimates required, this additional information would be extremely useful in implementing the technique. Finally, was the historical cost of equity giving rise to the risk premium estimate accurately and properly computed?

The Capital Asset Pricing Model (CAPM) Approach

The capital asset pricing model (CAPM) is a relatively new approach that has met with mixed reaction in the estimation of utilities' cost of equity capital. This method develops certain conceptual bases for the two parts of the risk premium method—the cost of debt and the risk premium. A recent survey found that two commissions (Oregon and South Carolina) actually had a preference for CAPM testimony, while only one (Texas) was generally against its use.[49] Some 38 states had seen CAPM testimony or had it under consideration. Attitudes and usage in regulatory proceedings appear to be changing, with CAPM becoming more acceptable. Still, no consensus regarding its proper role is apparent.

CAPM is based on the notion that investors generally hold portfolios of securities, not a single security, and therefore the riskiness of a security is viewed in terms of its contribution to the riskiness of the portfolio.[50] The basic assumptions of CAPM are these:

1. The market in which investors trade is highly efficient. Investors have ready access to all relevant information at no cost. Transaction costs are zero. Investors face no restrictions on trading and behave as if their trading activity will have no effect on prices (they are price takers).
2. Investors have homogeneous expectations regarding the expected return and risk of all securities.
3. Investors may borrow and lend at the risk-free interest rate, i.
4. Investors attempt to maximize expected utility of wealth and choose among alternative portfolios based upon their mean R_p and standard deviation σ_p.

The investor attempts to maximize the expected utility of wealth derived from the assets held. The investor, by diversifying into a number of securities not perfectly correlated with one another, can lower the risk of the portfolio relative to its return.

The total risk of a particular security (the standard deviation of its rate of return) may be broken down into two components. The first, called *systematic* (or *undiversifiable*) *risk*, is that part of a security's variability directly related to overall movements in economic activity. It is that risk all stocks have in common and thus cannot be diversified away. The second component of total risk, *unsystematic* (or *diversifiable* or *unique*) *risk*, is unique to a particular security, resulting from things like strikes, weather conditions, management, lawsuits, and input conditions. In a well-diversified

---

[49] Diana R. Harrington, "The Changing Use of the Capital Asset Pricing Model," *Public Utilities Fortnightly*, February 14, 1980, pp. 28–30.

[50] For more detail on virtually every aspect of CAPM, consult Eugene F. Fama, *Foundations of Finance* (New York: Basic Books, 1976).

portfolio of securities, this second component is eliminated by offsetting movements in the returns of individual securities, leaving only systematic risk. Thus, the relevant risk of a security in a CAPM context is its systematic risk. Investors require greater return for holding securities with higher systematic risk. The capital market in equilibrium establishes this relationship. The market in a CAPM environment does not reward unsystematic risk with extra return.

The measurement of systematic risk is accomplished by measuring the degree to which the security moves up and down with the market. This tendency to move with the market is measured by the security's *beta coefficient*, β. A beta of 1.0 means that if the market goes up 10 percent, the security's return will also go up by 10 percent. If beta is 1.5, a fall in the market of 10 percent will be accompanied by a 15 percent fall in the security's return. In general, a beta less than 1.0 is less volatile than the market and a beta greater than 1.0 more volatile. Technically, beta is defined as the covariance of the security's rate of return with the market's return divided by the variance of market returns. Almost all securities have a positive beta coefficient and thus tend to move with the market.

The relationship between risk and return in the CAPM framework, known as the *security market line* (SML), is given by the following equation:

$$R_j = i + (R_m - i)\beta_j \tag{1}$$

where:

$$\beta_j = \frac{\text{cov}(R_j, R_m)}{\sigma_m^2}$$

and where:

R_j = expected rate of return of security j

i = risk-free rate

R_m = expected rate of return or the market portfolio, the portfolio of all securities in the market

β_j = beta coefficient of security j

σ_m^2 = variance of returns for the market

$\text{cov}(R_j, R_m)$ = covariance between the returns for security j and those of the market portfolio

It is evident that the expected rate of return on security j is equal to the risk-free rate plus a risk premium which depends on the security's systematic risk as measured by its beta coefficient. The higher the beta, the higher the firm's expected return. The expected return of security *j* is the investors' required rate of return when the market is in equilibrium. The expected rate forms the basis for estimates of the required rate of the utility's equity holders or cost of equity capital.

Betas have been used in at least two ways in rate hearings. The first is to identify firms of equivalent risk. Once firms of equivalent risk are identified based on their betas, an average cost of capital for the group is determined. This is then used as a return guideline for the utility under consideration. Incidentally, the logic underlying the use of betas to identify firms of approximately equal risk is based on portfolio theory, not necessarily on the validity of the more elaborate CAPM.[51] Such betas generally show utility common stock to have significantly less risk than the market portfolio. Modern portfolio theory asserts that portfolio risk can be measured by the standard deviation of portfolio return, σ_p. For a particular security, risk is identified as its marginal contribution to σ_p. The marginal contribution of a particular security, say security *j*, is proportional to $\mathrm{cov}(R_j, R_P)$, the covariance between the return on security *j* and the portfolio return.[52] It follows from the definition of a beta coefficient that the firm's risk would also be proportional to β_{jp}, the beta of security *j* with respect to R_P. But note that the return on any well-diversified portfolio will be highly correlated with the market portfolio *M*. Therefore, in estimating the firm's risk by its beta, we are using the market portfolio *M* as a proxy for our standard portfolio *P*.

The second and more common use of beta is to apply CAPM and the security market line in the computation of the cost of equity capital. As the definitive methodology for estimating beta in this framework does not yet exist, the procedure that follows is only indicative. First, a beta for the utility in question is estimated using regression analysis or is purchased from a financial services company like Merrill Lynch. Using linear regression analysis, a firm's beta is often calculated via the empirical model:

$$R_{jt} = a_j + b_j R_{It} + e_{jt} \qquad (2)$$

where:

R_{jt} = security *j*'s rate of return in period *t*;

R_{It} = rate of return on market index (Standard and Poor's 500) in period *t*; and

e_t = error term

The firm's characteristic line is determined from the results of estimating

---

[51] Stewart C. Meyers, "The Application of Finance Theory to Public Utility Rate Cases," *Bell Journal of Economics and Management Science*, 3, 1 (spring 1972), 68.

[52] Meyers, "Application of Finance Theory," p. 68.

this equation. It is the line of best fit. The b_j coefficient from equation (2) is the estimate of beta for security j. Usually, realized weekly or monthly market rates of return are used in this calculation over a three- to five-year period. After the firm's beta is obtained, it is used in equation (1) along with estimates of i and R_m, the risk-free rate and the market rate, over the period to obtain the estimated cost of equity capital. The risk-free rate that is used in this computation should correspond to that interest rate or cost of debt in the risk premium method.

A highly simplified example of a CAPM-determined cost of equity capital is used for illustration. Suppose, using monthly data on Gamma Utility Company and Standard and Poor's 500 index over the last five years in equation (2), it is determined that Gamma's beta equals 0.82. Further, the present rate for 90-day Treasury Bills is 9 percent, while the expected rate on the market portfolio is 13 percent, giving rise to a market risk premium of 4 percent. The cost of equity estimate may be obtained from equation (1) as $R_{\text{Gamma}} = 9\% + (13\% - 9\%) .82 = 12.28\%$. Obviously, in obtaining this estimate, many of the complicating problems that must be faced in actually implementing CAPM are ignored.

In regulatory proceedings, the use of CAPM has not been endorsed wholeheartedly by academicians or practitioners. There are numerous conceptual and practical problems encountered in its use, and many of these difficulties are evident in a recent exchange in the *Financial Management* journal.[53] Among the problems that must be faced are the determination of appropriate period returns (which rates to use as observation over what period) and the risk-free rate, use of *ex post* data to predict *ex ante* return, instability of individual betas over time, and various biases in estimation, not the least of which is that resulting from the presence of unsystematic risk. In a recent paper by R. Litzenberger, K. Ramaswamy, and H. Sosin,[54] at least seven alternative versions of CAPM are set forth, each based on a modification of the basic CAPM assumptions. The most appropriate version of CAPM depends on which most accurately predicts the utility's cost of equity capital. But there are no definitive guidelines by which to judge this. Nevertheless, the authors indicate the types of adjustments necessary to remedy certain types of biases. As a final word of warning, the CAPM, like all models, must be used with great care if it is to be presented in rate hearings.

The questions raised about the precision of the CAPM, a conceptually complete method whose parameters have been estimated with varying degrees of success, cast serious doubts on the *ad hoc* versions of the risk

[53] Comments by various authors on "Use of the CAPM in Public Utility Rate Cases," *Financial Management*, autumn 1978, pp. 52–76.

[54] "On the CAPM Approach to the Estimation of a Public Utility's Cost of Equity Capital," *Journal of Finance*, 35, 2 (May 1980), 369–383.

premium method discussed above. Both are of this form:

$$\text{Rate of return} = \text{Interest rate} + \text{Risk premium}$$

The CAPM, even with its difficulties, has been tested statistically regarding the accuracy of the interest rate and risk premium used. The *ad hoc* versions of the risk premium method have not been so tested.

Study Questions

1. Define the elements of the rate-making equation. What is the role of the rate-making equation in the regulatory process?

2. How was the reasonableness of the rate base determined early in regulation? What problems were encountered under the standards of the Smythe case? How did the Hope case help?

3. What are the standards for a reasonable rate of return? What methods are used to determine the "fair" rate of return?

4. Why is the regulation of quality of service given short shrift in terms of the time and effort of regulators?

5. What do regulators consider discriminatory rates?

6. How is a cost-of-equity-capital estimate determined using the DCF approach? What are the advantages and shortcomings of this approach?

7. How is the allowed rate of return determined given the separate rates of return on debt, preferred, and common stock? Criticize this approach.

8. Utility ABC, Inc., has a cost of capital of 10 percent, gross utility plant of $200 million, a rate base of $100 million, operating expenses of $28 million, $2 million of taxes other than income taxes, a 50 percent income tax rate applicable to an equity cost of 6 percent of the 10 percent return, and an annual depreciation rate of 4 percent. What is the revenue requirement? What would the revenue requirement be if *pro forma* adjustments increased operating expenses by $5 million and decreased gross plant by $10 million? (Be careful, the latter adjustment is multifaceted.)

9. Examining a utility balance sheet, we find $400 million in common equity, $100 million in preferred stock, and $500 million in long-term debt. Calculation indicates a 9.5 percent rate for preferred stock dividends, and an 8.5 percent interest rate on long-term debt. Calculate the cost of capital if the cost of equity is 10, 12, 14, or 16 percent. What are the tax consequences of these different equity returns? Which equity return should be allowed if one witness testified that

industrial firms earned 16 percent on common equity last year, another testified that the earnings/price ratio was 14 percent for the utility, a third stated the dividend yield plus the expected growth in dividends equals 12 percent, and a final expert opined that like utilities earned 10 percent on common equity over the last three years? Write an opinion on the rate of return that might be included in a commission opinion. Cite court decisions, analyze the evidence, and give reasons for the return on equity finally selected.

10. Calculate the difference between straight-line depreciation expense and double-declining balance depreciation expense for a $1.5 million investment with a 15-year life. How do the tax deductions differ over the 15-year span using the two methods of depreciation?

11. What are the factors affecting the fair rate of return discussed in the Bluefield, Hope, and Permian Basin decisions? Do any of these decisions cite a specific technique for computing return on equity?

12. Criticize the view that common stock investors in utilities have faced stock prices that have not kept pace with inflation.

13. Calculate the utility bill for 1495 KWH using the following tariff.

Electric Tariff

Customer charge	$5
Energy charge	
7¢ per KWH for the first 250 KWH	
4¢ per KWH for each KWH over 250 KWH up to 1000 KWH	
3¢ per KWH for all KWH in excess of 1000	
Energy adjustment clause	
1.5¢ per KWH	

What factors could cause the energy adjustment clause to change?

14. Examine a public utility's annual report to stockholders. List the parts of the report that refer to utility regulation or its effects.

15. Examine the annual report of your state's utility commission.

16. Read a recent volume of *Public Utilities Reports*, a legal reporter of commission and court decisions. What traditional regulatory issues were before the commissions in these cases? Select one decision and outline the issues discussed.

17. List the areas in which public utility rates affect, directly and indirectly, your cost of living.

18. Are your utility rates fair? Give reasons for your opinion. Which utility

service costs you more—telephone, electricity, or gas? Does the lowest-cost service have the fairest rates?

Student Readings

FARRIS, M., AND R. SAMPSON.   *Public Utilities.* Boston: Houghton-Mifflin, 1973, chaps. 6, 7, 8.

GARFIELD, PAUL, AND W. LOVEJOY.   *Public Utility Economics.* Englewood Cliffs, N.J.: Prentice-Hall, 1964, chaps. 5–9, 12.

KAHN, ALFRED E.   *The Economics of Regulation,* vol. 1. New York: Wiley, 1970, chap. 2.

PHILLIPS, CHARLES R., JR.   *The Economics of Regulation,* 2nd ed. Homewood, Ill.: Irwin, 1969, pp. 128–32, chaps. 7–9.

Advanced Readings

BAUER, JOHN.   *Effective Regulation of Public Utilities.* New York: Macmillan, 1925.

BONBRIGHT, JAMES C., AND GARDINER C. MEANS.   *The Holding Company.* New York: McGraw-Hill, 1932.

BONBRIGHT, JAMES C.   *Principles of Public Utility Rates.* New York: Columbia University Press, 1961, chaps. 10–15.

CATALONO, PETER.   "Determining Utilities Cash Working Capital Allowances." *Public Utilities Fortnightly,* November 20, 1980, pp. 46–48.

COMMONS, JOHN R.   *Legal Foundations of Capitalism.* New York: Macmillan, 1924.

COPELAND, BASIL L.   "Alternative Cost-of-Capital Concepts in Regulation." *Land Economics,* 54, 3 (August 1978), 348–361.

DORAU, HERBERT B.   *Materials for Study of Public Utility Economics.* New York: Macmillan, 1930.

FREEMAN, HARROP A.   "Public Utility Depreciation." *Cornell Law Quarterly,* 32 (1946), 4–23.

GLAESER, MARTIN G.   *Outlines of Public Utility Economics.* New York: Macmillan, 1927.

GORDON, MYRON J.   "Rate of Return Regulation in the Current Economic Environment." In *Adapting Regulation to Shortages, Curtailments and Inflation,* ed. John L. O'Donnell. East Lansing: Michigan State University, 1977, pp. 15–28.

GORDON, MYRON J. *The Investment, Financing and Valuation of the Corporation.* Homewood, Ill.: Irwin, 1963.

IRWIN, MANLEY R., AND KENNETH B. STANLEY. "Regulatory Circumvention and the Holding Company." *Journal of Economic Issues*, 8, 2 (June 1974), 395–408.

JOSKOW, PAUL L. "Inflation and Environmental Concern: Structural Changes in the Process of Public Utility Price Regulation." *Journal of Law and Economics*, October 1974, pp. 291–327.

KAY, J. A. "Accountants, Too, Could be Happy in a Golden Age: The Accountants Rate of Profit and the Internal Rate of Return." *Oxford Economic Papers*, November 1976, pp. 447–460.

LERNER, EUGENE M., AND WILLARD T. CARLETON. "The Capital Structure Problem of a Regulated Public Utility." *Public Utilities Fortnightly*, July 8, 1965, pp. 24–32.

LEWIS, BEN W. "Public Utilities." In *Government and Economic Life*, vol. II, eds. Leverett S. Lyonn and Victor Abramson. Washington, D.C.: The Brookings Institution, 1940, pp. 616–745.

MACAVOY, PAUL W. "The Informal Work-Product of the Federal Power Commission." *The Bell Journal of Economics and Management Science*, spring 1971, pp. 379–395.

MAO, JAMES C. T. "Planning the Optimal Capital Structure." In *Quantitative Analysis of Financial Decisions*. New York: Macmillan, 1969, pp. 415–463.

MYERS, S. C. "The Application of Finance Theory to Public Utility Rate Case." *The Bell Journal*, 3, 1 (1972), 58–97.

MUMEY, GLEN A. "Earnings Probabilities and Capital Costs." *Journal of Business*, October 1967, pp. 450–461.

MUNDELL, ROBERT. "Inflation and Real Interest." *Journal of Political Economy*, June 1963, pp. 280–283.

OSTERYOUNG, JEROME S. "Franchise Fees Reexamined." *Public Utilities Fortnightly*, November 24, 1977, pp. 29–31.

RASMUSSEN, EUGENE F. "Investor Risk and Required Rate of Return in Regulated Industries: A Comment." *Nebraska Journal of Economics and Business*, autumn 1978, pp. 51–56.

"Recent Cases on Compensating Bank Balances." *Public Utilities Fortnightly*, January 20, 1977, pp. 48–49.

SCHMID, J. RICHARD. "The Statistician as Expert Witness: Forecasting Energy Sales—A Case History." *American Statistical Association 1976 Proceedings of the Business and Economics Statistics Section*. Washington, D.C.: American Statistical Association, 1976, pp. 583–588.

SOLOMON, E.   "Alternative Rate of Return Concepts and Their Implication for Utility Regulation." *The Bell Journal*, 1, 1 (1970), 65–71.

STAUFFER, THOMAS R.   "The Measurement of Corporate Rates of Return: A Generalized Formulation." *Bell Journal of Economics*, autumn 1971, pp. 434–469.

SUELFLOW, JAMES E.   *Public Utility Accounting: Theory and Application*. East Lansing: Michigan State University, 1973.

TOWERS, ROBERT G.   "CWIP—In Rate Base or Not?" *Proceedings of the Iowa State University Regulatory Conference, 1980*. Ames: Iowa State University, forthcoming.

"Utilities Fight to Escape a Tax-Credit Trap." *Business Week*, December 5, 1977, pp. 96–100.

VAN HORNE, JAMES C.   *Financial Management and Policy*. Englewood Cliffs, N.J.: Prentice-Hall, 1980.

Cases

Bluefield Water Works and Improvement Co. v. *Public Service Commission of the State of West Virginia*, 262 U.S. 67 L. ed. 1176.

Federal Power Commission et al. v. *Hope Natural Gas Company*, 320 U.S. 591 51 PUR(NS) 193.

Iowa State Commerce Commission, re: *Iowa Power and Light Company*, 6 PUR 4th 446.

Iowa State Commerce Commission, re: *Northwestern Bell Telephone Co.*, 97 PUR 3d. 447.

Market Street Railway Co. v. *California Railroad Commission et al.*, 324 U.S. 548, 58 PUR(NS) 18.

Missouri Ex Rel Sourthwestern Bell Telephone Co. v. *Public Service Commission*, 262 U.S. 276.

Permian Basin Area Rate Cases, 390 U.S. 747, 20 L. ed. 2d. 312.

New York Public Service Commission, re: *New York Telephone Co.*, 23 PUR 4th 554.

United Railways & Electric Co. of Baltimore v. *Harold E. West*, 280 U.S. 234, 74 L. ed. 390.

5

Independent Regulatory Commissions

This chapter provides some historical background and rationale for the regulation of public utilities by independent regulatory commissions. It also briefly reviews commission procedures and behaviors. Finally, the alleged advantages and shortcomings of commission regulation are presented.

——— ANTECEDENTS OF REGULATORY COMMISSIONS ———

JUDICIAL REGULATION

Our statute law is based on principles embodied in early English common law. Certain occupations were identified under common law as common callings. These industries were required to provide adequate service at reasonable rates without discrimination. An aggrieved party, one who was charged unreasonable rates, discriminated against, or denied service, had the right to sue. This right of legal redress through the courts was the customary method of handling these grievances until well into the nineteenth century.

Judicial regulation, as it is called, had many limitations: (1) litigation was slow and expensive; (2) courts lacked the required expertise for effective regulation; and (3) courts attempted to "right past wrongs," not to chart future behavior, which was the job of the legislature. These weaknesses made the courts ineffective regulators.

DIRECT LEGISLATIVE REGULATION

During the nineteenth century, in an attempt to cope with the problems of judicial regulation, direct legislative regulation of the public utility emerged as the dominant form. Initially, public utilities were incorporated by special legislative acts, under which a charter of incorporation was granted, specifying their special rights and privileges, such as the right of eminent domain. Fairly detailed regulatory provisions governing maximum rates or even the rate structure were also generally included in the charter. The corporation movement at the end of the nineteenth century prompted the enactment of general incorporation laws. These laws made it a routine matter for a firm to incorporate simply by filing the required application with the appropriate state office. Since these laws applied to all firms that were to be incorporated, they provided a charter which was broadly worded as to rates, condition of services, and security issuance. Both the special and the general legislative enactments were ineffective in their regulatory impact.

The difficulties with direct legislative regulation were many: Legislatures, like the courts, do not have the specialized knowledge required to regulate the public utility; direct legislative regulation lacked the flexibility required in the face of a changing corporate environment—adjustments required amendments to the law and violations required court action for enforcement—and, as a result, continuous regulation was impossible; there was an incentive for bribery and fraud in obtaining and maintaining special charters; without meaningful accounting information, rate regulation is extremely difficult. As one can imagine, attempts to enforce the regulatory provisions of these charters were meager and faced tremendous obstacles. Because of these inadequacies of direct statutory regulation, local franchise regulation became popular in the late nineteenth and early twentieth centuries.

LOCAL FRANCHISE REGULATION

Franchise contracts were the dominant form of public utility regulation at the turn of the century and, though steadily displaced by commission regulation, remained popular for many years. To operate within the municipality, the company had to obtain a franchise, which is nothing more than a contract between the city and the company specifying the special privileges and duties of the public utility. The rights granted to the firm might include for example, eminent domain, use of city streets and property for its pipes, poles, and tracks, and exclusive right to supply the designated service for some period of time. Among the accompanying obligations were provisions covering the type and conditions of service, the level and structure of rates, the term of the franchise, taxes, and accounting.

The duration of the franchise could be classified as perpetual, limited term, or indeterminate. The perpetual franchise has no expiration date, and since it yields to the utility substantial power and lacks flexibility, it is no longer issued. The duration of the limited-term franchise ranges from 5 to 50 years, which permits renegotiation and adjustment upon expiration. The shorter-term franchisee often faced the difficulty of obtaining low-cost financing for expansion, while the longer-term franchisee may feel so secure in its position as to provide less than adequate service. The limited-term franchise is also inflexible in that it does not provide a mechanism for a rate change other than renegotiation of the contract. The indeterminate franchise remained in effect until terminated by the city. If the franchise was terminated, the city generally could acquire the property for reasonable compensation. This form of contract thus provides an inducement to the utility to provide adequate service, without the problems of orderly expansion as the expiration date approaches and of renegotiation of contracts.

The shortcomings probably outweigh the advantages of local franchise regulation, at least for most areas. Franchise regulation was ineffective because of its inability to respond to a rapidly changing environment—the franchise terms could not be readily altered. Second, it faced jurisdictional problems as utilities outgrew city boundaries and state regulation became desirable. Finally, cities lacked and failed to provide the administrative machinery required for effective regulation. These inadequacies ultimately led to state commission regulation.

Local franchise regulation has again developed in the cable television area, and difficulties similar to those of franchise regulation of other public utilities are presently being reported.[1]

COMMISSION REGULATION

Prior to 1870, state commissions were principally advisory in nature, and federal commissions did not exist. Then, with the consumer-oriented Granger movement, came a push for strong regulatory commissions. By 1874, commissions in Illinois, Iowa, Minnesota, and Wisconsin were empowered to set maximum rates for and prevent discrimination by the railroads. These commissions did not survive intact. Minnesota and Iowa reestablished commissions that set rates in 1885 and 1887, respectively. The Massachusetts Gas and Electric Commission was established in 1885. In 1887, Congress created the Interstate Commerce Commission to regulate

---

[1] "TV Cables in a Tangle," *Newsweek*, August 4, 1980, pp. 44–45.

interstate rail service. Responding to numerous abuses, stronger state commissions with expanded regulatory powers and jurisdiction over public utilities were created in New York, under Governor Charles Evans Hughes, and in Wisconsin, under Governor LaFollette, in 1907. During this period, the public ownership movement was strong and commission regulation blunted its attack. These more potent commissions served as models of regulation for other states; by 1920, two-thirds of the states had commissions, though some had relatively limited powers. Today there is a regulatory commission in each state, and the Federal Energy Regulatory Commission and Federal Communication Commission, commissions established in 1977 and 1934, respectively, regulate interstate public utility activities (see the appendix to this chapter).

COMMISSION ACTIVITIES

OVERVIEW OF PROCEDURES

The regulatory agencies are charged with the protection of the public interest. In the furtherance of this objective, they regulate prices, entry, and conditions and quality of service. Their rulings must be consistent with statutory law and due process and are subject to judicial review.

Procedures followed by state and federal commissions vary, but not greatly. Regulatory commissions have the authority under their governing statutes to adopt rules and regulations that have the force of law. Some rules set forth the regulatory procedure; others give specific content to the general wording of the statute, specification of proper accounting standards being an example of the latter. Public hearings are often used for the adoption of important rules.

Adjudicated cases are those involving a formal proceeding, open to the public, at which the commission gathers evidence, evaluates it, and rules on a contested issue. These include rate hearings, service complaints, and proposed changes of the nature and scope of the utility's activities, such as adding or abandoning service, mergers, and plant expansions. Adjudication may be initiated by the utility, an outside party such as customers, or the commission. When a formal case is initiated, the commission sets a date for the public hearing and gives notice to all parties concerned so that they have time to develop evidence to represent their interests. The rules governing the testimony of witnesses or evidence follow those of courtroom proceedings, but are generally not quite as strict. All parties have the opportunity to present evidence, to cross-examine opposition testimony, and to present rebuttal testimony. A verbatim record is kept of the proceedings. Finally, a decision is rendered by the commission. This decision becomes binding if the parties to it do not apply for a rehearing on the grounds the decision is in error, new evidence has been found, or conditions affecting the decision have changed substantially during the proceeding. If the application for a rehearing is refused, the aggrieved party may seek judicial review.

NATURE OF COMMISSION ACTIONS

Commissions act in a quasi-judicial and quasi-executive fashion. The separation of powers doctrine is not one of the basic tenets of regulation; commissioners are asked to be good judges (and jurors), legislators, and administrators. They act in a quasi-judicial manner when hearing evidence and rendering decisions. Commissioners' actions are quasi-legislative when they prescribe detailed standards and rules for the utility to follow. Finally, their behavior is administrative in nature when they investigate rates and service and enforce orders.

THE RATIONALE FOR COMMISSION REGULATION

Why this form of regulation? Thomas M. Cooley established the blueprint for regulation by his administration of the Interstate Commerce Commission in its first years. The quasi-judicial review by commissions of utility management and operations was established. The alleged advantages of this form include independence, continuity and expertise, and collegiality.

INDEPENDENCE

The members of a commission are presumed to have a high degree of autonomy from the executive and other branches of the government. Several factors lead to this independence. First, appointive commissions are invariably bipartisan in nature, with no more than a simple majority from one political party. Second, commissioners hold lengthy terms of office, ranging from 4 to 10 years, which extend beyond the term of office of the individual appointing them. Finally, it is extremely difficult to remove a commissioner from office—he or she cannot be removed simply because of an unpopular decision. In practice, however, all three branches have some influence on commission behavior: the legislative, control over authority and funding; the executive, appointment power and budget control; and the judicial, power to interpret statutes and to determine whether a commission has exceeded its authority and whether its findings are based on adequate evidence.

Continuity and Expertise

Because of their lengthy term in office, commissioners' expertise may be enhanced; they may gain in knowledge and judgment over time. Moreover, the staggered terms of commissioners promote continuity of policy. Finally, since the range of commission activity is limited, commissions are able to focus on and become experts in regulatory matters.

Collegiality

A ruling is generally not a single individual's decision; rather, commission decisions are made by a group. This promotes deliberation and results in decisions that are not capricious or arbitrary.

So the potential advantages include impartiality, flexibility, continuity, and expertise.

——— THE LIMITATIONS OF COMMISSION REGULATION ———

Commission regulation is not without shortcomings. Commissions have a tendency to be passive, reactive bodies rather than leaders. The salaries are often said to be inadequate to attract high-caliber commissioners and staff. The legislation governing commission behavior does not always provide sufficient direction for commission activities. The complexity of regulation and inadequate staffs can lead to indecision, long proceedings, and a regulatory lag. The lack of separation of functions (administrative, legislative, and judicial) makes it difficult to act objectively and provides no balance of power.

The independence and collegiality of commissions may create problems. Independence may make commissions unresponsive to overall governmental policy, resulting in conflict in governmental actions. The federal government had in 1969 nineteen separate agencies involved in activities directly relating to electric power:

1. Department of Agriculture
   Rural Electrification Administration
2. Commerce Department
   Environmental Science Services Administration (Weather Bureau)
3. Department of Defense
   Corps of Engineers, Department of the Army
4. Department of Interior
   Bureau of Reclamation
   Bureau of Indian Affairs
   Bonneville Power Administration

> Southeastern Power Administration
> Southwestern Power Administration
> Geological Survey
> Bureau of Mines

5. Department of Justice
6. Department of State
    International Boundary and Water Commission—United States and Mexico
    International Joint Commission—United States and Canada
7. Executive Office of the President
    Bureau of the Budget
8. Atomic Energy Commission
9. Federal Power Commission
10. St. Lawrence Seaway Development Corporation
11. Tennessee Valley Authority
12. Water Resources Council.[2]

These agencies carried out seven major functions:

1. Licensing of non-federal use of public lands and navigable waters of the United States
2. Regulation of power moving in interstate commerce
3. Construction, operation, and maintenance of federal projects and marketing of the power produced at such projects
4. Actions in connection with development of power in international streams
5. Research and development aimed at stimulating the use of atomic energy
6. Loan programs to stimulate the use of electricity to better living conditions
7. Collection of basic data on water resources for power operations[3]

The creation of the federal Department of Energy brought several, but not all, of these functions into one agency and sought to coordinate energy policy. Included in the Department of Energy are these areas:

1. Atomic energy defense activities and uranium enrichment
2. Energy research and development
3. The Federal Energy Regulatory Commission—formerly the Federal Power Commission
4. The Energy Information Agency
5. The Power Marketing Administration

---

[2] Theodore M. Schad, "Federal Agencies Involved with Electric Power," in *Hearings Before the Senate Committee on Government Operations on S.607, The Utility Consumers' Counsel Act of 1969*, part 4 (Washington, D.C.: U.S. Government Printing Office), pp. 1148–1153.

[3] Ibid., p. 1148.

Among the commissions and agencies remaining outside were the Nuclear Regulatory Commission and the Rural Electrification Administration.

Collegiality may weaken the overall administration of the commission and its staff by creating conflicting authorities. David M. Welborn found that the role of the chair on federal commissions, with the exception of the FCC, has been enlarged in the last decade to provide interagency coordination and to provide administrative control of the commission staff.[4] This type of organizational change appears to be an attempt to integrate the staff organization of the commission with the traditional line organization of government and business. Traditional governmental agencies have an organization that follows the more conventional line structure. An agency head makes policy decisions and issues directives, and subordinates in the chain of command carry out the policy. If not, the department head in the organization takes remedial action. Regulatory commissions, on the other hand, tend to have a staff organization. Specialized professionals—with their own professional alliances, standards, and views—review rate and service filings by utilities and other parties, and police compliance with legislation rate orders, service standards, and accounting requirements. The staff then reports its findings both formally and informally to the commission. Control of staff organizations generally is less effective, a result seen in regulatory commissions. But criticisms that propose line organization for regulatory commissions may have limited effect; studies that draw upon staff organizations are sorely needed.[5]

SUMMARY

Early regulation of utilities during the 1800s and early 1900s took three major forms: judicial regulation, direct legislation, and local franchise regulation. First, under judicial regulation, effective regulation was lacking, since an aggrieved party had to use the court system for legal redress. Second, regulation via direct legislation of maximum rates, rate structure, and the like as set forth in the corporation's charter suffered from difficulties in making changes to the original charter and lack of specialized knowledge on the part of the legislatures. The third form, granting a franchise, was also ineffective because it was inflexible and lacked an administrative mechanism for effective regulation. Because of the inadequacies of these early forms and the perceived successes of commissions, commission regulation became the dominant form of utility regulation during the 1900s.

---

[4] David M. Welborn, *Governance of Federal Regulatory Agencies* (Knoxville: University of Tennessee Press, 1977), pp. 131, 147.

[5] Additional criticisms will be covered in a more detailed fashion in Chapter 6.

To protect the public interest, commissions regulate prices, entry, and conditions and quality of service. In formal proceedings, the commission gathers evidence, evaluates it, and renders a decision on major issues, much like in a courtroom proceeding. Commissioners are asked to be good judges, legislators, and administrators. Commissions act in a quasi-judicial fashion when hearing evidence and rendering decisions; in a quasi-legislative fashion when prescribing standards and rules; and in an administrative fashion when investigating rates and enforcing orders. Commission regulation thus lacks separation of powers.

The alleged advantages of commission regulation include independence (commission members are assumed to be largely independent of the executive and other branches of government), continuity and expertise (commission members have a long term of service that presumably enhances their expertise), and collegiality (decisions of a multimember commission are based on deliberate and reasoned judgment and therefore are not likely to be capricious or arbitrary). These advantages may be restated as impartiality, flexibility, continuity, and expertise.

The disadvantages of commission regulation are numerous. The complexity of regulation and inadequate staffs can lead to indecision, long proceedings, and regulatory lag. The lack of separation of functions—judicial, legislative, and administrative—impedes objective action and provides no balance of power. Commission independence may result in unresponsiveness to overall governmental policy, while collegiality may lessen the effectiveness of administration by creating conflicting authorities within the commission.

Appendix

Federal Regulatory Agencies – Public Agencies

Commission	Year Established	Primary Regulatory Function
Civil Aeronautics Board	1938	Regulates passenger fares and subsidizes air transport.
Federal Communications Commission	1934	Regulates rates for interstate and foreign services of telephone and telegraph carriers and licenses civilian radio and television communication.
Federal Energy Regulatory Commission	1977[a]	Regulates rates and practices of sales for resale, interstate electricity transmission, and transmission of natural gas.

Commission	Year Established	Primary Regulatory Function
Interstate Commerce Commission	1887	Regulates rates, routes, and practices of railroads, truck and bus lines, oil pipelines, domestic water carriers, and freight forwarders.
Nuclear Regulatory Commission	1975	Regulates the construction and operation of nuclear power plants.
Postal Rate Commission	1970	Regulates rates of the U.S. Postal Service.
Securities and Exchange Commission	1934	Regulates financial disclosure of publicly held firms, and certain practices of mutual funds investment advisors and public utility holding companies.

[a] A predecessor, the Federal Power Commission, was created in 1920.

SOURCE: National Association of Regulatory Commissioners, *1978 Annual Report on Utility and Carrier Regulation of the National Association of Regulatory Utility Commissioners.*

State Regulatory Agencies — Public Utilities

Alabama Public Service Commission
Alaska Public Utilities Commission
Arizona Corporation Commission
Arkansas Public Service Commission
California Public Utilities Commission
Colorado Public Utilities Commission
Connecticut Public Utilities Control Authority
Delaware Public Service Commission
District of Columbia Public Service Commission
Florida Public Service Commission
Georgia Public Service Commission
Hawaii Public Utilities Commission
Idaho Public Utilities Commission
Illinois Commerce Commission
Indiana Public Service Commission
Iowa State Commerce Commission
Kansas State Corporation Commission
Kentucky Energy Regulatory Commission
Kentucky Utilities Regulatory Commission
Louisiana Public Service Commission

Maine Public Utilities Commission
Maryland Public Service Commission
Massachusetts Department of Public Utilities
Michigan Public Service Commission
Minnesota Public Service Commission
Mississippi Public Service Commission
Missouri Public Service Commission
Montana Public Serice Commission
Nebraska Public Service Commission
New Hampshire Public Utilities Commission
New Jersey Board of Public Utilities
New Mexico Public Service Commission
New York Public Service Commission
North Carolina Utilities Commission
North Dakota Public Service Commission
Ohio Public Utilities Commission
Oklahoma Corporation Commission
Oregon Public Utility Commissioner
Pennsylvania Public Utility Commission
Rhode Island Public Utilities Commission
South Carolina Public Service Commission
South Dakota Public Utilities Commission
Tennessee Public Service Commission
Texas Public Utility Commission
Texas Railroad Commission
Utah Public Service Commission
Vermont Public Service Board
Virginia State Corporation Commission
Washington Utilities and Transportation Commission
West Virginia Public Service Commission
Wisconsin Public Service Commission
Wyoming Public Service Commission

SOURCE: National Association of Regulatory Commissioners, *1978 Annual Report on Utility and Carrier Regulation of the National Association of Regulatory Utility Commissioners.*

Study Questions

1. What difficulties were found with the early attempts to regulate public utilities?

2. Carefully trace the American regulatory experiments from judicial regulation to commission regulation. Did each successive form evolve out of the inadequacies of that preceding it?

3. How might each of the alleged advantages of commission regulation also be criticized as disadvantages?

4. Evaluate the criticisms that have been levied at commission regulation.

Student Readings

FARRIS, M., AND R. SAMPSON. *Public Utilities.* Boston: Houghton Mifflin, 1973, chap. 5.

GARFIELD, P., AND W. LOVEJOY. *Public Utility Economics.* Englewood Cliffs, N.J.: Prentice-Hall, 1964, chaps. 3 and 4.

GLAESER, MARTIN G. *Outlines of Public Economics.* New York: MacMillan, 1927, part II.

PHILLIPS, CHARLES F., JR. *The Economics of Regulation,* 2nd ed. Homewood, Ill.: Irwin, 1969, chap. 4.

6

A Critique of
Public Utility Regulation

The complex nature of regulation in these industries, particularly the relationship between the regulatory commission and the public utility, has been the subject of considerable criticism over the years. Although the level of utility service typically has been more than adequate, opponents of public utilities have mounted numerous attacks on, among other things, the nature and effectiveness of regulation, the appropriateness of incentives, and resource allocation in utility industries. Such criticisms are hardly new. Much of Henry Carter Adams' 1887 classic essay, "Relation of the State to Industrial Action," responded sharply to the extreme laissez-faire opponents of governmental control of commerce.[1] Over a half-century later, Horace M. Gray spoke out on the public utility concept:

> Originated as a system of social restraint designed primarily, or at least ostensibly, to protect consumers from the aggressions of monopolists, it has ended as a device to protect the property, i.e., the capitalized expectancy, of these monopolists from the just demands of society, and to obstruct the development of socially superior institutions.[2]

A discussion of public utilities would not be complete without mention of these classic criticisms.

---

[1] Henry C. Adams, "Relation of the State to Industrial Action," *Publications of the American Economic Association* (Baltimore: Guggenheim and Weil, 1887).

[2] Horace M. Gray, "The Passing of the Public Utility Concept," in *Readings in the Social Control of Industry* (Philadelphia: Blakiston, 1942), p. 294.

INAPPROPRIATE INCENTIVES

It is frequently argued that the regulatory pricing mechanism is essentially a "cost plus" system, providing the utility with no incentive to economize on its use of resources. This view is reflected in the rate equation, wherein the utility is allowed to recover its costs plus a return to owners for the use of their capital. Apart from being an average-cost pricing system and using the wrong costs (historical costs), it is argued that the cost-plus system provides no incentives to lower costs since these, low or high, will be recovered by utility revenues. The introduction of cost-saving technology is discouraged because the profits a utility might obtain from such undertakings are too often quickly eliminated by regulators.

A counterargument is that, in the presence of regulatory lag, the utility firm does have an incentive to reduce or at least hold the line on costs and to innovate. This is true for both inflationary and deflationary periods. In a period of high inflation such efforts may not result in an economic profit, but still serve to offset rapidly rising costs and provide a reasonable return.

RESOURCE DISTORTIONS

Price Exceeds Marginal Cost

One possible type of distortion in the public utility field where economies of scale are important is the reduced output and resource usage resulting from the higher than marginal-cost price. That is, since prices are based on average costs, not marginal costs, in the absence of enlightened regulatory surveillance resources may be underallocated to a decreasing-cost industry. This occurs because the wrong price signals are given to consumers—i.e., prices exceed marginal costs.

The advocacy of setting utility rates equal to marginal costs is more than an *ad hoc* view of rate making. The marginal cost position is coherent and has been offered extensively as a substitute, at least in part, for traditional rate-making methods. Such an important economic criticism needs extensive coverage, which is given in Chapter 7.

Dynamic World—Static Regulation

Since regulation is essentially a static phenomenon, largely based on past events with little attention to the future, distortions occur. First, the argument goes, future costs are the appropriate costs on which prices should be based for resource allocation. But future considerations, plans, and forecasts are often given short shrift in rate proceedings. Accounting costs are the past costs that are used in rate cases. Moreover, commissions seldom give adequate consideration to demand elasticity in setting rates; they frequently assume demand is completely inelastic. In periods of rising costs, this means service prices will be set too low, and utility earnings will inadequate even on the date of the increased rate award. More frequent rate hearings are thereby required. The proponents of this argument claim that more prompt forecasting of ongoing changes in costs, technological change, and demand is required in regulatory proceedings.

Various commissions have adopted forecasted test periods to offset regulatory lag. Others have adopted automatic adjustment clauses or have permitted interim rates to be collected subject to refund.

Forecasts, opponents argue, are likely to be self-serving and speculative rather than objective and forward-looking. The opponents of forecasting point out that regulation is dynamic. Concomitant increases in investment, sales, and profits, though not forecasted, do occur and serve as an incentive to utility management. Forecasts, on the other hand, provide an inefficient incentive, a target for utility management to aim at, whether the objective is efficient or not.

The alleged accuracy of forecasts is seen as illusory by its opponents. Revenues, expenses, and investment cannot be matched by forecasts. Increased sales generally create opportunities for new investment that embodies up-to-date technology, creates operating efficiencies, and reduces maintenance. Changes in customer mix, which alter the profit margin on sales and the returns on investment, cannot be forecasted accurately given the state of the art. Also, the fair rate of return for a utility does not trend closely with inflation; rather, the return rises to a different nominal, though constant, rate. Given these difficulties, the resulting forecasting error relative to any alleged shortfall in profits is much too high for regulatory commissions to rely on forecasts. The commissions cannot gamble on the accuracy of a forecast with the consumers' money. The investor, in any case, is not guaranteed a return, but only a reasonable opportunity to earn a profit, which traditional rate-making practices provide.

The Averch-Johnson Thesis

Some claim that the nature of rate of return regulation distorts public utility incentives so that use of capital becomes relatively more attractive than variable production factors such as labor, resulting in a misallocation of resources. This alleged misallocation effect is often referred to as the *Averch-Johnson (A-J) effect*, after Harvey Averch and Leland Johnson, who described it in their classic 1962 article, "Behavior of the Firm under Regulatory Constraint."[3] This work led to a stream of articles discussing various features of their thesis.

While the A-J paper is an extremely interesting application of economic concepts, the basic conclusions of A-J are unproved in the real world. As we will note, the results of the empirical work are mixed, and many of the theoretical refinements and extensions contradict the conclusions of the original model. Despite its unsettled nature, the A-J model and subsequent developments are an excellent illustration of the development and use of economic theory. It is in this spirit that we highlight the theory and empirical work relating to the A-J controversy.

The A-J effect contemplates a monopoly model with a profit-maximizing objective. The rate of return on assets is assumed to be constrained by regulators below the profit-maximizing level but above the purely competitive level. This condition surely existed for many utilities during the late 1950s and 1960s, when this position spawned much economic research. It is also assumed there is no regulatory lag. The most interesting implications derived from this model are these: (1) The capital-labor ratio adopted by the constrained monopoly (the regulated utility) will exceed that which would minimize cost at the output level selected by the firm; and (2) there is an incentive for the regulated utility to enter secondary regulated markets, even if revenue falls below the incremental cost of serving these markets.[4]

The rationale behind the first implication is that rate regulation amounts to an effective factor price change for the utility. Given the factor prices determined in the market, P_L for labor and P_K for capital, the unconstrained firm will operate on the minimum isocost line for any given output level. The slope of the isocost line is the negative ratio of prices, $-P_K/P_L$. In Figure 6.1, the unregulated firm would thus operate on isocost line AB using L_1 units of labor and K_1 units of capital to produce an output of X_1; to produce X_2, the firm would operate on CD using L_2 and K_2, etc. The expansion path I is determined by these cost-minimizing combinations of capital and labor for any given output level; it is the series of tangency points between the isocost lines and isoquants. But for the firm under rate regulation, the effective cost of capital is lower than the market cost of capital. On each additional unit of capital, the constrained firm is permitted a return in excess of the market cost of capital—it is permitted "profit" on each unit. This effectively lowers the price of capital by an amount equal

---

[3] *American Economic Review*, 52, 6 (1962), 1053–1069. Another early article which found this phenomenon is S. H. Wellisz, "Regulation of National Gas Pipeline Companies: An Economic Analysis," *Journal of Political Economy*, 71, 1 (February 1963), 30–43.

[4] A third proposition often associated with the A-J thesis is that utilities will pay inflated prices for plant and equipment. See Fred M. Westfield, "Regulation and Conspiracy," *American Economic Review*, 55, 3 (June 1965), 424–443.

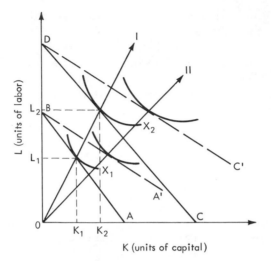

FIGURE 6.1 A–J Effect on the Output Expansion Path

to this unit "profit," and the effective isocost lines, $A'B$ and $C'D$, have a new slope. The firm is induced to move along expansion path II, rather than path I where costs are minimized, so as to maximize profits. The regulated firm therefore selects a capital-labor ratio greater than the one that minimizes cost at the chosen output level.

The effect of A-J overcapitalization is shown in Figure 6.2. $LRAC_1$ is the firm's long-run average cost curve without the inefficient shift toward capital. P_1 and X_1 are the regulated price, slightly above costs, and the output level. After the firm's response to the rate of return constraint, the firm's average cost curve, $LRAC_2$, is higher and profits are increased. The price and output level after the switch are P_2 and X_2.

The second proposition, that regulated firms may attempt to enter secondary regulated markets even though unprofitable, is best illustrated with an example. The idea is that by entering secondary markets the firm can increase its rate base, obtaining additional revenues from the primary market that more than compensate for the losses in the secondary markets. The primary assumptions of Table 6.1 are that the investment in the secondary market is included in the overall rate base, the allowed rate of return exceeds the cost of capital, and the demand in the primary market is perfectly inelastic.

The numerical example indicates why firms may have an incentive to enter secondary markets even though incremental costs in these markets exceed incremental revenues. The partially unexploited monopoly position in the primary market may be exploited more fully by entering secondary markets, thereby including in the rate base the investment in these markets and obtaining the additional revenues in the primary market to meet the

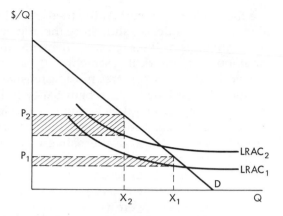

FIGURE 6.2 A–J Effect on Profits and Output

expanded constraint. In this example, if only $18 million can be earned in the secondary market, additional revenues of $2 million will be allowed in the primary market to obtain the total of $20 million allowable in the secondary market, or $90 million for the two markets combined. It should be noted that this is only an assertion and cannot be proved generally, because the results depend on the particular cost and demand curves chosen.

TABLE 6.1 The Averch-Johnson Thesis: Illustration of the Incentive to Enter an Unprofitable Secondary Market[a]

	PRIOR TO ENTRY		AFTER ENTRY
Revenues	Primary Market	Secondary Market	Combined
Rate base $(V-D)$	$200	$50	$250
Allowed rate of return (R)	10%	10%	10%
Fair return	20	5	25
Operating cost $(O + t)$	50	15	65
Allowable revenues (RR)	70	20	90
Actual revenues	$ 70	$18	
Costs			
Cost of capital	8%	8%	8%
Capital costs	16	4	20
Operating costs $(O + t)$	50	15	65
Total costs	$66	$19	$85
Profit	$ 4	$(1)	$ 5
Minus: Profit prior to entry			$ 4
Additional profit from entering secondary market			$ 1

163

[a] All figures are in millions of dollars.

How valid are the A-J implications? At the theoretical level under the constraints specified, the A-J model is valid. Since the original paper, there have been numerous attempts at theoretical refinements and extensions, but only a modest amount of empirical research.

On the theoretical side, perhaps the most extensive study of the implications of the model was done by Elizabeth Bailey in her book, *Economic Theory of Regulatory Constraint.*[5] Bailey explores the implications of a variety of alternative assumptions including regulatory lag, increasing cost of capital, peak load demand, and alternative objective functions.[6] Since the implications of the model depend on the assumptions, it is no wonder that the results under various assumptions at times are at odds with the A-J effect. With the objective of sales maximization, for instance, the firm *under*capitalizes instead of overcapitalizes.

The early empirical evidence was of a casual nature. For example, in the original paper, A-J noted that AT&T was earning 11.7 percent on its monopoly telephone services but only 2.6 percent on its "competitive" telegraph services. Other examples are given by Leland Johnson in a subsequent paper titled "Behavior of the Firm under Regulatory Constraint: A Reassessment."[7] More recent empirical studies of the electric utility industry have been performed with conflicting results. The studies by Robert Spann and Leon Courville seem to confirm the A-J effect.[8] Courville found that for 1962, its inefficient production added $436.5 million to the costs of electricity. This result is based on plant data, but the firm data did not support the A-J thesis. On the other side, Boyes found no A-J capital bias.[9] He argues that in the 1950s electrical industries faced few constraints to expansion, while in the 1960s they faced increasing factor prices and more difficulty in expansion. Thus, a sample drawn from 1950s might yield an A-J effect, while one drawn from the 1960s might give a negative A-J result. Boyes's sample, drawn from the late 1950s and early 1960s, mixing essentially different periods, found no evidence of an A-J effect.

A more recent study by Baron and Taggart, using a model that accounts for price setting by commissions and the uncertain demand faced by utilities on a cross-sectional sample of 48 investor-owned electric utilities

[5] *Economic Theory of Regulatory Constraint* (Lexington, Mass.: D. C. Heath, 1973).

[6] A study of the A-J thesis under alternative objective functions is found in E. Bailey and J. Malone, "Resource Allocation and the Regulated Firm," *The Bell Journal*, 1, 1 (spring 1970), 129–140. A thorough theoretical discussion of the implications of the A-J thesis is contained in W. Baumol and A. Klevorick, "Input Choices and Rate of Return Regulation: An Overview of the Discussion," *The Bell Journal*, 1, 2 (autumn 1970), 162–190.

[7] *American Economic Review*, 63, 2 (1973), 90–97.

[8] R. Spann, "Rate of Return Regulation and Efficiency in Production: An Empirical Test of the A-J Thesis," *The Bell Journal*, 5, 1 (spring 1974), 38–52. Leon Courville, "Regulation and Efficiency in the Electric Utility Industry," *The Bell Journal*, 5, 1 (spring 1974), 53–74.

[9] W. J. Boyes, "An Empirical Examination of the Averch-Johnson Effect," *Economic Inquiry*, 14 (March 1976), 25–35.

of the year 1970, suggests that undercapitalization rather than overcapitalization is present.[10] In separate studies, Sudit and Vinod found that the Bell System over the period 1950–1971 was not overcapitalized.[11]

A series of unsettled questions emerge from the A-J discussion. Does allowed rate of return actually exceed the cost of capital? If not, the A-J conclusions are invalid. Are utilities primarily profit maximizers or are other goals equally important? If utilities face essentially an uncertain demand, does the A-J thesis hold? The effect of regulatory lag has been shown under certain conditions to diminish the A-J effect (Bailey and Malone, 1970), but how general is this conclusion? What effect did regulatory lag have in maintaining rates in the 1960s in the face of possible rate reductions? Does it hold under different model specifications? Was the rapid adoption of capital-intensive nuclear power plants in the 1960s and early 1970s spurred on by an A-J effect? Do dynamic models give different results?[12] To evaluate these questions adequately and others concerning the A-J effect, further theoretical and empirical work is needed.

REGULATION IS INEFFECTIVE

Several econometric studies have attempted to determine the effectiveness of utility regulation. The results of these studies have not been sanguine. However, the studies are not the final word; effective regulation by certain commissions at specific times has been identified, such as the Michigan Public Service Commission regulation of telephone rates during post-World War II period.[13]

Stigler and Friedland

George Stigler and Claire Friedland in a 1962 article titled "What Can Regulators Regulate? The Case of Electricity,"[14] hypothesized that regulation is ineffective and unnecessary. Since the primary roles of public utility commissions are to control the rate level and rate structure, Stigler and Friedland (S-F) looked at the effects of regulation on rates and returns in the electric utility industry in the years 1912, 1922, 1932, and 1937. First,

---

[10] D. Baron and R. Taggart, Jr., "A Model of Regulation under Uncertainty and a Test of Regulatory Bias," *The Bell Journal*, 8, 1 (spring 1977), 151–167.

[11] E. Sudit, "Additive Nonhomogeneous Production Functions in Telecommunications," *The Bell Journal*, 4, 2 (autumn 1973), 499–514. H. Vinod, "Nonhomogeneous Production Functions and Applications to Telecommunications," *The Bell Journal*, 3, 2 (autumn 1972), 531–543.

[12] E. Davis, "A Dynamic Model of the Regulated Firm with a Price Adjustment Mechanism," *The Bell Journal*, 4, 1 (spring 1974), 270–282.

[13] C. Emery Troxel, "Telephone Regulation in Michigan," in W. G. Shepherd and Thomas G. Gies (eds.) *Utility Regulation* (New York: Random House, 1966), pp. 141–186.

[14] *Journal of Law and Economics*, 5, 2 (October 1962), 1–16.

regarding the overall rates, S-F regressed population, price of fuel, proportion of power from hydroelectric sources, per capita income, and regulation (as a dummy variable, 0 for a state without a regulatory commission, 1 for a state with) on the average electricity price to see if state regulatory commissions were effective in reducing rates. They found that the regulatory variables was insignificant in all but one year (1937), and concluded that commission regulation had little or no effect. Second, regarding the rate structure, two possible influences were explored. The first is the question of whether commissions keep the relative rates of the many smaller consumers low so as to gain greater political popularity. The relative prices based on the consumption of electricity turned out to be unaffected by regulation. The second influence S-F considered is the effect of regulation on the relative rates of domestic and industrial consumers. They hypothesized that the relative rates to domestic consumers would be lower in states with regulatory commissions to reduce price discrimination and curry political support. The relative rates were found to be opposite to those expected. Again, no regulatory effect was discovered. Finally, the question of whether investors in utility firms not regulated by state commissions did better than those with state regulation was examined. No discernible pattern in market values of stocks was found, again supporting their thesis of ineffective regulation.

Why might these negative findings be expected and regulation be unnecessary? S-F argue that electric utilities have no long-run monopoly power and face competition from other sources of power, such as natural gas, coal, and oil. Thus prices will not be lowered by regulation, and regulation is unnecessary. They noted that if the elasticity of long-run demand is -8.0, then utility rates of return will exceed competitive rates by only 3.5 percent. Moreover, they argue that regulators are incapable of controlling all the dimensions of service needed to bring about the desired result. In this regard, S-F point to the use of inadequate accounting information, dimensions of service still under the utility's control (once the price is set, utilities may lower the quality of service, through slower repairs and installation, less peak-load capacity, and so on), and finally, regulatory lags.

The Stigler and Friedland article has not been accepted without criticism. First, very few observers have ever believed that early public utility regulation was effective. And since the results are based on data at least 50 years old, the study may have little relevance for today. Second, because a state does not have a regulatory commission does not necessarily mean utilities in that state were not subject to regulation; most were subject to local regulation. Third, in light of the empirical demand studies mentioned in Chapter 2, their assumption of -8.0 for long-run demand elasticity is extremely high—it is probably more like -1.5 to -2.0. In this case, rates of return exceed competitive levels by from 25 to 50 percent, not 3.5 percent.

Finally, the study covers an entirely different era in the utility industry—
the holding company period—before effective interstate regulation, during
the fair value era and before utility rates were lowered into the inelastic
portion of the demand curve to promote usage and realize economies of
scale.

T. G. Moore's Study

The question of effectiveness of regulation was analyzed empirically
by T. G. Moore in a study entitled "The Effectiveness of Regulation of
Electric Utility Prices."[15] Moore first computed the short-run marginal cost
of both public and privately owned electric utilities from FPC data on
production costs. Next, the demand functions were estimated. Finally, the
monopoly price was computed by equating marginal cost and marginal
revenue. When the monopoly price was compared to the price actually
charged, Moore found that the monopoly price was not significantly in
excess of the regulated price for privately owned utilities and only slightly
higher for publicly owned utilities. Rates for privately owned utilities were
probably not reduced by more than 5 percent from the monopoly level,
and 10 percent for publicly owned utilities. Moore's conclusion: Regulation
apparently is ineffective.

Charles G. Moore's Study

In his 1975 paper, "Has Electricity Regulation Resulted in Higher
Prices? An Econometric Evaluation Utilizing a Calibrated Regulatory Input
Variable," C. G. Moore concludes that electricity regulation actually increased prices during the 1947–1966 period.[16] His model, which is similar
to the Stigler-Friedland model, postulates that the regulated price is a
function of cost and demand conditions and regulatory input. The *a priori*
expectation is that the larger the regulatory input the lower the price, all
else being the same. Instead of the dummy variable used by Stigler and
Friedland, Moore used a calibrated input variable. The dummy variable
technique is unworkable for testing the regulatory effect in recent years
because virtually all states have regulatory commissions. The two regulatory input variables used instead were the amount of a state commission's
(a) annual expenditures and (b) staff time devoted to regulation of electric
utilities. The correlation between the regulatory variable and electric utility
prices is significant and positive, not negative as was expected. The implication is that states spending a greater amount on electric utility regulation pay higher prices for electricity. Again, regulatory failure.

---

[15] *Southern Economic Journal*, 36, 4 (1970), 365–375.

[16] *Economic Inquiry*, 13, 2 (1975), 207–220.

Certainly, this relationship could result from increased political activity when utility prices rise substantially and greater political apathy when relatively low prices prevail. Regulatory activity over the last two decades would support such a view. According to Moore, these negative findings are primarily attributable to cross-subsidization efforts of regulators. As regulators attempt to reduce rates to the smaller residential consumers with an inelastic demand, the rates to the larger industrial users must be greater than they otherwise would be. In consequence, total quantity demanded declines because the consumption reduction of the elastic industrial group is greater than the additional consumption of the inelastic group. Thus, economies of scale are not achieved as fully as in more heavily regulated states, and electricity prices are higher. Of course, other factors may also contribute to this effect. For example, regulatory lag in carrying out rate reductions during the period studied was substantial.

The Federal Power Commission's Effectiveness: MacAvoy's Study

The FPC, now the Federal Energy Regulatory Commission, is often thought to have been one of the most efficient and effective of the federal regulatory commissions. In the late 1930s and 1940s aggressive regulatory actions were undertaken. During the 1950s, lack of regulatory action led to a complete turnover of the commission under President Kennedy. The Landis Report[17] recommended significant change. Under Chairmen Swidler and White, more aggressive regulation was initiated in the regulation of the field price of natural gas and expanded jurisdictions over wholesale electric sales, based upon the Phillips decision[18] and the Colton decision,[19] respectively. Subsequent commissions have retreated from forceful regulation, until now the effort, begun in 1954, to deregulate the wellhead price of gas has been in part successful.

An important study by Paul MacAvoy, titled "The Effectiveness of the Federal Power Commission," bodes ill for the Federal Power Commission.[20] An overview of the results of this study follow. When compared to the costs of regulation, the gains appear very small. During the 1960s, the administrative costs of the FPC ranged from $31 to $95 million per year, averaging about $35 million. What did this buy? Pipeline prices were not lowered as a result of regulation. Gas-producer price regulation had

---

[17] James M. Landis, *Report on Regulatory Agencies to the President-Elect*, Committee Print, U.S. Senate Committee on the Judiciary, 85th Cong., 2nd Sess., Washington, D.C., 1960.

[18] *Phillips Petroleum Co. v. Wisconsin*, 347 U.S. 672 (1954).

[19] *Federal Power Commission v. Southern California Edison Co.*, and *City of Colton, California v. Southern California Edison Company*, 276 U.S. 205 (1964).

[20] *The Bell Journal*, 1, 2 (autumn 1970), 271–304.

a negative benefit; wellhead prices were set too low, resulting in reserve and production shortages. The lower prices to residential consumers were probably more than offset by the hardships imposed by these shortages. The FPC's planning and coordinating of electricity production had an insignificant effect on the consumer. Another study suggests that FPC regulation of wholesale electric sales was also ineffective.[21] All in all, the costs of its primary activities clearly outweighed the benefits derived. The MacAvoy study added support to the growing concern about the effectiveness of commission regulation.

PROCEDURAL AND
—————————— OPERATIONAL DEFICIENCIES ——————————

INADEQUATE PERSONNEL AND BUDGET

A common criticism of commissions is that they have inadequate staffs in relation to their workload. Their budgets do not allow for enough adequately trained personnel. Moreover, the commissioners themselves often come under fire as being appointed or elected for political favors, not talent. The backgrounds of commissioners are varied, though lawyers predominate, and they frequently are untrained in the economic aspects of regulation. On the other hand, an economist in this position might not understand some of the political and legal dimensions of the job .

COMMISSION LIFE CYCLE

Many observers believe that commissions move through four phases, with the commission ultimately being dominated or captured by the industry. During the first stage, *incipiency*, the commission attempts to determine the parameters of its mandate; it is groping for its mission, its identity, and thus is not particularly effective. The second phase, *youth*, is characterized by aggressive behavior favoring consumers and by a strong feeling of public responsibility. In the third phase, called *maturity*, commissions lack consumer orientation and aggressiveness. There are fewer conflicts with utilities; they work more closely together. Procedures are established, but regulatory effectiveness has peaked. Commissions are completely inadequate in the final stage, *old age*. They have become very close friends with, and speakers for, the utilities they regulate. Commission decisions now run consistently in favor of utilities.

---

[21] Eugene F. Rasmussen, *Federal Power Commission Regulation of Wholesale Electric Sales: A Case Study of Policy Initiation,* unpublished Ph.D. dissertation, 1976, University of Nebraska-Lincoln.

THE ADMINISTRATIVE PROCESS

It is frequently charged that the regulatory process is too slow, cumbersome, and expensive. In Illinois, cases must be heard within 11 months of when they are filed; in many states this lag is longer. The proceedings can be dragged out by any of the parties to the action. In an attempt to avoid controversy and the scrutiny of the legislature, commissions negotiate, seek reasonable compromises, and often condone these delaying tactics. The squeaky-wheel analogy is relevant in this process.

In addition to being slow and expensive, the administrative process may be dominated by the utility. If utilities have greater resources and wield more power than do intervenors and commissions, one-sided decisions may result from a one-sided record in a case. Moreover, as mentioned in Chapter 5, the process as currently constituted places excessive strains on the fairness of regulators. It is extremely difficult for commissions to be impartial in the many functions they perform. They are asked to be judge and jury as well as administrator and legislator, and yet be reelected or have their sponsor reelected.

ORGANIZATIONAL PROBLEMS

In 1971, a presidential study group called the Ash Council recommended that, instead of commissioners, federal regulatory agencies be directed by a single administrative head responsible to the president. In addition, many of the adjudicative functions of commissioners would be performed by a new administrative court. This would free some of the administrators' time to develop general policy. These changes presumably would improve the accountability and functioning of commissions.

GEORGE STIGLER'S "NEW" THEORY OF REGULATION

Under the traditional view, scant attention is given to the supply side of regulation. The typical assumption is that regulation is costless. Therefore, when faced with a market failure, the usual reaction is "let's regulate" to regain some of the benefits, in terms of wealth or fairness, lost to society. Regulation is initiated in the public interest.

In an interesting article by George Stigler, "The Theory of Regulation," an alternative view is set forth:

> Regulation may be actively sought by an industry, or it may be thrust upon it. A central thesis of this paper is that, as a rule, regulation is acquired by the industry and is designed and operated primarily for its benefit.[22]

---

[22] *The Bell Journal*, 2, 1 (spring 1971), 2–21.

In light of the recent evidence on regulatory failure, traditionalists are hard pressed to rationalize the particular beneficiaries and patterns of regulation. Stigler's alternative is to view regulation as a product whose allocation is determined by the forces of supply and demand. The focus then is on the benefits *and* costs of regulation.

The principal benefit of regulation (over entry and rates) is the transfer of wealth. The value of regulation to an industry thus is related to the additional profits obtainable over alternative arrangements, such as cartelization. Regulation also requires political action. But several interested parties have a stake in the regulation of an industry. The political authority whose assumed goal is to obtain votes and contributions is in a sense an arbitrator among competing interest groups who seek to obtain the benefits of regulation. The political process of "selling" regulation or determining the winning group may be influenced at a lower cost by some groups than others. The nature of the political process is such that it is difficult and costly to make the preferences of a group known. Moreover, it is expensive to discover the effects of a particular political decision. Thus, the strongly felt preferences of majorities and some minorities are implemented by the political process, while weakly felt preferences are ignored.

Industries seeking regulation must offer the appropriate political body the things it wants. These are votes and resources, with the latter including campaign funds, contributed services, jobs upon retirement, and bribes of various sorts. The costs of obtaining favorable legislation probably increase with industry size. The larger the industry, the greater the cost to society of regulation, and the more political opposition to overcome. Also, the larger the industry, the more difficult to persuade those in the industry that regulation is beneficial. There is also the problem of those not party to the agreement getting a "free ride." Thus, the smaller the number of participants to the agreement, the smaller the coordinating and enforcement costs. The winning group vying for the spoils of regulation will be a minority. Accordingly, Stigler's view is that regulation typically is sought by and operated for the benefit of the minority constituency (industry), as opposed to consumers.

Sam Peltzman has formalized and extended the Stigler model in a recent paper entitled "Toward a More General Theory of Regulation."[23] In this important work, the maximizing behavior of the political authority is analyzed as various parameters are varied, such as the cost and demand conditions in the industry. This analysis yields testable implications for the pattern of regulation among industries and for regulated output and prices.

Although the Stigler theory has something in common with the capture theory of the political scientists, it is more precise, yielding testable

---

[23] *Journal of Law and Economics*, 19, 2 (1976), 211–240.

implications, and it makes widely accepted assumptions about individual behavior, such as that individuals rationally act in their own self-interest. After all is said, however, it must be admitted that this is a relatively new and untested theory; it has not yet been "debugged." Yet it does redirect our attention to an important element of regulation. As Stigler so aptly put it,

> So many economists, for example, have denounced the ICC for its pro-railroad policies that this has become a cliché of the literature. This criticism seems to me exactly as appropriate as a criticism of the Great Atlantic and Pacific Tea Company for selling groceries, or as a criticism of a politician for currying popular support. The fundamental vice of such criticism is that it misdirects attention: it suggests that the way to get an ICC which is not subservient to the carriers is to preach to the commissioners or to the people who appoint the commissioners. The only way to get a different commission would be to change the political support for the commission, and reward commissioners on a basis unrelated to their services to the carriers.[24]

THE ALTERNATIVES

OTHER SYSTEMS

Some alternatives to commission regulation as presently instituted are the following.

Abandonment of Regulation.   Given the imperfections of government regulation and its tendency to spread, several economists, including the Nobel laureate Milton Friedman, would prefer that regulation of public utilities be abandoned.[25] They point to the fact that some competition, though limited, does exist and that technological change will eventually erode the unregulated private monopolists' profits. Historically, unregulated utilities have been tried and rejected.

Government Ownership.   There is some support for government ownership of utilities. In most countries of the world, with the United States, Japan, and Sweden the notable exceptions, government ownership predominates. In the United States, Nebraska, Tennessee, and the state of Washington are the notable exceptions that have public ownership of electricity. Presumably, under government ownership, the inefficiencies of regulation would be eliminated. But many would argue that the inefficiencies of a government-supplied service with its bureaucracy and lack of market incentives may be far greater than any of the alternatives. Fur-

---

[24] Stigler, "The Theory of Regulation," pp. 17–18.

[25] Milton Friedman, *Capitalism and Freedom* (Chicago: University of Chicago Press, 1962), p. 28.

ther, government political control of citizens is increased with public ownership.

Reorganized Utility Regulation. Under this view, commissions would be reformed to improve their efficiency and effectiveness. The possible reform alternatives include larger budgets, improved personnel, a clearer and expanded mandate, and structural changes, perhaps along the lines recommended by the Ash Council.

IMPROVING COMMISSION REGULATION

The critics of public utility regulation rely in part on Milton Friedman's dual observation that private monopoly is short-lived and is, in any case, preferable to a publicly sanctioned monopoly. Trebing has observed that critics derive their views from neoclassical economics, while institutional economists, such as Henry C. Adams, John R. Commons, B. H. Meyer, and others, developed regulatory practices regarding rate base, cost-of-service, and rate discrimination.[26] This observation is reminiscent of an 1887 comparison of laissez-faire advocates to advocates of government activism toward industrial practices.[27] Trebing sees the perspective of the critics to be

1. A shift in emphasis from concern over private monopoly to concern over the political power exercised by government
2. Policy proposals which place government in a passive role relative to the enterprise and the consumer
3. A continuing effort to preserve the efficacy of the market mechanism, even in the face of major structural imperfections
4. A reliance on a high level of abstraction for purposes of analysis and policy prescriptions
5. A belief that the consumer, unassisted by government control or regulation, should be the final arbiter on matters of pollution, abusive practices, and the mix and level of output.[28]

Thus, many economic criticisms of public utility regulation are criticisms of regulatory legislation as well as the methods of economics. The antagonism between institutional and orthodox views of economics has been described this way:

> In general the institutional interest has been tied to reform movements of one sort or another and has been antipathic to economic explanations running

---

[26] Harry M. Trebing, "Realism and Relevance in Public Utility Regulation," *Journal of Economic Issues*, 8, 2 (June 1974), 210.

[27] Henry Carter Adams, "Relation of the State to Industrial Action," *Publications of the American Economic Association* (Baltimore: Guggenheim and Weil, 1887), p. 493.

[28] Harry M. Trebing, "The Chicago School vs. Public Utility Regulation," *Journal of Economic Issues*, 10, 1 (May 1976), p. 104.

in terms of uniform self-interest, static economic relationships and a stable institutional structure.

. . .

The institutionalists believe that while the equilibrium concept and the marginal method may be found useful for some subordinate purposes of analysis fundamentally correct explanations of economic phenomena are possible only by reference to the nature and prescriptive force of social institutions.[29]

Orthodox economics, with no positive notion of government itself, is predisposed to develop critiques of public utility regulation that rely upon an activist or positive notion of government. The orthodox economist, who finds market failure less costly than governmental action, is no longer satisfied with government regulation of market forces. Institutional economics, on the other hand, sees a positive role for government. Administrative agencies such as regulatory commissions achieve democratic and constitutional objectives.

Comparing the views of a notable proponent and an opponent of natural gas field price deregulation can show the difference in emphasis. The Federal Power Commission regulation of natural gas wellhead prices began after the 1954 Phillips case. Deregulation nearly succeeded in 1956 and was partially accomplished in the 1970s. This case provides a clear juxaposition of the opposing orthodox and institutional economic methods. While the orthodox economist sees a precise opportunity cost of regulation in dollars and cents per thousand cubic feet, the institutional economist sees the quite visible hand of monopoly, the monopoly power of the OPEC cartel and the lack of workable competition in natural gas production.

Trebing contrasted the views of Breyer and MacAvoy with that of Schwartz, adherents of the orthodox and institutional economists, respectively. Trebing writes:

One group holds that the FPC is still depressing price below the equilibrium price that would prevail in a producer market that is considered competitive. The second holds that the producer market is tightly oligopolistic and that the FPC policies have been ineffectual in coming to grips with the power of the producers to withhold gas in anticipation of higher profits.[30]

The orthodox economist sees the economy as a set of market clearing prices set by supply and demand. A monopolized market is no less able to equalize supply and demand than is a competitive market, albeit the monopoly market is clearly at a different price and supply. It is well known that predictions of the orthodox economic model of the market cannot discrim-

---

[29] Paul T. Homan, "The Institutional School," *The Encyclopedia of the Social Sciences,* vol. V (New York: MacMillan, 1931), pp. 387, 392.

[30] Harry M. Trebing, "Broadening the Objectives of Public Utility Regulation," *Land Economics,* 53, 1 (February 1977), 113.

inate between imperfect and perfect competition. Whether the supply curve reflects competitive quasi-rents, monopoly profits, or dynamic windfall gains and losses is irrelevant to the econometric study.

On the other hand, the institutional economist looks at the actual conditions and transactions that make up a market and compares these conditions and transactions to an ideal, workable competition. Whether competition can exist and regulate the market, without regulation, is investigated. From this perspective, David Schwartz observed market concentration; interlocking relationships between gas producers, both major and minor, and between producers and pipelines; major bidding combines for acquisition of offshore leases; involvement of major petroleum companies and conflicting functions of major producers as both intrastate purchasers and interstate sellers of gas.[31] All these conditions indicate a lack of arms-length bargaining, a vertically integrated or intertwined natural gas industry, conditions we can hardly describe as workably competitive.

Breyer and MacAvoy see a different market, where

> Decentralization of ownership is as prevalent in gas production as it is in many workably competitive American industries,[32]

and

> to try to limit producer rents and windfalls. . . . is what the [Federal Power] Commission has been trying to do.[33]

When we turn from orthodox critiques toward improving commission regulation, the emphasis shifts. Trebing suggests that the three regulatory objectives of "the control of monopoly profits, the prevention of excessive price discrimination, and the assurance of adequate service on a continuing basis to all classes of users"[34] should now be supplemented by several additional objectives:

1. The promotion of that form of industry structure most conducive to superior performance
2. Formal recognition of equity and income distribution
3. The establishment of national and regional priorities for allocating available supplies of energy and communication during periods of curtailment and shortages
4. The recognition and control of social costs[35]

---

[31] David S. Schwartz, "Pricing and Competition in the Regulated Energy Industries," in Harry M. Trebing (ed.), *New Dimensions in Public Utility Pricing* (East Lansing: Institute of Public Utilities, 1976), p. 571.

[32] Stephen G. Breyer and Paul W. MacAvoy, *Energy Regulation by the Federal Power Commission* (Washington, D.C.: The Brookings Institution, 1974), p. 60.

[33] Ibid., p. 66.

[34] Trebing, "Broadening the Objectives of Public Utility Regulation," p. 106.

[35] Ibid., p. 119.

The validity of government action has been debated since nineteenth-century laissez-faire advocates contested the right of government to protect the public interest. Recent criticism of utility regulation continues this old debate. Advocates of regulation propose the practical reform of direct administrative regulation.[36] Traditional property rights enforced by government that permit the withholding of property from others are no less government regulation. But critics see this form of governmental regulation to be superior to direct administrative regulation. Criticism of direct administrative regulation, as well as the defenses and proposed reforms, will continue. Direct administrative regulation will expand in certain utility industries and recede in others as criticisms, defenses, and reforms come to the attention of regulators and legislators.

Study Questions

1. How does the presence of a regulatory lag, itself an infirmity, offset the "cost plus" nature of public utility pricing?

2. Give the two primary implications of the Averch-Johnson thesis. Briefly explain how each of these implications follows from the basic model.

3. Give two actual examples of utility decisions that may have been biased by the A-J effect. Why are you not sure the decisions were made with the A-J effect in mind?

4. Would equal nationwide average interstate toll rates result in telephone service in high-cost secondary toll markets?

5. Show graphically the A-J effect.

6. Stigler and Friedland have charged that regulation is ineffective and unnecessary. Outline their arguments.

7. What evidence supports Stigler and Friedland's charge? Might regulation still be worthwhile?

8. List the main procedural and operational deficiencies of commission regulation. Give counterarguments.

---

[36] Examples of such reform recommendations can be found in Harry M. Trebing, "Structural Change and Regulatory Reform in the Utilities Industries," William H. Melody, "Radio Spectrum Allocation: Role of the Market," and Thomas K. Standish, "State Initiatives in State-Federal Relations," in *The American Economic Review*, 70, 2 (May 1980), pp. 388–392, 393–397, 398–402.

9. Outline Stigler's view of regulation. Given this view, would the remedy of the procedural and operational defects listed under question 8 vastly improve regulation?

10. Compare and contrast Stigler's view of regulation with the traditional view and the "capture theory" of the political scientists.

11. What are the alternatives to commission regulation? Which would you prefer, and why?

Student Readings

AVERCH, H. A., AND L. JOHNSON. "Behavior of the Firm under Regulatory Constraint." *American Economic Review*, 52, 6 (1962), 1053–1069.

BREYER, S., AND P. MACAVOY. *Energy Regulation by the Federal Power Commission*. Washington, D.C.: The Brookings Institution, 1974.

CRAMTON, R. C. "The Effectiveness of Economic Regulation: A Legal View." *American Economic Review*, 54, 2 (1964), 182–191.

FARRIS, MARTIN, AND R. SAMPSON. *Public Utilities*. Boston: Houghton Mifflin, 1973, chap. 10.

HILTON, G. W. "The Basic Behavior of Regulatory Commissions." *American Economic Review*, 62, 2 (1972), 47–54.

JOHNSON, L. "Behavior of the Firm under Regulatory Constraint: A Reassessment." *American Economic Review*, 63, 2 (1973), 90–97.

MACAVOY, P. "The Effectiveness of the Federal Power Commission." *The Bell Journal*, 1, 2 (1970), 271–304.

PHILLIPS, CHARLES F. *The Economics of Regulation*, 2nd ed. Homewood, Ill.: Irwin, 1969, chap. 18.

POSNER, R. "Theories of Economic Regulation." *The Bell Journal*, 5, 2 (1974), 335–358.

POSNER, R. "Taxation by Regulation." *The Bell Journal*, 2, 1 (1971), 22–50.

SCHERER, F. M. "Are the Averch-Johnson Postulates Consistent with Reality?" In *Industrial Market Structure and Economic Performance*. Chicago: Rand McNally, 1970, pp. 533–537.

STIGLER, GEORGE J. "The Theory of Economic Regulation." *The Bell Journal*, 2, 1 (1971), 2–21.

STIGLER, G., AND C. FRIEDLAND. "What Can Regulators Regulate? The Case of Electricity." *The Journal of Law and Economics*, 5 (1962), 1–16.

TREBING, HARRY M.   "Broadening the Objectives of Public Utility Regulation." *Land Economics*, 53, 1 (February 1977), 106–122.

WEIN, H.   "Fair Rate of Return and Incentives—Some General Considerations." In *Performance under Regulation*, ed. Harry M. Trebing. East Lansing: Michigan State University, 1968, pp. 39–67.

Advanced Readings

BAILEY, E.   *Economic Theory of Regulatory Constraint.* Lexington, Mass.: D. C. Heath, 1973.

BAILEY, E., AND J. MALONE.   "Resource Allocation and the Regulated Firm." *The Bell Journal*, 1, 1 (1970), 129–140.

BARON, DAVID P., AND ROBERT A. TAGGERT, JR.   "A Model of Regulation under Uncertainty and a Test of Regulatory Bias." *Bell Journal of Economics*, 8, 1 (1977), 151–167.

BAUMOL, W., AND A. KLEVORICK.   "Input Choices and Rate of Return Regulation: An Overview of the Discussion." *The Bell Journal*, 1, 2 (1970), 162–190.

BAWA, V. S., AND D. S. SIBLEY.   "Dynamic Behavior of a Firm Subject to Stochastic Regulatory Review." Bell Laboratories Economic Discussion Paper 38, September 1975.

BOYES, W. J.   "An Empirical Examination of the Averch-Johnson Effect." *Economic Inquiry*, 14 (March 1976), 25–26.

COREY, GORDON R.   "The Averch and Johnson Proposition: A Critical Analysis.: *The Bell Journal of Economics and Management Science*, 2, 1 (1971), 358.

COURVILLE, L.   "Regulation and Efficiency in the Electric Utility Industry." *The Bell Journal*, 5, 1 (1974), 53–74.

DAVIS, E.   "A Dynamic Model of the Regulated Firm with a Price Adjustment Mechanism." *The Bell Journal*, 4, 1 (1974), 270–282.

DAYAN, DAVID.   "Behavior of the Firm under Regulatory Constraint: A Reexamination." *Industrial Organization Review*, 3 (1975), 61–76.

McNICOL, P. L.   "The Comparative Statics Properties of the Theory of the Regulated Firm." *The Bell Journal of Economics and Management Science*, 4, 2 (1973), 428–453.

MOORE, CHARLES G.   "Has Electricity Regulation Resulted in Higher Prices? An Econometric Evaluation Utilizing a Calibrated Regulatory Input Variable." *Economic Inquiry*, 13, 2 (1975), 207–220.

Moore, T. C.   "The Effectiveness of Regulation of Electric Utility Prices."
Southern Economic Journal, 36, 4 (1970), 365–375.

Peltzman, Sam.   "Toward a More General Theory of Regulation." *Journal
of Law and Economics*, 19, 2 (1976), 211–240.

Perrakis, Stylianos.   "Rate of Return Regulation of a Monopoly Firm with
Random Demand." *Economic Review*, 17, 1 (February 1976), 149–162.

Petersen, H. C.   "An Empirical Test of Regulatory Effects." *The Bell Journal*, 6, 1 (spring 1975), 111–126.

Spann, R.   "Rate of Return Regulation and Efficiency in Production: An
Empirical Test of the A-J Thesis." *The Bell Journal*, 5, 1 (1974), 38–52.

Sudit, Ephraim F.   "Additive Nonhomogeneous Production Functions in
Telecommunications." *The Bell Journal*, 4, 2 (autumn 1973), 499–514.

Vinod, H. D.   "Nonhomogeneous Production Functions and Applications
to Telecommunications." *The Bell Journal*, 3, 2 (autumn 1972), 531–543.

Zajac, E. E.   "A Geometric Treatment of Averch-Johnson's Behavior of
the Firm Model." *American Economic Review*, 60 (March 1970), 117–125.

7

Pricing – The Regulation of Consumer Demand

This chapter presents pricing problems, such as marginal cost pricing, peak load pricing, and price discrimination. We will describe common pricing practices in each major utility industry in some detail to illustrate how pragmatic and imperfect solutions are found to meet competing objectives in the pricing of public utility services. Incorporated in the discussion is a comparison of the marginal cost pricing concepts advocated by many economists and traditional utility pricing practices, such as cost based and value of service pricing. Because utility services differ and jurisdictions vary, we will examine a number of pricing practices. For example, the methods and objectives of federal regulatory commissions often differ from those of state commissions. Furthermore, the character and costs of utility services vary, resulting in different pricing practices both within and among the various sectors of the utility industry. As we will see, there is no definitive mechanism for setting specific public utility prices.

THE ROLE OF PRICES IN A MARKET ECONOMY

Despite the differences between the American mixed economy and a pure market economy, there is a distinct similarity in the role prices play. The basic function in both settings is the allocation of scarce resources among the competing uses. For instance, what amount of coal will be allocated to steel production and what amount to electricity production; how much lumber for building homes and for making paper products? An extreme but interesting contrast is the Soviet economy, where generally "Prices depend upon administrative decisions rather than on supply and demand factors."[1] Prices apparently are used, but for different purposes, even when free markets do not exist.

This resource distribution role of prices may be further subdivided into the following subclassifications:

a.   *What* things will be produced and in what quantities
b.   *How* they will be produced and by whom
c.   *To whom* the products will go

These questions may be answered once we understand how free market prices are determined.

The price in a free market, which implies a given set of conditions, such as level of technology, individual preferences, and income, is determined by the interaction of supply and demand. Suppliers (firms) attempt to maximize profits and compete with one another to obtain sales. Demanders (consumers) attempt to allocate their limited incomes over the available goods and services so as to satisfy their preferences. As these two groups interact under the given market conditions, an equilibrium price is established. It acts as a balancing mechanism to ration or allocate scarce economic resources. As the demand for some product increases, in a pure market economy the price increases, all else being the same. Production will increase and more resources will flow into the industry. Consumers, on the other hand, have an increased incentive, the higher the price, to cut back on consumption of the product. Essentially, the converse holds for a reduction in demand—production will decline and resources will be released for more profitable use elsewhere.

The assumptions of a purely competitive market are (1) perfect information, knowledge, and foresight; (2) perfect resource mobility so that firms can enter and leave the industry; (3) a homogeneous product; and (4) a sufficiently large number of buyers and sellers so that the market agents are price-takers. A traditional distinction is between perfect and pure competition: perfect competition includes three assumptions of the former but excludes the first assumption, perfect information.[2] Dropping the assumption of perfect information implies that a series of unique prices can exist in the perfectly competitive market at all points in time, but only in the long run will the results converge to the purely competitive solution.

---

[1] George Garvy, *Money, Financial Flows, and Credit in the Soviet Union* (Cambridge, Mass.: Ballinger, 1977), p. 48.

[2] George J. Stigler, "Perfect Competition, Historically Contemplated," in *Essays in the History of Economics* (Chicago: The University of Chicago Press, 1965), p. 263.

Too little is made of this distinction today, and the discussion is typically framed in terms of the competitive or market setting, usually implying the purely competitive model. In this chapter, we will show the reliance of marginal cost pricing upon the assumption of *pure* competition or perfect knowledge.

The reader, of course, is aware that perfect and pure competition are static, theoretical constructs which, as defined, do not and cannot exist in the real world. Nevertheless, these concepts are useful in illustrating the nature and direction of change in prices and quantities that one would expect in response to a change in economic conditions, such as technology, taxes, and resources, for industries at the competitive end of the business spectrum.

In the competitive model, the questions regarding allocation are easily answered. The long-run equilibrium of the firm and the market is shown in Figure 7.1. Note the equilibrium price equals the average cost (AC) and the marginal cost (MC) at the profit-maximizing quantity of output Q^*, where $MR = MC$. The equilibrium price occurs where the supply curve intersects the demand curve. At this price the quantity offered by all those wishing to sell equals the quantity desired by all those wishing to buy; there is no excess demand or excess supply. Those things will be produced which consumers, based on their preferences and income, believe are important, and the quantity produced will correspond to the intersection of supply and demand, where the marginal value to consumers equals the marginal cost of resources employed in producing the last unit. Competition in the industry means the firms employing the most efficient techniques of production will remain, while the less efficient producers will be driven from the market. Consumers, owning the resources used in production—land, labor, capital, and so on—receive incomes for the use of these resources. These incomes are used to purchase the goods and

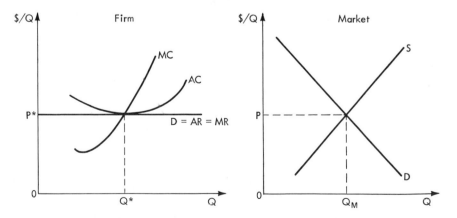

FIGURE 7.1   The Long-Run Equilibrium of the Firm and the Market

services in the market. An individual's ability to purchase the output of the economy is directly proportional to his or her income.

While questions regarding resource distribution in the competitive setting have definite and convenient answers, many economists argue that the competitive system is desirable in a larger sense—essentially a normative view. Under the competitive system, resources will be allocated most efficiently, and production will occur at the lowest possible cost to society. The consumer will judge the quality and quantity of the products to be supplied through his or her payment for these products. Prices will efficiently ration consumer demand, allowing maximum freedom of choice while limiting wasteful use of resources. Finally, in market transactions a desirable amount is transferred from buyer to seller—the amount equals the cost of production, no more, no less. In sum, consumers get the types of services in the amounts desired, consistent with the provision of service at the lowest cost to society, and the value of resources transferred for the service equals the value of resources used in the production of the service. For these reasons and others, some have argued that we should let our real world economy approximate as closely as possible the competitive price system. This is a point to which we will return later in the chapter.

OTHER MARKET STRUCTURES

MONOPOLY

At the opposite end of the spectrum of business organization is *monopoly*. The pure, unregulated textbook monopoly rarely, if ever, exists in the real world. Nevertheless, the monopoly concept is useful in organizing our thoughts and in predicting certain types of responses that are predominantly monopolistic in nature.

The salient features of an industry characterized by monopoly are these:

a. There is a single supplier in the industry.
b. The firm's demand curve equals the market demand curve, which is downward sloping.
c. Because of (b), MR lies below AR.
d. If the firm produces at all, price will be above MC.

A graph that represents the monopoly is presented in Figure 7.2. The profit-maximizing monopolist will restrict output and charge a higher price than would result under pure competition. Price exceeds marginal cost at Q^*, the firm's optimum where $MC = MR$, implying that consumers would be willing to pay more than the marginal cost of allocating additional resources to this industry.

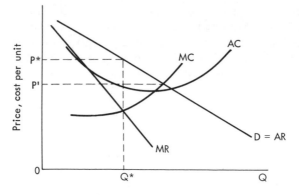

FIGURE 7.2   The Monopolist's Optimum

OLIGOPOLY

A more realistic middle ground between the extremes of perfect competition and monopoly is *oligopoly,* a form of business organization more
readily recognized in the real world. The distinguishing characteristic of
the oligopoly is the relatively small number of relatively large firms in the
industry. The fewness of suppliers and the relatively large share of the
market per supplier means that in making a decision, each firm must take
into account the other firms' possible actions and reactions to that decision.
This interdependence in pricing, product, advertising, and other decisions
is the important feature of oligopoly. And a high degree of unpredictability
in these areas makes static analysis either difficult or inadequate. Economists have devised a multitude of conceptual schemes to explain oligopolistic behavior. Some of the models work fairly well in explaining certain
types of behavior in particular industries, but none is reliable in the sense
that it can explain the wide range of behavorial responses possible in these
industries. Among these models are the dominant firm, price leadership,
and kinked demand models. These models, discussed in detail in most
intermediate microeconomic theory texts, will not be discussed here.

MONOPOLISTIC COMPETITION

Under *monopolistic competition,* probably the most common form of business
organization in the real world, there are many firms selling similar but
slightly differentiated products. Such products are close substitutes. However, the lack of perfect substitutability results in a downward-sloping
demand curve. The remainder of the assumptions of the model are the
same as those of the perfectly competitive model. The differentiation of
the product may be real or apparent and may result from patents, trade-

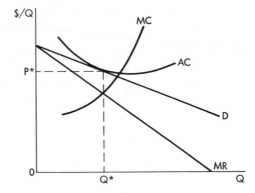

FIGURE 7.3 Long-Run Equilibrium in Monopolistic Competition

marks, package designs, brand names, or courteous service, among other reasons. In the short run, the monopolistically competitive firm can earn profits or losses. But in the long run the profits of the firm will be zero, owing to the entry or exit of rival firms. This is shown in Figure 7.3, where $P^* = AC$ at the firm's preferred output Q^*.

The profits in the short run, represented in Figure 7.4 by the shaded rectangular region, will be eliminated in the long run by increased costs and/or reduced revenues resulting from entry of rival firms to the point where profits are zero. The long-run equilibrium position is characterized in Figure 7.3, where $P = AC$ at the profit-maximizing output, Q^*, where $MC = MR$.

The monopolistically competitive firm is similar to the competitive firm in that both have zero profits in the long run. Like the monopolist, however, its optimum occurs where price (equals AC) exceeds the marginal cost of production, implying an underallocation of resources to the industry from society's viewpoint, all other things being equal.

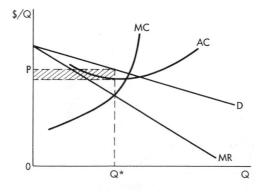

FIGURE 7.4 Short-Run Equilibrium in Monopolistic Competition

Of the standard economic models, empirical evidence suggests that the monopoly model with long-run decreasing costs and government regulation probably comes closest to the public utility setting. Figure 7.5 illustrates this situation. At least three distinct prices are possible given this model.

    a.   What price would the *unregulated*, profit-maximizing public utility select?
    b.   What price might society adopt? And to what end?
    c.   What price do regulators select?

The answer to (a) is obviously the monopoly price, P_m, with the associated quantity Q_m obtained from the $MR = MC$ profit-maximization condition. The answer to (b) which many economists would choose is the price P_{mc}, which corresponds to the point where price or AR equals marginal cost. Professor Bonbright cites marginal cost pricing as economically efficient as early as 1928.[3] Here the price or consumer's marginal benefit reflects the sacrifice consumers make in terms of the goods and services that could have been produced with these resources—the marginal cost of production. Prices above this level, such as the monopoly price, overstate the sacrifice and result in underconsumption. The converse holds for prices below P_{mc}. The answer to (c) is less certain, though we would suspect it to be between P_m and P_{mc}. If we interpret the costs involved in the rate-making equation as economic costs and assume regulators are able to monitor and adjust rates accordingly, a price (AR) equal to average costs is the answer, P_{ac}. This follows from the observation that allowed revenues equal costs of service, $(O + T + R(V - D) = RR)$, or total revenue equals total cost. Divide by quantity where this condition holds, and we have $P = AR = AC$.

From a resource allocation point of view, pricing where $MC = P$, called marginal cost pricing, may be the superior alternative. But if P_{mc} is the price established, the total costs of the firm are not being covered. With losses in the industry, resources will be withdrawn and service will be inadequate. A government subsidy to the utility financed by tax proceeds has been proposed as a solution,[4] but we have no assurance that such a plan would work, since the taxes imposed introduce other distortions in the economy. The point is that without the subsidy, the twin objectives of efficient resource allocation and maintenance of utility service

---

[3] James C. Bonbright, "Railroad Valuation with Special Reference to the O'Fallon Decision," *American Economic Review*, 18 (1928), 196.

[4] Harold Hotelling, "The General Welfare in Relation to Problems of Taxation and of Railway and Utility Rates," *Econometrica*, 6 (1938), 242–269.

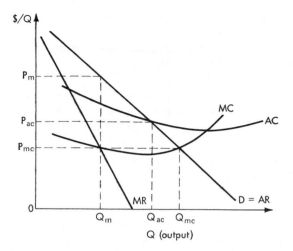

FIGURE 7.5 Monopoly with Long-Run Decreasing Costs and Government Regulation

cannot be achieved simultaneously. Multipart rates or economic price discrimination, discussed later in the chapter, is another proposed solution to this problem, a solution that creates distortions like those of the excise tax.

PROBLEMS IN UTILITY PRICING: AN EVERYDAY MARGINAL COST

Marginal cost is the additional cost associated with producing one more unit of output. Perhaps a nonutility example with which nearly everyone is familiar will reveal some of the complex ideas and intricate reasoning that underlie marginal cost pricing. The example is of an automobile. First, what is an automobile? What are its important characteristics? In order to specify the marginal cost, the output must also be specified. The automobile is some combination of horsepower, color, passenger and cargo capacity, and other factors. A subcompact and a full-sized automobile are each one unit of different outputs. To derive the marginal cost, we look at the costs associated with the marginal output and its assembled characteristics. These characteristics can then be related backward through the production process to the associated resources and their costs.

The costs flow from the opportunity costs of resources through the production process to the opportunity cost of the output. The production process, through the marginal product, gives rise to the marginal cost. Put very simply, the marginal cost equals the resource cost divided by the marginal product, as indicated in Table 7.1. The presence of economies of scale in the production process gives rise to decreasing marginal costs of output, since marginal product rises with output.

Before we proceed, the economic concept of *cost* should be clarified. The problem develops because the economic concept of cost need not correspond to the business's or consumer's ideas of costs, which are really outlays of money or money value. Outlays are reasonably objective and are the actual costs of owning and operating the automobile. The economic concept of cost is subjective, depending upon the resource owner's valuation of the worth of other alternative uses for the resources. If a purely competitive market exists for the resources, the objective outlay and subjective opportunity cost would be equal. Even in the economist's perfectly competitive market, a lack of perfect knowledge and foresight may cause objective outlays and subjective opportunity costs to diverge. For example, during a recession, many automobile workers are unemployed. The subjective opportunity cost of the workers, their desired wage, exceeds the objective outlay the automobile manufacturers are willing to pay during a recession. Perfect knowledge is lacking, and uncertainty prevails among the workers regarding their market wage. Certainly, the automobile industry is not even perfectly competitive. The oligopolistic nature of automobile manufacturing and the proverbial used car salesman who practices the maxim of *caveat emptor* (let the buyer beware) drive a further wedge between the subjective opportunity cost and the outlay for an automobile. *Shadow prices* or *imputed costs* will frequently be estimated by economists to represent subjective opportunity costs where opportunity costs and outlays differ.

Having illustrated the idea of output, production process, and cost, we can proceed to a more practical determination of marginal cost itself. We use the monetary amount of the opportunity cost. For example, the short-run marginal cost would be computed as follows for a consumer who owns a large, low-mileage car but who would prefer a high-mileage subcompact. The short-run marginal cost is the out-of-pocket costs of gasoline, maintenance, and other incidental charges for the large automobile. The long-run marginal cost of the subcompact is the long-run marginal cost to the consumer. Included are the out-of-pocket expenses for the subcompact plus the capital charges—depreciation, interest, and *ad valorem* taxes—for the subcompact, but not for the actual car owned, the full-sized automobile.

TABLE 7.1 Derivation of Marginal Cost

Resource Use (Units)	Resource per Cost Unit	Total Production (Units)	Total Cost	Marginal Product per Resource Unit	Marginal Cost per Unit of Product
1	$10	10.0	$10	10.0	$1.00
2	10	21.0	20	11.0	0.91
3	10	33.5	30	12.5	0.80
4	10	48.0	40	14.5	0.69
5	10	65.0	50	17.0	0.59

The day-to-day operation would be determined by the short-run marginal cost. The question to be answered is this: Is the trip worth the short-run marginal cost? The trade-in decision of the present owner of the full-sized auto can be explained by use of marginal analysis. The full-sized auto will be traded in when its short-run marginal cost exceeds the long-run marginal cost of the subcompact preferred by the consumer. Should the short-run marginal cost of the full-sized automobile be less than the subcompact's long-run marginal cost, the present value of the cost savings will exceed the trade-in *value* of the full-sized automobile.

In the parlance of marginal cost pricing, the trade-in value would be called *current value*. The current value would only coincidentally be equal to the financial outlay or principal outstanding. Only at the initial purchase, when the outlay equals the purchase price, at retirement to the scrap heap, when both values are zero, or if economic depreciation is charged will the financial outlay track the current value. If the full-sized automobile had originally been purchased for $5000, this equality at the original date of purchase and at the terminal date is shown in Table 7.2. The failure of current value to equal the "remaining balance" of the "financial cost" indicates in the example a difference in timing of "consumer outlays" and "total economic cost." This difference in timing is compensated by the cost of money or the time value of money. The reader should verify that the present value when discounted at a 10 percent cost of capital of both the "consumer outlays" and the "total economic cost" equals $5000, the purchase price. The consumer outlays need not correspond at each point in time to the economic cost so long as the time value of the money is properly computed on the balance outstanding.

If one expects inflation, the result holds and noncash appreciation must be recognized. Assume the 10 percent cost of money is made up of a 5 percent real time value of money and a 5 percent inflation premium, as in Table 7.3. As time passes, and assuming expectations are realized, the "current value" rises. Inflation may increase the current value, but no

TABLE 7.2 Comparison of Economic Cost with Financial Cost

	ECONOMIC COST				FINANCIAL COST	
Year	Current Value	Economic Depreciation	Economic Cost of Money	Total Economic Cost	Consumer Outlays	Remaining Balance*
0	$5,000	$ —	$—	$ —	$1,000	$5,000
1	3,000	2,000	500	2,500	1,262	4,000
2	2,000	1,000	300	1,300	1,262	2,190
3	1,000	1,000	200	1,200	1,262	1,147
4	0	1,000	100	1,100	1,262	0
Total		$5,000		$6,100	$6,048	

* Assuming a 20 percent down payment and a 4-year installment note at 10 percent.

TABLE 7.3 Comparison of Economic Cost and Financial Cost under Inflation

		ECONOMIC COST			FINANCIAL COST	
Year	Current Value	Economic Depreciation	Economic Cost of Money	Total Economic Cost	Consumer Outlays	Remaining Balance*
0	$5,000	$ —	$ —	$ —	$1,000	$5,000
1	3,150	2,100.00	250.00	2,350.00	1,262	4,000
2	2,205	1,102.50	157.50	1,260.00	1,262	2,190
3	1,158	1,157.25	110.25	1,267.50	1,262	1,147
4	0	1,215.90	57.90	1,273.80	1,262	0
Total		$5,575.65		$6,151.30	$6,048	

* Assuming a 20 percent down payment, a 4-year installment note at 10 percent, and 5 percent inflation.

adjustment is called for in the financial cost. The financial cost, based upon the 10 percent nominal cost of capital, adequately compensates for the real time value of money and for inflation. By considering the time value of money along with the various consumer outlays over time, the opportunity cost of an investment is covered without having the "remaining balance" track "current value." Exactly this circumstance arises when our consumer finances a new automobile with a trade-in and an installment loan. When the role of finance is introduced into the marginal cost concept, the need for consumer outlays to conform to changes in current value and interest on current value is overcome. Not having periodically to appraise a used car is a great advantage. In the absence of an actual free market transaction, the various appraisals one obtains for any given automobile are varied at best, and inaccurate at worst. Fortunately, financing arrangements for consumer outlays that do not require use of current value or set outlays equal to economic cost are available.

A time-of-use pricing problem does exist, a problem that has little to do with inflation or current value. It exists even if no inflation is expected, as in Table 7.2. This problem has been called the *free-rider problem*, a name well suited to our automobile example. Consider the problem of an acquaintance who borrows your car, drives 400 miles, empties the gas tank, and offers you nothing. This is the real time-of-use pricing problem. It is not a problem confined to periods of inflation and rising current value or peak use such as on weekdays. Rather, the real economic problem is that costs are not attributed to the user.

Several other economic concepts can be illustrated using the automobile example—statics, comparative statics, and dynamics. In the *static* economy, the ratio of the price of the full-sized car to the price of the subcompact would remain constant. This circumstance has not been true in recent years. As a point in time is attained where the price of a subcompact exceeds the price of many full-sized automobiles, a comparison may be made to when the price of a subcompact was less than the price of full-sized automobiles. This is an example of *comparative statics*, the comparison of two different relative prices. *Dynamics* is concerned with the pattern of relative price movements, the path by which the price of sub-compacts attains the higher level. Dynamics would consider the recession and its effect upon American automobile manufacturing, the implications of the Chrysler fiasco, and the impact of foreign imports and consumer credit.

The automobile illustration introduces many of the complex ideas and reasoning that underlie marginal cost pricing. These include:

1. How should output be specified?
2. What does the production process imply about economies of scale?
3. Are objective outlays equal to the subjective costs? Or must shadow prices be used?
4. Which marginal cost is important? Short-run marginal cost? Long-run marginal cost?
5. Which capital costs are we to look at? Current value? Financial outlays?
6. How should the free-rider problem be dealt with?
7. Are we interested in a static, comparative static, or dynamic analysis of the prices?

A similar variety of conceptual problems is encountered in attempting to define marginal cost in utility pricing. Is the appropriate cost concept the long run, where all costs are viewed as variable, or the short run, where some costs are fixed? Along what dimension is output to be meas-ured? The addition of one more passenger on a half-empty plane has a very low marginal cost, but if the plane is full perhaps the flight itself should be viewed as the unit of output. Likewise, what is the marginal cost of a new electric customer? How are common or joint costs to be allocated with marginal cost pricing between the production of two prod-ucts using the same production facilities?

In addition to these problems, numerous difficulties must be faced in implementing marginal cost pricing. First, the calculation of marginal cost frequently is not feasible, uneconomic, and impossible. Second, mar-ginal cost is not stationary, but constantly changing as output varies. To charge a continually varying price based upon marginal cost would be extremely annoying to consumers and administratively difficult. Finally, pricing according to marginal cost in the long run or the short run often leads to revenues that are inadequate to meet total costs. For these reasons, the concept of long-run incremental cost has been advanced as a reasonable and achievable alternative for pricing. *Long-run incremental cost* is the ad-ditional variable costs and fixed cost, both viewed as future costs, attrib-utable to the production of a particular *block* of output. It is, in effect, an average marginal cost.

In recent years, regulators have given a great deal of attention to the rate structure of utilities. Charging different rates to different segments of service raises additional possibilities for pricing. One of the questions of concern is how different classes of customers should be charged for capacity costs when the usage of service is markedly uneven for different user groups. Typically, one group buys when the system is producing at its peak, while another group consumes during an off-peak period. The utility must install enough capacity to meet peak demand; off-peak demand does not require additional capacity.

STABLE PEAK

The principle mentioned above that users should bear the marginal cost of providing service, including capacity costs, is applied in Figure 7.6. The off-peak demand, D_1, is less than capacity. This group does impose certain costs on the utility—namely, the noncapacity variable costs of serving them, including such things as fuel costs, metering, and billing costs. The appropriate price to charge this group is P_1, which covers the marginal cost of serving them. These peak users, with the demand D_2, are responsible for the capacity costs. A marginal increase or decrease in usage by off-peak users does not affect capacity costs, whereas a change in usage by peak users alters the need for this level of capacity and for incurring these costs. Consequently, capacity costs are properly attributable to peak

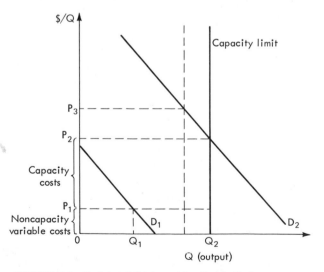

FIGURE 7.6 Peak Load Pricing with a Stable Peak

users. The price to this group should be P_2, which covers all marginal costs, including marginal capacity costs.

The graph in Figure 7.6 depicts the long-run solution to the problem, since capacity is adjusted to demand and revenues cover costs. If we view the vertical dashed line in the figure as the present capacity limits, however, P_3 should be charged to peak users so that demand is rationed to the capacity limits and marginal costs are covered. Here revenues exceed costs, and the long-run solution requires additional capacity and a lower price. Conversely, if at the price that equates usage to capacity revenues fall short of costs, the utility should move toward a smaller capacity and charge higher rates.

Some might argue that it is unfair to have the peak users pay for the capacity costs. After all, off-peak consumers are using the capacity too. If we increase the off-peak users' rates and reduce the peak-users' rates, a larger capacity is required to meet peak demand, while off-peak users are consuming a smaller amount. Here price to the off-peak user is inflated and overstates the sacrifice (marginal cost) of additional consumption. The existing capacity is used less and consumer satisfaction is lower than before, yet additional capacity is needed for peak users. A smaller investment in plant and equipment and greater utilization could result with peak-load pricing.

SHIFTING PEAK

In Figure 7.7, the peak is shifted as a result of charging a lower price to off-peak users. At a price of P_1, added capacity is required to serve off-peak users. As they press on capacity limits, off-peak users should be required to pay a portion of capacity costs. In this case, prices of P_3 and P_2 should be charged to off-peak and peak users, respectively, correspond-

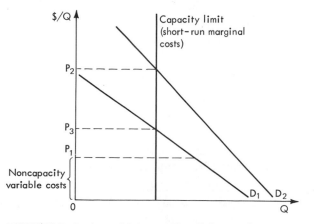

FIGURE 7.7 Peak Load Pricing with a Shifting Peak

ing to short-run marginal costs and fully utilizing capacity. Again, if revenues exceed costs, plant should be expanded and prices lowered. If revenues are inadequate to cover costs, capacity should be reduced and rates increased. The long-run solution requires that the sum of the different rates does not exceed the marginal cost of serving the two groups and that each price is set so that it clears the market; the quantity demanded equals the quantity supplied.[5]

Although commissions are hesitant to rely entirely on peak users for capacity costs, many commissions are moving in this direction. Several electric utilities charge lower rates in winter than in summer. Long distance telephone rates vary depending, among other things, on the time the call is placed, with the highest rates on normal business hours, the peak calling period. Natural gas rates for interruptible service, which is terminated during peak periods, is lower than other types of service. Airlines offer special reduced rates under various plans for travel during off-peak periods or on partially filled planes. Flying stand-by is analogous to interruptible service. Peak-load pricing suggests better utilization of existing capacity, the installation of the optimal capacity, lower plant costs than other pricing schemes, and economically efficient prices—prices based on marginal costs.

HETEROGENEOUS CAPITAL AND PEAKS

Peak-load pricing has been advocated as a rationale for allocation of capital charges exclusively to peak users. For example, the allocation of electric generation charges to summer peak users, thereby weighing most heavily on residential air-conditioning use, has been suggested. When heterogeneous plants are considered, it can no longer be concluded that off-peak users would not contribute to capital charges.

Assuming an electric utility which has both base-load, Q_1, and peak-load, Q_2, generation capacity, base-load capacity is generally running and available, except for maintenance, all year because of a lower operating cost, $SRMC_1$. Peak-load capacity is scheduled only as needed because of a more expensive operating cost, $SRMC_2$. Off-peak demand, D_1, will be willing to pay a price P_1, which exceeds the base-load short-run marginal cost, $SRMC_1$, but forestalls use of the peaking unit and its associated costs, $SRMC_2$—costs that exceed the worth of the off-peak users. As Figure 7.8 shows, off-peak users may contribute to capital charges. Similarly, with D_1 and D_2 as the demand today and the demand in a future year in a growing system, the same conclusion would hold. Earlier users would still

---

[5] For more elaboration, see Alfred Kahn, *The Economics of Regulation,* vol. 1 (New York: Wiley, 1970), chap. 4.

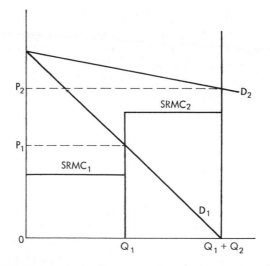

FIGURE 7.8 Peak Allocation with Heterogeneous Capital

contribute to the capital charges associated with excess capacity in the earlier years of the system.

Once we leave the simple cases of marginal cost pricing and peak-load pricing, the seemingly straightforward economics become extraordinarily complicated. In the Figure 7.8 example of a base-load unit and a peaking unit, a practical problem of first magnitude rears its head. How does one calculate the appropriate capital charge for each group of consumers? If a free market existed for utility capital, the capitalized value of the capital could be determined. In the above two-period example, where D_1 represents demand one year in the future and D_2 demand two years in the future, at which time the capital is worthless, this capital value would be

$$V = \frac{(P_1 - SRMC_1)Q_1}{(1 + r)^1} + \frac{(P_2 - SRMC_1)Q_1 + (P_2 - SRMC_2)Q_2}{(1 + r)^2}$$

The cost of capital is r, and the time periods for discounting are one and two years, but fractions of a year may be used for peak and off-peak analysis.

Marginal cost pricing in such a framework requires prior knowledge of the market clearing price and, in fact, a knowledge of demand curves. Given the present state of econometric analysis, ex post estimates of demand are only occasionally known, as we saw in Chapter 2. Ex ante estimates of demand functions have not been made, much less on the comprehensive basis utility rate making would require. Without such information on the capital-intensive public utilities, capital valuations in marginal cost pricing remain judgmental at the least, and speculative at the worst. Public utility regulation went through bad times when fair value appraisals reigned. To renew the era of capital appraisals with scanty econometric information, despite even the best of motives, would be ill-advised. Even today, practitioners of marginal cost methods have found their greatest problem to be the determination and allocation of current capital values— not a surprising difficulty, given the history of valuation of public utility capital.

PRICE DISCRIMINATION

Price discrimination is generally defined as price differences not based on differences in costs. As we saw in Chapter 2, price discrimination is possible and profitable for the firm with market power where there exist clearly definable user groups with different price elasticities and where the resale from one group to another can be substantially restricted by market segmentation. For the unregulated, profit-maximizing firm, we found that lower rates will be set for the group with the greater elasticity.

Price discrimination is commonplace in public utilities. For example, electric utilities generally charge lower rates to industrial users than to residential or commercial users. These lower rates are due in part to the higher consumption of industrial users and the lower direct costs associated therewith. ELCON, an association of industrial users, has stated:

Cost of Service Pricing

The price of electricity sold to industry is related to the cost to the utility of supplying that electricity. Lower volume prices to industry are possible for the following reasons:

1. Electricity is delivered more efficiently at high voltage than at low voltage. (Industrial consumers can take power ranging from 12,500 volts to 130,000 volts or higher, far beyond residential and commercial requirements.)
2. Large factories usually pay for and maintain substations and in-plant electrical distribution systems. Utilities must buy and maintain substations and transformers needed to step down high voltage to 220- or 110- volt house currents; extensive distribution systems are needed to take electricity to individual homes and apartments.
3. Fewer miles of power lines and towers must be maintained (routinely or during storms) to serve factories than are needed to deliver the same amount of electricity to many individual homes.
4. Metering and billing charges are less for selling the same amount of electricity to large industrial consumers as compared to residential consumers.
5. Use of electricity by residential and commercial consumers is more variable than use by industry; variability adds to costs.

In summary: it costs more to bring one kilowatt hour of electricity to a single family home than to a large factory.[6]

Nevertheless, industrial consumers typically have more power options available to them, including the possibility of self-generation of power. The remaining overhead expenses and investment could, however, with a higher industrial elasticity of demand, be expected to be allocated less toward industrial customers—e.g., by using the peak allocation method or by assigning residual costs to residential consumers.

Recent events in the gas industry also reflect such price discrimination. Under the Natural Gas Policy Act, incremental gas pricing establishes rates for certain industrial and large-volume users at a price competitive with that for fuel oil. This pricing reflects the ability of these customers to switch to alternative fuels—i.e., the elasticity of demand.

Certain of the price differentials we see in the public utility field are not based on differences in cost. Consider the example depicted in Figure 7.9. The firm is assumed to be able to separate two markets with the demand curve, D_2, for the second group having its zero quantity at Q_1. A uniform price, P_1, which would cover costs could be charged to the first group. This would justify a plant size corresponding to $SRAC_1$. But a segment of the first group and most of the second group who are willing to pay a price equal to, or even above, the marginal cost of serving them are not being served. If a lower price, P_2, is charged the second group, the costs of serving them are completely covered. This would justify a larger plant, and as a result of economies of scale, would reduce average costs to P_3. With a price of P_1 to the first group and P_2 to the second, the first

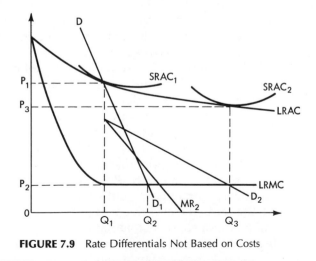

FIGURE 7.9   Rate Differentials Not Based on Costs

---

[6] Electricity Consumers Resource Council, *Profiles in Electricity Issues*, 1, 2 (June 1977), 2.

group is not made worse off, but the second group is better off by virtue of the consumer surplus obtained and a more efficient plant being used.

The D_1 group, which is being discriminated against, might actually be benefited if the P_2 price generates more than enough to cover the costs of serving the second group. If we view these as short-run cost curves, the additional revenues from group 2 make a contribution to overhead which the first group would otherwise have to bear alone. With these as long-run curves, any additional revenues from group 2 could be used to lower the rates to group 1. But strict regulation is required to achieve this result.

There are appropriate bounds within which this price discrimination may be acceptable in regulated industries, but price discrimination is not acceptable in all circumstances. In the long run, the industry must be subject to economies of scale. Price discrimination has no place in a constant or increasing cost industry except in the case of social overhead capital, where utility growth can confer external benefits over time to certain customer classes. Because of a large unit size, price is based on demand conditions rather than cost. In the short-run setting, there must be ample excess capacity to justify reducing rates to some group, which would otherwise not be served, so that fixed costs can be spread over a greater output. The bounds of the discriminatory rates are well established. The rate to the group with the inelastic demand would never be more than the average costs of serving them alone, and the rate to the elastic group would never be lower than the additional costs of serving them.

The effectiveness of third-degree discrimination found in rate-making rules requires enforced segregation of customer classes. Two examples of rate-making rules associated with third-degree price discrimination are the inverse elasticity rule, discussed in Chapter 2, and the proportionality rule, which sets rates based on some multiple or fraction of marginal costs. The strength of the discrimination underlying these rules is no more than an assumption. Realistically, economic discrimination may not be particularly enforceable or meaningful. Furthermore, much discrimination in practice probably reduces to arbitrary discrimination. Upon closer examination, we find that customer classes for which rates are set are based upon historical practice and for administrative convenience, rather than being based upon homogeneous groups of demand functions and demand elasticities. The implied assumption of third-degree price discrimination is that the number of customers in the classes can be enforced. This is true only if resale of utility services is prohibited or no competitive suppliers exist. If utility customers can leave the class, the effectiveness of the price discrimination is reduced. For example, industrial customers of electricity or natural gas have available self-generation and alternative fuels, respectively. The telephone terminal equipment, long-distance message, and private line markets are now competitive for certain customers. A ceiling thus exists on the discriminatory pricing to such customers. This ceiling will be no higher than the average cost of the alternative available to the customers.

If the price discrimination rule, either the proportionality or the inverse elasticity rule, suggests a price higher than the relevant average cost, customers will drop out and choose what is in effect an inefficient means of production. Discrimination thus leads to the violation of an assumption of marginal cost pricing that only efficient production take place. Accordingly, price discrimination, under realistic conditions, may degenerate into a form of monopoly pricing.

The monopoly customers that lacked alternative technologies because of need, size, or inability to cooperate would pay a higher price. Technically, the customer with other, albeit inefficient, options could threaten and feign derived demand curves with greater elasticities. But monopoly customers would not be able to so influence their own price. Such a utility rate-making scheme, in which lack of knowledge of customer demand curves and interdependence of these demand curves and the rate schedules exist, would not produce a single unique set of rates. A number of methods have been proposed to determine the unique rates—notably, the proportionality rule, the inverse elasticity rule, and the fully distributed cost or cost to serve methods. The former two are based on marginal cost pricing and economic welfare economics, and the latter on business practice and actual or embedded costs. Each is designed to provide the utility with the opportunity to recoup the cost of service, something marginal cost pricing alone cannot guarantee.

MARGINAL COST VERSUS FULLY DISTRIBUTED COST

The pricing methods we are now prepared to discuss are marginal costs adjusted by the proportionality rule or the inverse elasticity rule, and fully distributed costs. These sets of pricing methods can best be described as quasi-marginal cost and quasi-average cost. The bases for both methods, marginal cost and average cost, are adjusted by methods that allocate overhead and capacity charges. Such allocations are necessary so that prices are sufficient to cover total costs. The proportionality rule sets different prices at some fraction or multiple of marginal cost, while the inverse elasticity rule sets prices in relationship to marginal cost in proportion to the demand elasticities. The fully distributed cost method, which is a quasi-average cost method, uses a weighted average of financial outlays of the utility and over an extended period approximates the same result as does economic average-cost pricing. The weights used in the averaging process allocate capital investment among customer classes at a point in time and over time. Various accounting and engineering data are used to allocate the investment at a point in time, while straight-line depreciation, original cost rate base, and the nominal cost of capital jointly allocate investment and capital charges over time.

Welfare economics is unable to provide a definitive justification for quasi-marginal cost pricing; rather, an argument by analogy is adopted. The result of pure competition would be marginal cost pricing. Minimal deviation from the results of pure competition should be acceptable. This is a rather weak analogy, since quasi-marginal cost pricing is also consistent with socialist planning.[7] The classical liberal preference is the competitively governed free market, an end not necessarily achieved by quasi-marginal cost pricing in a mixed economy.[8] Rather, rate and service regulation and monopoly markets persist under quasi-marginal cost pricing, with the important element of competition still lacking in several areas. The absence of a compelling justification in welfare economics for quasi-marginal cost pricing raises important questions for rate-making practice, especially with regard to the current value versus actual cost methods.

ECONOMIC WELFARE, INCLUDING SECOND-BEST CONSIDERATIONS

A reasonable question economists, and the public generally, occasionally ask is this: What objective ought public utility prices to pursue? Welfare economics provides a standard by which economists judge whether the result of economic policy is proper or not. Welfare economics looks at the value of economic policy to individuals and society. Two methods have been used: the old welfare economics, and the new welfare economics. The old welfare economics looks at the cumulative economic surplus from a policy. So long as consumers are willing to pay more than the marginal opportunity cost of providing goods and services, the economic surplus is increased by increasing production and sales. In effect, the economic surplus, which could be measured in dollars, serves as a measure of utility, the economist's fundamental measure.

The new welfare economics objects to attempts to measure utility, either indirectly by economic surplus, as Alfred Marshall and A. C. Pigou proposed, or directly, as earlier utilitarians such as Jeremy Bentham advocated. The new welfare economics proposes a much simpler method. All consumers and producers in the economy would be polled to see whether each is better or worse off under the proposed policy. The only acceptable economic policy is that which is not blackballed by any con-

---

[7] A. P. Lerner, *The Economics of Control* (New York: Macmillan, 1944).

[8] Alan T. Peacock and Charles K. Rowley, "Pareto Optimality and the Political Economy of Liberalism," *Journal of Political Economy*, 8, 3 (May–June 1972), part I, 476–490.

sumer or producer. Unanimity or consensus among individuals thus establishes economic well-being.

Using the methods of the old or the new welfare economics, the conclusion can be reached that price ought to equal marginal cost. One of the key assumptions of this conclusion is perfect knowledge and foresight—a primary condition of pure competition.[9] Perfect competition, let alone monopolistic competition, oligopoly, duopoly, and monopoly, does not meet this assumption. The reason why perfect knowledge is necessary at any point in time and perfect foresight into the future is necessary is that otherwise consensus cannot be reached on what the marginal costs are. For example, if consumers believe a new power plant will last 35 years while the utility investors believe only a 25-year life is likely, the marginal capital charge sought by investors will exceed that which consumers are willing to pay. Also, agreement and accurate foresight are necessary on salvage value, the technology that will be available, and the cost of capital throughout the life of the project.

The condition of perfect knowledge and foresight is usually euphemistically stated to mean regulation must be forward-looking. In practice, forward-looking regulation has been applied by surveying utility managers, forecasting utility data, and reviewing utility budgets. Restricting attention to such measures of utility activity tends to emphasize only the subjective view of utility management. But there are other things to look at. For example, a survey of consumers' subjective knowledge and foresight is also required by welfare economics.

Other factors make agreement on the true marginal cost difficult. These difficulties are caused by externalities. Other markets or segments of the economy often do not set prices based on marginal cost. Most significantly, government uses majority voting and taxes, which are not associated with the costs of the public services or goods provided. Imperfect competition prevails in other markets, such as suppliers of utilities affiliated with the utility. Classic externalities such as air and water pollution affect the electric, gas, and water utilities; radio and microwave frequencies, so important to telecommunications, are an unpriced but limited resource; and the process of innovation and patents are not priced at marginal cost.

As was pointed out earlier, simply put, the marginal cost equals the marginal resource cost divided by the marginal product of the resource. Where the marginal resource cost is not an accurate social marginal cost itself, the marginal cost of the utility service itself can hardly be accurate. When marginal resource costs are inaccurate, the *second-best* problem is

---

[9] E. Malinvaud, "The Analogy between Atemporal and Intertemporal Theories of Resource Allocation," in *Readings in Modern Theory of Economic Growth,* eds. Joseph E. Stiglitz and Hirofumi Uzawa (Cambridge, Mass.: MIT Press, 1969), p. 468.

J. Wiseman, "The Theory of Public Utility Price—An Empty Box," *Oxford Economic Papers,* 9, 1 (February 1957), 68.

said to exist. Unless agreement can be reached on what the accurate shadow price or marginal social resource cost truly is, the marginal cost is unlikely to be accurate and to reflect the proper economic policy. Other agreements are also necessary. The short-run and long-run marginal products differ, and unless agreement is reached on the degree of resource changes to consider, the marginal costs are not accepted by all economic parties.

Marginal cost pricing further requires that only the marginal unit sold be priced at marginal cost. Other nonmarginal units sold, so-called *inframarginal* units, are permitted to be sold at discriminatory prices. First-degree or perfect discrimination, charging each individual a different price, is no less acceptable than charging each customer the same price, the marginal cost. First-degree discrimination would be adverse to the consumer. By charging a price equal to the maximum price the consumer is willing to pay, the maximum price indicated by the demand curve, the consumer gives up all the surplus. Alternatively, the price could be set to favor the consumer: it could be set at a minimum necessary to elicit a supply. Each unit sold would be sold at exactly the marginal cost of that quantity supplied. Further, any price between the maximum and minimum might be set. In Table 7.4, the possibility of price discrimination requires that only the fourth unit be priced at marginal cost, $7. The marginal cost principle does not indicate that a specific price is required for the first, second, or third units sold. This fuzzy specification in marginal cost pricing has led to the proportionality and inverse elasticity rules. Since marginal cost pricing is unlikely to generate revenues equal to the revenue requirement, price discrimination using these rules has been suggested to recover or return the revenue differences and recover the overhead, common, or joint costs.

The proportionality rule is proposed as an application of perfect or first-degree discrimination. The demand curve must be totally inelastic for this to occur. Then the quantity consumed is no less or no more as price is set at some fraction or multiple of marginal cost. Resource allocation is not changed. Since elasticity is apparent in utility demand and perfect discrimination is very costly to practice or undesirable, the proportionality concept has given way to the inverse elasticity rule. Perfect discrimination

TABLE 7.4   Price Range from Demand Price to Marginal Cost under Marginal Cost Pricing

Quantity (Units)	Demand Price		Marginal Cost
1	From $10	to	$8.5
2	From 9	to	8.0
3	From 8	to	7.5
4	From 7	to	7.0
5	From 6	to	6.5

is replaced by third-degree or intergroup discrimination. Sales at the quantity where price equals marginal cost are replaced by so-called optimal departures from optimal quantities by quasi-marginal cost pricing. The price to the inelastic customer class is raised or reduced more than that to the elastic customer classes to minimize the *reduction* in economic welfare, by varying total sales only a small amount, while at the same time recovering the revenue requirement. The reader should be aware that optimality no longer is achieved. It is interesting that the quasi-optimal marginal-cost-based price for a single output firm is at average cost.[10] Effective price discrimination may not in fact be achieved and desired, and average cost pricing may become a reasonable practice.[11]

As the discussion of marginal cost pricing and price discrimination indicates, this pricing method is indifferent to the distribution of income and wealth. The charges for inframarginal units could range from high to low. The quasi-marginal cost methods affect more than the allocation of resources. Some individuals are made poorer and some richer. There is no agreement about the result of some being poorer and some richer. Conservative economists claim making investors richer spurs investment; liberal economists point out that making consumers poorer restricts demand. Brown and Heal conclude

> A traditional argument is that, provided the losses can be covered in a non-distortionary fashion these [regulated increasing-returns industries] should price at marginal cost, insuring, in a first-best world, an efficient allocation of resources. It should now be clear that this argument is incorrect, and not merely because it neglects second-order conditions. Endowments may be such that there is no way of achieving global Pareto optimality by marginal cost pricing.[12]

Perhaps the most telling criticism of quasi-marginal cost methods is by Pareto. The same Pareto, who was an early developer of marginal cost pricing, wrote:

> Note, however, that this determination certainly is not for the purpose of arriving at a numerical calculation of prices. Let us make the hypothesis most favorable to such a calculation; assume that we have overcome all the difficulties in the way of acquiring knowledge of the data of the problem, and that we know the Ophelimities [utilities] of all the goods for each individual, all the particulars pertaining to the production of the goods, etc. This is

---

[10] William J. Baumol, "Quasi Optimality: The Price We Must Pay for a Price System," *Journal of Political Economy*, 87, 3 (June 1979), 584.

[11] I. M. D. Little, *A Critique of Welfare Economics*, 2nd ed. (London: Oxford University Press, 1957), p. 214.

[12] Donald J. Brown and Geoffrey Heal, "Equity, Efficiency and Increasing Returns," *The Review of Economic Studies*, 46 (4), 145 (October 1979), 584–585.

already an absurd hypothesis, and yet it still does not provide us with the practical possibility of solving the problem. We have seen that in the case of 100 individuals and 700 goods there would be 70,699 conditions (in reality a great number of particular details, which we have disregarded so far, would increase this number further); then we would have to solve a system of 70,699 equations. As a practical matter, that is beyond the power of algebraic analysis, and it would be still further beyond it if we considered the fabulous number of equations which a population of forty million individuals, and several thousand goods would entail. In that case the roles would be changed; and it would no longer be mathematics which would come to the aid of political economy, but political economy which would come to the aid of mathematics. In other words, if all these equations were actually known, the only means of solving them would be to observe the actual solution which the market gives.[13]

Given the thousands of telephone equipment items, hundreds of telephone, electric, and gas utilities, and millions of utility customers in the United States, without enumerating the number of suppliers and employees and governmental jurisdictions, the marginal cost pricing problem soon becomes of vast dimensions.

At one important point in utility rate making, the market does not aid the mathematics of marginal cost pricing. This point is seen in the value of capital. Invariably, marginal cost methods must rely upon some shadow price for capital, the so-called current value or cost.

CURRENT VALUE VERSUS ACTUAL COST

Current capital costs are cited as appropriate economic costs and actual embedded costs as inappropriate economic costs. Such a conclusion is not accurate, for embedded costs and current costs rest upon the same economic concept—the time value of the capital.

Consider the current cost or present value of capital to be a function of the discounted future income to investors:

$$PV_n = \frac{R_1}{(1 + R)} + \frac{R_2}{(1 + r)^2} + \cdots + \frac{R_{h-1}}{(1 + r)^{h-1}} + \frac{FV_h}{(1 + r)^h}$$

where PV_t, R_t, r, and FV_t are current cost, future income, cost of capital, and future value, respectively. The time periods, indicated by the subscript t, range from now, n, through times 1, 2, to a time hence, h. The future value, FV_h, can be shown by the same equation upon which supporters of forward looking or future cost must rely to be the remaining original cost for which investors have not been compensated. This is shown by multiplying the equation above by $(1 + r)^h$ and solving for FV_h:

---

[13] Vilfredo Pareto, *Manual of Political Economy*, trans. Ann S. Schwier (New York· Augustus M. Kelley, 1971), p. 171.

$$FV_h = PV_n(1 + r)^h - R_1(1 + r)^{h-1}$$
$$- R_2(1 + r)^{h-2} - \cdots$$
$$- R_{(h-1)}(1 + r)$$

It is unlikely that the future value will equal the current cost, but the embedded costs that result (the Rs) cover both depreciation and the return investors receive. For current value henceforth to equal future value, re-production cost appraisals and observed depreciation methods would be necessary. Both were the bane of regulation for many years. For rate-making purposes, the significant differences between current capital costs and embedded capital costs is that the former is essentially unworkable, time-consuming, and virtually unmeasurable, whereas the latter is both functional, realizable, and accurately ascertainable. Further, attempting to equate the current cost henceforth with the future value and to equate depreciation with economic depreciation derives from the same profit maximization motive as does the monopoly pricing rule.[14] The monopolist is helped by applying the current value rule to maximize cumulative excess profits, but the consumer is not so helped. History has shown that, without perfectly competitive entry and exit of firms or the absence of cross-subsidization by the monopolist, use of current value is not an effective control on rates. Current value would amount to even less control than the old "fair value" rate base. With the "fair value" rate, at least reproduction and replacement cost studies were verified minimally by the existence of the plant and the equipment. With current value, there is only speculation about what plant and equipment might be used in the future. Under the current value method, one cannot even kick the telephone pole to see if it will fall over, as one could under fair value methods.

Marginal cost methods also convert current capital values to capital charges by a capital recovery annuity formula:

$$Q = (V) \times \cfrac{r}{1 - \cfrac{1}{(1 + r)^n}}$$

where Q = annuitized quasi-rent payment for capital

V = current capital value

r = cost of capital

n = time period length

Such an annuity implies a unique and precise rate of economic depreciation and a series of expected capital values in the future. This expected capital

---

[14] Harold Hotelling, "A General Mathematical Theory of Depreciation," *Journal of the American Statistical Association*, September 1925, p. 341.

value series has not been checked for accuracy of prediction. The precision of the expected capital values that result is unlikely to be an accurate representation of subsequent current values, especially during inflation. Noncash appreciation, which is significant during inflation, does not track the inflation rate in this capital recovery series.[15] The real price of utility service, all other things being equal, declines with this formulation over time. It is unlikely that the current cost of capital is tracked; rather, a substitute financial outlay is used—a substitute not unlike that used in embedded costs.

Welfare economics does not provide a compelling basis for the adoption of marginal cost pricing. This basis is reduced even more for quasi-marginal cost pricing, since third-degree or intergroup price discrimination departs from the desired economic value for the commonwealth. Applying marginal cost pricing piecemeal to separate utility and customer classes has little support in economics because of second-best problems. This is especially true since only shadow prices can be used for capital values. The history of "fair value" rate-base regulation suggests that capital values based on appraisals are likely to be inaccurate, self-serving, expensive, and time-consuming to measure. For example, electricity transmission and distribution costs, which depend upon specific locational features and current cost appraisals, have been often replaced by trended original cost, not current cost, in marginal cost studies.

The fully distributed cost method, an actual cost method, is based upon the return on investment concept of business. This method relies upon available accounting data, is used widely in business as a means of financial control, and is compatible with revenue determination. The return on investment (ROI) approach uses the following accounting relationship for each class of service:[16]

$$ \text{ROI} = \frac{\text{Net income}}{\text{Sales}} \times \frac{\text{Sales}}{\text{Investment}} $$

---

[15] U.S. Nuclear Regulatory Commission, *Treatment of Inflation in the Development of Discount Rates and Levelized Costs in NEPA Analyses for the Electric Utility Industry* (Washington, D.C., January 1980), pp. 8–9.

[16] Revenues = Operating expense + annual depreciation + taxes + (gross investment − accumulated depreciation) × rate of return, or $RR = O + D + T + (V - D)\text{ROI}$.

Dividing by quantity, Q, gives average price,

$$ P = \frac{RR}{Q} = \frac{O}{Q} + \frac{d}{Q} + \frac{T}{Q} + \frac{(V - D)}{Q}\text{ROI} $$

Return on a class of service is developed as

$$ \text{ROI} = \frac{P - \dfrac{O}{Q} - \dfrac{d}{Q} - \dfrac{T}{Q}}{\dfrac{V - D}{Q}} $$

This equation states that ROI is the product of the net profit margin and the capital turnover ratio. In addition to directly attributable investment and out-of-pocket costs, net income is reduced by an allocation of some portion of overhead expenses. Investment includes a portion of overhead investments. Each of the overhead costs is a weighted average. For example, in telephone rate making the investment weights are often direct investment; in electric and gas rate making, they are often coincident peak demand, noncoincident peak demand, the "average and excess" demand, and KWH or MCF usage. The intertemporal allocation of capital is reflected by annual depreciation expense and net investment after a depreciation reserve ratio is used to reduce total plant in service. When the returns on investment for the various classes of service are set, rates recover both direct and overhead operating expenses. Also, investment costs such as depreciation, income taxes, and operating income are recovered.

An increase in an expense, such as general corporate expense, gives rise to an increase in the operating ratio—a decrease in operating efficiency. If nothing else changes, the return on investment for the class of service would decline below the designated rate unless utility rates are raised proportionately. As another example, suppose that the investment to serve a class of service increases. In this case, two possibilities present themselves. If this added investment sufficiently increases the quantity sold or decreases the operating ratio, the ROI may be maintained without a rate revision; otherwise rates must be adjusted.

The rate of return formula can be reformulated as follows:

$$\text{ROI} = \left(1 - \frac{\text{Operating expense}}{\text{Sales}}\right)\left(\frac{\text{Sales}}{\text{investment}}\right)$$

Let operating expense be indicated by the equation $OE = F + aQ$; investment by the equation $I = G + bQ$; and sales by the equation $S = PQ$,

---

Then,

$$\text{ROI} = \frac{P - \dfrac{O}{Q} - \dfrac{d}{Q} - \dfrac{T}{Q}}{P} \times \frac{P}{\dfrac{(V - D)}{Q}},$$

$$\text{ROI} = \frac{\text{Net income}}{\text{Sales}} \times \frac{\text{Sales}}{\text{Investment}}$$

or

$$\text{ROI} = \left(1 - \frac{\dfrac{O}{Q} + \dfrac{d}{Q} + \dfrac{T}{Q}}{P}\right) \times \frac{P}{\dfrac{(V - D)}{Q}}$$

$$\text{ROI} = (1 - \text{operating ratio}) \times \text{capital turnover ratio}$$

with price P and quantity Q. Fixed costs are F and G, and aQ and bQ are variable costs.

A number of fully distributed cost study methods exist. The first identifies variable costs and distributes lump sum fixed costs, resulting in

$$\text{ROI} = \left(1 - \frac{F + aQ}{PQ}\right)\left(\frac{PQ}{G + bQ}\right)$$

Alternatively, the entire cost is treated as variable costs including fixed costs. The resulting equation becomes

$$\text{ROI} = \left(1 - \frac{F/Q + a}{P}\right)\left(\frac{P}{G/Q + b}\right)$$

The corresponding average utility rate is indicated by the slope of the line OB in Figure 7.10 for both methods. The first equation is much like fully distributed cost studies in the telephone and railroad industry. The second exemplifies the fully distributed cost studies in the gas and electric utility industry. Observe that the slope of the tangents to the long-run cost, LRC, and the short-run cost, SRC, are the long-run and short-run marginal costs, respectively.

The approximations to short-run and long-run marginal cost are generally no more accurate than average costs. Out-of-pocket costs have been used to approximate short-run marginal cost. The line OC in Figure 7.10

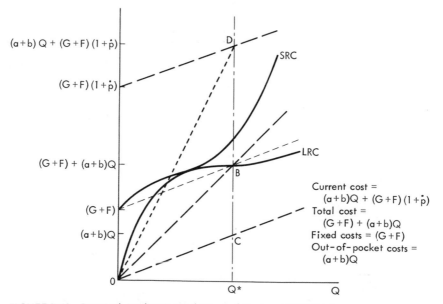

FIGURE 7.10 Practical Applications of Marginal Cost and FDC Pricing

represents the price that corresponds with out-of-pocket costs and the equation

$$\text{ROI} = \left(1 - \frac{a}{P}\right)\left(\frac{P}{b}\right)$$

As line *OC* is parallel to line $(G + F)$ *B* and is not tangent to *LRC*, marginal costs are not approximated by out-of-pocket costs. Long-run marginal cost estimates rely upon the current capital costs. Thus, the inflation index, $(1 + \dot{p})$, raises investment costs so that

$$\text{ROI} = \left(1 - \frac{F + aQ}{PQ}\right)\left(\frac{PQ}{G(1 + \dot{p}) + b(1 + \dot{p})Q}\right)$$

The line $(G + F)(1 + \dot{p})D$ has a slope equal to the slope of the line $(G + F)B$. Variable costs again do not approximate either short-run or long-run marginal costs. Alternatively

$$\text{ROI} = \left(1 - \frac{F/Q + a}{P}\right)\left(\frac{P}{(G/Q + b)(1 + \dot{p})}\right)$$

This gives rise to the rate embodied in the line *OD*. Again, the approximation to marginal costs is poor. There is no *a priori* reason why the tangents to short-run or long-run costs or both at quantity, Q^*, equal the rate for the line *OD*. Current cost adjustments do not bring one closer to marginal cost pricing.

Rather than attempting to justify the fully distributed cost approach by a holistic welfare standard, as quasi-marginal cost pricing is justified, a case-by-case approach is applied. Available information on such matters as operating efficiency, service quality, and rate levels may be heard and considered by the commission. The fully distributed cost method thus follows the incremental method of control and decision making, which advocates a piecemeal approach to policy questions. It balances effective control of monopoly pricing through average cost pricing, as against the only weakly supported gains in economic welfare from marginal cost pricing. It recognizes that utility pricing makes some richer and some poorer, a result which simply cannot be ignored in setting just and reasonable rates. Average cost pricing by commissions is a solution that cannot be judged *a priori*, but only by its practical results in each case.

VALUE OF SERVICE PRICING

Value of service is a concept long used in rate design. Unfortunately, it is used to mean several different things. Frequently, this term connotes nothing more than price discrimination, as discussed earlier. Another meaning of the term for the single product is simply the monopoly price, "charging what the traffic will bear" to the extent permitted by the regulatory agency. Finally, the value of service is used as a standard of rate making to mean anything other than cost-of-service pricing. In this sense, the term encompasses the other two meanings, but also takes into account additional factors, such as equity considerations, expansion objectives, and social and political constraints, in some unspecified and incalculable way.

Examples of rates based on value of service considerations follow. Different rates are charged different classes of users based on the elasticity (or inverse elasticity) of demand differences. Rates in different telephone exchanges vary according to the size of the town. Higher rates are charged in larger cities because individuals value the service more, since a greater number of individuals may be called; and the average incomes of city dwellers, and thus their ability to pay, are greater. Rates may be the same for different consumers, but costs may vary widely. For example, telephone rates over a range of distance are largely the same for all long distance calls, though the costs can vary substantially depending upon origin and destination. Additional examples will be given in the following discussions of telephone and electricity pricing.

A recent variant of value of service pricing is *lifeline rates.* Under lifeline rates, some minimum level of utility service is to be priced at a low rate. The original lifeline rates, as the name suggests, were for residential telephone service, but the concept has been extended to include residential electric and gas service. California is the state most noted for its legislatively mandated lifeline rates, but the District of Columbia at an early point also had such rates. The Public Utilities Regulatory Policies Act calls for all state commissions regulating electric rates to consider lifeline rates. Two reasons have been given:

1. The poor will be made financially advantaged by such a quasi-welfare program.
2. All people are entitled to access to a necessary minimum level of utility services.

Since lifeline rates are not designed to cover the costs of the lifeline level of service, particularly the customer and demand charges, the uncompensated costs are recovered in the rates charged for use in excess of the lifeline level and by nonresidential users.

In overturning a Colorado Public Utility Commission order to offer discounted gas rates to low-income elderly and low-income disabled persons, the Colorado Supreme Court discussed the value of service nature of lifeline rates. The court stated:

> [T]he PUC ordered the utility companies to provide a lower rate to selected customers unrelated to the cost or type of service provided. . . . In this instance, the discount rate benefits an unquestionably deserving group, the

low income elderly and low income disabled. This, unfortunately, does not make the rate less preferential.[17]

In a dissent, Justice Carrigan stated an opposing view:

> High costs of utility service may effectively result in total denial of gas service to customers who cannot afford those high rates. Such a denial of natural gas service in the homes of elderly and disabled poor persons would have a serious, adverse impact on the health, safety, and comfort of that class of customers to whom the PUC proposes to offer lower rates.[18]

The connection between low utility use, ability to pay, and need has been questioned. ELCON, an association of industrial electricity consumers, points out that there is a weak relationship between electricity consumption and income, that many eligible consumers are likely to be missed and end up paying the higher rates, that certain high-income but low-consumption customers will benefit, and that alternative public assistance is available.[19]

The fundamental economic question raised by lifeline rates is whether government ought to subsidize certain utility uses and tax other utility uses or, alternatively, to make general income transfers financed through general tax revenues. Conventional economic analysis would favor the latter type of transfer payment.

The ethical dilemma of an economic analysis of lifeline rates is the same as that for marginal cost rates: Is the benefactor's level of well-being greater, equal to, or less than the recipient's? One cannot look at income alone, because individuals' ages and earning potentials differ. Within like ages, earnings may differ because, though money income is equal, benefits in kind differ. Many elderly, though they have low income, for example, may reside in their own homes and make no housing payments. The working poor may, because of age, income, and health, be ineligible. On the other hand, the consumer-benefactors may receive an external benefit knowing that their money goes to pay for necessities for the needy. Another question is whether the administrative costs of lifeline rates are sufficiently low relative to other alternatives. And a related question is this: What are the ethical costs of corporations collecting personal information on customers?

Another form of value of service pricing developed in recent years is sumptuary utility rates and service requirements. *Sumptuary rates and*

---

[17] *Mountain States Legal Foundation* v. *Colorado Public Utilities Commission et al.,* 28 PUR 4th 611 (1979).

[18] *Mountain States Legal Foundation* v. *Colorado Public Utilities Commission et al.,* 28 PUR 4th 616 (1979).

[19] Electricity Consumers Resource Council, *Profiles in Electricity Issues,* 7 (February, 1980).

service requirements are designed to discourage or prevent so-called extravagant and frivolous use of utility services. It includes certain inverted and flat rate designs and service requirements. Sumptuary service requirements include the federally mandated maximum winter and minimum summer temperature requirements, the insulation and energy conservation requirements for new utility hookups, the elimination of outdoor gas decorative lighting, and the banning of lawn watering and filling swimming pools during droughts.

Of course, telephone value of service pricing and sumptuary utility rates and service requirements can be analyzed within the same framework as that applied to lifeline rates. Telephone value of service relies heavily on the view that the benefactor receives external benefits from the communications access provided by universal service and larger calling areas. In effect, telephone service is priced as an "option good" for the service the consumer might choose to use, even if not actually used.

INDUSTRY PRICING PRACTICES

Marginal cost pricing and, most frequently, fully distributed costs have been the basis for pricing in telephone, electric, gas, and water services. In certain areas of telephone pricing, value of service pricing has prevailed. Much attention has been given the two cost concepts by regulatory commissions.

TELEPHONE SERVICE

Incremental cost is the additional cost incurred by the firm of supplying some segment of service. Those costs directly related to another service and those costs both services have in common, though not attributable to either, such as certain fixed or overhead costs, are excluded from this measure of cost. *Fully distributed costs* include variable costs plus some portion of the common, unattributable costs. Terms referring to analogous concepts are *out-of-pocket costs* for incremental costs and *fully allocated costs* for fully distributed costs.

An illustration of these concepts and their rationale is given by Baumol and Walton in their article, "Full Costing, Competition and Regulatory Practice."[20] Following their illustration, Table 7.5 gives three alternative plans for the construction of a plant. The incremental cost of producing B, for example, is obtained by comparing plans 1 and 3; the addition of B to plan 1 adds $5 to total cost, as given in plan 3. A comparison of the

---

[20] *Yale Law Journal*, 82, 4 (March 1973), pp. 639–655. A more mathematical treatment is found in J. Kay, "Recent Contributions to the Theory of Marginal Cost Pricing: Some Comments," *Economic Journal*, 81, 322 (June 1971), 366–371.

TABLE 7.5 Illustration of Incremental Cost

Plan	Production of	Total Cost	Incremental Cost
1	A	$ 7	$4
2	B	8	5
3	A and B	12	9

incremental costs of both ($9) with the total cost of producing both ($12) shows that $3 of total costs is not directly attributable to either. Under a fully distributed cost standard, this $3 must be distributed between the production of A and B on some basis. One of the many possible bases for this allocation is the relative proportion of incremental costs of each. Under this method, approximately $5.3 [(4/9 × 3) + 4] is the fully distributed cost for A, and $6.7 [5/9 × 3) + 5] is the cost of B.

The argument for a fully distributed cost calculation is that selling a segment of service subject to competition below "full cost" leads to inadequate revenues which must be recouped from monopoly services. The customers of the monopoly service subsidize the low price, which drives competitors out of the industry. It is argued that prices based on fully distributed costs prohibit this internal subsidization.

The counterarguments are that rates based on incremental costs can benefit both consuming groups, those in B, the competitive service, and those in A, the monopoly service. Any revenues obtained from sales of B exceeding incremental costs must benefit the customers of A under strict rate regulation. In the example given, suppose the competitive rate for B is $6.2. At the fully distributed cost of $6.7, the firm would not be permitted to sell B, and the users of A must pay for the entire $3 unattributable costs. But if B can be sold at the competitive rate of $6.2, users of A need only pay $1.8 of the common costs, while B's users contribute $1.2. Thus, rather than to their detriment, the consumers of A benefit by permitting the firm to produce both. The test of subsidization is whether A's users are made worse off by the production of B. But if B's revenues more than cover their incremental costs, a contribution is made to "overhead."

Another argument for incremental costs is that prices based on fully distributed costs protect less efficient rivals. The added resources required from society in the production of B, reflected by incremental costs, may very well be higher for the rival firm, even though its fully distributed costs are lower. A price based upon the minimum of fully distributed costs allows the rival producer, using more of society's resources, to survive. It is true the rival may not be driven from the market under fully distributed costs, but this result is obtained at a cost to consumers of higher prices than would result under true competition. Those firms with higher incremental costs but lower fully distributed costs, therefore, tend to be the primary advocates of full-cost prices.

There are several arguments against incremental costs.

1. The measurement of incremental costs is imprecise because of shifts in and movement along the cost curves from one point in time to the next. Also, the appropriate length of the run is not obvious; short-run, long-run, or some intermediate run may be used in principle.
2. The allocation of contributions to cover overhead may approximate monopoly pricing because there is no single acceptable method of allocation of contributions. These allocations tend to be arbitrary.
3. Incremental costs are understated because common costs, which may be attributed to individual services, are omitted and instead are met by contribution. Only joint costs may not be attributed directly to individual services.
4. Revenues based on incremental costs may not provide sufficient quasi-rent because of excess capacity to enable the firm to stay in business. This is particularly so where substantial excess capacity exists, a prevalent public utility condition. Typically, bankruptcy or predatory competition results.
5. The structure of the industry, if imperfectly competitive, does not give rise to appropriate quasi-marginal cost pricing and contribution.

Next we will review the use of incremental cost pricing and fully distributed cost in the telephone industry. We will present arguments for and against each pricing method. The telephone industry provides competitive services in addition to monopoly basic services. The pricing issues for these services are different.

Competitive Services

The Federal Communications Commission in a series of decisions opened up three parts of the telephone industry to competition: private lines, terminal equipment supply, and common carrier service. The Bell System has argued that a burden test based upon incremental cost analysis be applied to determine the adequacy of competitive rates. The *burden test* reduces to a condition that total revenue from a new service exceed the changes in revenues from cross-elastic effects of other services, less the decrease in revenue requirement without the service, offset by the increased revenue requirement from providing alternative services. That is to say, the adjusted net revenues from a new service must exceed adjusted incremental cost. Thus, the Bell System, consistent with the Baumol-Walton position, argued that the competitive service should make some positive contribution toward overhead costs.

The FCC rejected the burden test and a long-run incremental cost analysis in favor of a fully distributed cost analysis. The Bell System's fully distributed cost studies show significant differences in rates of return on investment by line of service. Some classes of service even show losses. Table 7.6 shows the results of a fully distributed cost study computed by AT&T that was provided to the FCC. It indicates that fully distributed cost method 7 was used in the cost study. The Federal Communications Com-

TABLE 7.6 AT&T's Reported Rates of Return by Line of Service for Bell System Interstate Services Using Fully Distributed Cost Method 7 for Year Ended December 31, 1978

Line of Service	Return on Investment
(1) Message telecommunications service (MTS) domestic, offshore, Canada and Mexico	8.7%
(2) MTS overseas/international	23.0
(3) Outward wide area telecommunications service	16.8
(4) Inward wide area telecommunications service	11.6
(5) Private line telephone channels	16.6
(6) Private line telephone other	5.2
(7) Private line telegraph channels	3.1
(8) Private line telegraph other	5.9
(9) TELPAK	9.1
(10) Television program transmission commercial	8.5
(11) Television program transmission other	−4.4
(12) Audio/program transmission commercial	8.3
(13) Audio/program transmission other	−4.4
(14) DATAPHONE digital service	6.3
(15) Private line overseas/international	20.4
(16) Other	11.3
(17) Facilities for other common carriers	−0.5
Total interstate services	10.1

SOURCE: Federal Communications Commission, "Inquiry Concerning AT&T's Earnings on Interstate and Foreign Services During 1978," *Federal Register*, 44, 194 (October 4, 1979), p. 57208.

mission has reviewed a number of fully distributed cost methods. In 1965, the Seven-Way Cost Study was developed. Seven categories of service were studied: message toll service (MTS), wide area telephone service (WATS), teletypewriter exchange service (TWX), private line telephone service, private line telegraph service, TELPAK, and all others. Adding service categories and other allocation methods resulted in cost methods 1 through 7. These methods rely upon relative use for individual service categories and direct unit investment costs to allocate investments directly to the individual service categories. The telephone system includes significant investments in facilities for future growth. AT&T has allocated this plant to service categories based upon service forecasts to reflect the historical cost causation principle contemplated in method 7. Method 7 relies upon historical cost causation; method 1 assigns plant based on experienced relative use.[21] The FCC found

> 5. . . . that Bell's use of LRIC and, generally, its basic service philosophy do not satisfy the constructs of true marginal cost pricing principles. Indeed, we note that it is not possible to make a strict translation from neoclassical

---

[21] Federal Communications Commission, "Inquiry Concerning American Telephone and Telegraph Co.'s Manual and Procedures for Allocation of Costs," FCC 79-562, *Federal Register*, 44, 194 (October 4, 1979), 57211–18.

marginal costing theory to the pragmatic world of telecommunications. On the basis of these determinations, we have concluded that no "optimal" social welfare or beneficial public interest characteristics should be imputed to Bell's costing methodology. To the contrary, we find Bell's basic service philosophy merely a variant of a full costing approach.

6. We determine that an FDC costing approach is more consistent with our objectives and responsibilities under the Act, and should be the basic standard by which the justness and reasonableness of rates will be judged. Of the seven FDC methods of record, Method 7's historical cost causation basis of allocating costs is determined to be most consistent with our mandate to ensure just, reasonable, and nondiscriminatory rates. However, we recognize that such factors as demand fluctuations and varying growth patterns between services could cause distortions between historical causation and actual cost patterns. For this reason, we require that revised Method 1 data be filed concurrent with Method 7. . . . We find that in Method 1 and Method 7, full cost data currently available from the record provide an adequate "zone of reasonableness" for purposes of drawing conclusions concerning the lawfulness of Bell's past and present rate levels.[22]

The Federal Communications Commission chose a fully distributed cost test to ascertain whether the monopoly services of AT&T were providing cross-subsidies to the three competitive areas: common carrier service, private line service, and terminal equipment service. The FCC's concern in each of the areas evolved over a number of years in a series of decisions. In 1959, the Above 890 decision[23] allocated microwave frequencies to large communication users to permit development of consumer-owned and -used microwave systems. The Hush-A-Phone decision[24] overturned telephone tariff provisions that prohibited any customer-owned terminal equipment from being attached to the telephone system. With the 1968 Carterfone decision[25] the FCC itself pursued a policy of promoting competition in the terminal equipment market. The authority of the FCC to control joint interstate and intrastate terminal equipment use was not upheld in the courts until nine years later.[26] The FCC then began certifying customer-provided equipment that could be electrically connected directly into the telephone network. In the intervening period, common carriers competing for toll service were permitted when the 1969 MCI decision was issued.[27] Finally, the courts in 1977 overturned the FCC and upheld the right of MCI to interconnect with its customers through telephone company owned local exchange loops.[28]

---

[22] Revisions of Tariff FCC No. 26, Private Line Services, Series 5000 (TELPAK), Docket No. 18128, October 1, 1976, 61 FCC 2d, pp. 58–90.

[23] 27 FCC 359 (1959).

[24] *Hush-a-Phone* v. *U.S.*, 238 F. 2d 266 (1956).

[25] *Carterfone*, 13 FCC 2d 420 (1968).

[26] *North Carolina Utilities Commission* v. *FCC*, 552 F. 2d 1036 (1977).

[27] *In re Application of Microwave Communications, Inc.*, 18 FCC 2d 953 (1969).

[28] *MCI Telecommunications Corporation* v. *FCC*, 561 F. 2d 365 (1977).

In 1980, the Federal Communications Commission issued a decision intended to unbundle the terminal equipment rate from the local exchange access loop, switching network, and transmission system charge. The economic burden created by telephone companies' tying the terminal equipment charge together with local exchange service to be sold as a single service was to be removed by this order. At the same time, the regulatory treatment of terminal equipment rates was modified to de-tariff, but not deregulate, terminal equipment rates. The terminal equipment market structure was modified by establishing equipment and enhanced service subsidiaries for AT&T.[29]

Much of the rate effort, especially in the terminal equipment area, has been at the state commission level. In the pricing of thousands of particular terminal equipment or telephone services, fully distributed cost has an analog, fully allocated cost. Fully allocated costs add to those costs which can be attributed directly to the particular terminal equipment or telephone service a markup to cover allocated overhead costs. The California Public Utilities Commission has used a fully allocated cost method.[30] The Bell System marginal cost analog is a type of incremental cost analysis. The out-of-pocket cost of the service plus the current capital charges for both return on and depreciation of investment serve as the marginal cost floor, to which is added a contribution based upon what the market will bear, or value of service. The New York Public Service Commission rejected the Bell System incremental cost method and developed its own incremental cost method based on a fully allocated cost study of terminal equipment adjusted to reflect current costs.[31]

Basic Service

Several practices strongly influence the existing pattern of telephone prices within a given jurisdiction (see Appendix A for a schedule of Illinois Bell rates). Traditionally, business users pay higher rates than residential users; long-haul users pay higher rates in relation to costs than short-haul users; and large exchanges are charged higher rates than smaller rural exchanges. An attempt has been made to satisfy these basic goals using three general pricing concepts: nationwide or statewide pricing, value of service, and subsidization.

Prices are set on a statewide basis for Bell operating companies so

---

[29] Second Computer Inquiry, Docket No. 20828, 47CFR Part 64, *Federal Register*, 45, 94 (May 13, 1980), 31319.

[30] Paul Popenoe, Jr., "Terminal Equipment Rates: Costs and Rate Base Treatment," *Proceeding of the First NARUC Biennial Regulatory Information Conference* (Columbus, Ohio: The National Regulatory Research Institute, 1978), p. G-60.

[31] Richard Stannard, "Pricing Telephone Service in the Face of Competition," *Proceedings of the First NARUC Biennial Regulatory Information Conference* (Columbus, Ohio: The National Regulatory Research Institute, 1978), p. G-46.

that total revenues equal total costs. Many towns served and some segments of service are priced so that revenues do not cover costs, but rates for all towns and all segments of service collectively are designed to cover costs. This permits small rural towns with extremely high costs to be provided with low-cost service.

Value of service pricing or price discrimination is frequently encountered in the telephone industry. As mentioned earlier, basic exchange service is priced on the basis of the size of the town, with customers in large towns paying higher rates. Long distance service is priced according to the time of day the call is placed, and there is a weekend versus business day differential. Here weekend and evening calls receive the lower rates. Costs are not ignored, however, in designing these rates. Night rates versus day rates, for example, might be justified on a peak versus off-peak basis as well as value of service. Business and residential rate differences are established largely on differences in elasticities, not on cost differences, with higher rates going to business users.

The relationship among various levels of local service is called a *relative level factor*. This factor shows the ratio of the rate for one class of service to the rate for another. For example, the ratio of the one-party business service rate to the one-party residential service rate in the same size exchange is one relative level factor. Local exchange service traditionally has been based upon a flat rate design. With a flat rate, a fixed amount is paid each month for unlimited local calling. In certain large urban areas, a flat rate for a maximum number of calls plus a per unit rate for measured service in excess of this maximum has been available. Recently, experimental rates have tested wider use of measured service rates.

Toll rates are a measured message rate. Interstate and often intrastate toll rates are set at nationwide average toll rates. These rates vary with the distance between the parties calling and the length of time of the call. The cost increases over greater distances and larger times, albeit at decreasing rates. Flat-rate toll services do exist in the form of WATS service or extended area service between two local exchanges.

Supplemental services and equipment, like Touch-Tone and Centrex or even basic terminal equipment, are offered by other suppliers in addition to the telephone company. On these items, the telephone company has set a profit-maximizing price which, of course, is determined partly by the elasticity of demand for the items, with the higher-elasticity items receiving the lower price. In competitive markets, subsidies directed toward extending service might be diverted by the telephone company to maintain its market share. Accordingly, a cross-subsidy must be guarded against in terminal equipment rates.

Subsidization of one service by others has been common and has been considered appropriate in certain instances by regulators. The rationale is that these low, subsidized rates foster development of telephone service or achieve certain social goals. Examples in this category include low service connection charges, large versus small exchange rate differentials, free directory assistance, and the 5-cent coin telephone in New Orleans (though it is likely that excessive directory assistance will be removed from this category soon). Value of service pricing and subsidization have recently received decreased support among regulators, certainly at the behest of scattered competitors. Particularly outside the area of basic transmission service by the telephone company, the ancillary equipment and service charges have been unbundled, with the rates based more on the associated costs. Value of service pricing, with cross-subsidization, has become more restricted to the charges for exchange access, switching, and interexchange transmission.

ELECTRIC SERVICE

Typically, customers of electricity service are divided into three classifications: residential, commercial, and industrial. The rates for each class are based in large part on price elasticity differences, with the highest rate to residential and the lowest to industrial consumers (see Appendix B for a partial set of Commonwealth Edison's rate schedules; it serves a large segment of Illinois, including the Chicago area).

With a particular classification, rates decline in steps as a function of energy taken. An example is given in Table 7.7. The decline in rate reflects in part the fixed KW demand charge spread over an increased energy usage. In addition, there is often a separate monthly customer charge or minimum bill of some amount intended to cover billings, meter readings, and so on. For nonresidential users, the rate is separated into two components. In addition to the energy charge, measured in kilowatt hours, there is a demand charge based upon the maximum amount of energy consumed at one time, measured in kilowatts. Both are decreasing step functions. The demand charge is designed in relation to the consumer's peak load, so that the investment costs of holding this capacity available are covered by those demanding it. This type of rate schedule is called a *Hopkinson demand schedule*. A simplified example is given in Table 7.8. A *Wright demand rate* is also used. As indicated in Table 7.9, the Wright rate depends upon the customer's load factor. A higher load factor will increase the number of kilowatt hours taken per kilowatt of demand and lower the rate.

TABLE 7.7 Typical Residential Rate Schedule

First 100 KWH	4.18¢ per KWH
Next 100 KWH	3.25¢ per KWH
All additional KWH	3.03¢ per KWH

TABLE 7.8 Hypothetical Nonresidential Rate Schedule

Demand Charge	
$3.60 per kilowatt for the first	200 KW
3.30 per kilowatt for the next	1,000 KW
2.90 per kilowatt for all over	20,000 KW
Energy Charge	
3.60¢ per KWH for the first	2,000 KWH
3.15¢ per KWH for the next	3,000 KWH
3.00¢ per KWH for the next	15,000 KWH
2.50¢ per KWH for all those over	20,000 KWH

The demand charge is based on the kilowatts of maximum consumption for a month. This charge is designed to penalize the user for erratic use—high usage at one point and low at another. For any two nonresidential consumers with the same electricity consumption, the one with the lowest load factor pays the higher average rate. The *load factor* is defined as the average load over some period of time (KWH taken divided by the hours in the period) divided by the peak load of the period (maximum KW consumed). The load factor is intended to measure volatility in consumption, with a lower load factor indicating a more erratic usage.

This is no assurance, however, that a rate system designed to even out a user's consumption will steady the usage or improve the load factor over the entire system. In fact, it may do just the opposite, as illustrated by Figure 7.11. The upper portion represents the hypothetical system load over a 24-hour period, while the lower line represents the user's load over the period. The heavier lines represent the load pattern before and the lighter lines represent the pattern after the consumer's response to the Hopkinson schedule. The user reacted by reducing his individual load and thus reduced his average rate. But the response increased the system peak and increased the capacity requirements of the system. Conversely, a shift that improves the system peak but worsens the customer's load is penalized. If all consumers had a 100 percent load factor, so would the system, but this is the extreme case. The interest in a particular consumer's distribution of demands should be as it relates to the demand pattern of the *whole system* if investment costs are to be minimized.

Frequently, a separate schedule with higher rates will be used for summer months. This practice relates to placing a portion of capacity costs on peak users. Also, monthly or quarterly fuel cost adjustments, reflecting

TABLE 7.9 Wright Rate Design

First 100 KWH per KW of demand per month	6¢ per KWH
All over 100 KWH per KW of demand per month	3¢ per KWH

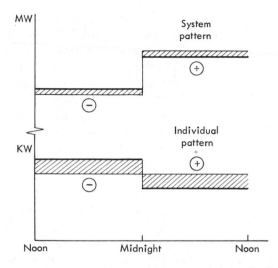

FIGURE 7.11 The Individual's Demand Pattern Relative to the System's Pattern

price charges to the utility, are common additions to utility bills. Moreover, there is a variety of special service charges, discounts, and rate schedules. The rate schedules mentioned above are currently dominant in the sale of retail electricity, although historically, other tariff designs have been used. The oldest was the flat rate, under which a fixed sum was paid each billing period for an unlimited amount of use. Fixture rates were used where the charge depended upon the end use of the power. For example, a fixed rate for each light fixture was charged. When meters were installed, step rates preceded block rates, which were discussed above as unit rates that declined in blocks based on usage. With step rates, the charge per kilowatt hour was constant each billing period and was based upon the block into which the usage level happened to fall. The larger the block, the lower the rate. Therefore, under the step rate it was possible to reduce the total bill by consuming—often wasting—more kilowatt hours if normal usage was near the upper end of the block cutoff. Because of their cumulative nature, block rates remedied this problem.

Recently, suggestions to replace declining block rates with uniform or inverted (increasing) block rates have been made. The rationale is that energy demand and plant construction would be reduced by such rates. With inflation, it is argued that the rates of all consumers would be kept lower. Opponents of uniform or inverted rates point out that growth in electricity demand depends upon many factors, of which price is only one. Also, the stability of utility revenues depends in part upon the use of declining block rates. Finally, the load factor of small users is frequently less and has higher associated demand costs.

The Federal Energy Regulatory Commission regulates wholesale sales of power by and among investor-owned electric utilities. These rates represent Hopkinson designs. They are based on fully distributed costs rather than incremental costs. Incremental costs for wholesale power are unlikely to be optimal or efficient. The retail rates charged by the resale utilities are not marginal-cost-based, in part because residential demand metering is costly. The second-best solution at the wholesale level is unlikely to justify marginal cost rates in this circumstance. For example, raising the peak wholesale rate to the incremental cost of a costly peaking unit might cause the wholesale customer to install its own peaking capacity. Alternatively, because of diversity, the wholesale utility could more efficiently add baseload units and reduce the peaking capacity.

The Federal Energy Regulatory Commission sets wholesale rates that reflect antitrust law as well as utility cost. In 1976, the Conway decision[32] prohibited the practice of a price squeeze by wholesale utilities that also sell retail power. The utility's wholesale rates cannot be higher than the utility's own industrial rates. Since the wholesale utility competes at the retail level with its wholesale customers for industrial load, a price squeeze would not permit the downstream utility to attract industrial customers on a competitive basis with the wholesale utility.

Retail electric rates regulated by state commissions generally are set by fully distributed cost methods. In 1974, the Wisconsin Public Service Commission in its Madison Gas and Electric decision[33] determined that "the appropriate benchmark for the design of electric rates in the case is marginal cost as represented by the practical variant, long-run incremental cost. If electric rates are designed to promote an efficient allocation of resources, this is a logical starting point."[34] The Ontario Energy Board, on the other hand, in its 1979 report stated:

> Efficient allocation and use of resources in producing and distributing electrical energy (engineering efficiency) should be encouraged. The validity of economic efficiency, advanced by witnesses for Ontario Hydro as the theoretical support for marginal cost pricing, is rejected by the Board as not being a measurable, achievable, or valid goal for Ontario Hydro. But efficiency in the technical or operating sense is a realistic objective that would minimize the unit cost of power and the rate levels.[35]

The Federal Energy Regulatory Commission now requires electric utilities periodically to supply rate design data. Both marginal cost and fully distributed cost data are required. Proposed voluntary guidelines issued in

---

[32] 426 U.S. 271, 48 L. Ed. 2nd 626.

[33] 5 PUR 4th 28.

[34] 5 PUR 4th 35.

[35] Ontario Energy Board, *Report to the Minister of Energy on Principles of Electricity Costing and Pricing for Ontario Hydro*, H.R. 5, December 20, 1979, p. viii.

1980 by the U.S. Department of Energy stated:

> Marginal cost-based pricing will encourage the proper amount of end-use conservation. . . . Utility efficiency will be furthered. . . . Finally, the equitable rates purpose is also furthered.[36]

The cost of service rate controversy the Public Utilities Regulatory Policies Act of 1978 placed before the state commissions entailed much debate between proponents of marginal cost pricing and proponents of fully distributed cost pricing. The reluctance of many state commissions to embrace marginal cost pricing is based not on a stodgy, unresponsive attitude, but rather on a legitimate concern about marginal cost concepts and practices. In practice, marginal cost rate making has been reduced to a current cost–fully distributed cost analysis. The surrogate for long-run marginal cost is a capital charge annuity based on the current cost of capital plus average out-of-pocket costs. This formulation has much in common with a fully distributed reproduction or replacement cost analysis. It is the formula for average cost-new, a formula James Bonbright criticized in 1928 as not being marginal cost.[37]

In addition to the capital valuation problem, the allocation problem of capital cost between customer classes remains unsolved. Fully distributed cost methods have relied upon three methods of allocating capital costs: (1) coincident peak responsibility method, (2) noncoincident peak responsibility method, and (3) average and excess method. The noncoincident peak method is not much used for allocating generating plant, but generally used for allocation of transmission lines. A coincident peak responsibility allocation distributes demand costs by the percentage a customer class contributes to peak demand. The noncoincident peak allocation distributes demand costs by the percentage the independent noncoincident peak demand of each customer class is to the sum of noncoincident peak demands. The average and excess method allocates a proportion of plant equal to the load factor as a function of energy or KWH used. The remaining plant costs are allocated on the basis of peak responsibility. The allocation of plant determines the amount of depreciation and return cost allocated to a class. The costs of maintaining such facilities are included in the demand charge.

Marginal cost methods have tended to allocate electric plant using a peak responsibility method or a probabilistic variation thereof, the loss of load probability. Allocation of electric plant costs have remained an integral part of marginal cost pricing.

---

[36] Department of Energy, "Voluntary Guidelines for the Cost of Service Standard under the Public Utility Policies Act of 1978 Proposed Guidelines and Public Hearing," *Federal Register*, 45, 173 (September 4, 1980), 38762.

[37] James C. Bonbright, "Railroad Valuation with Special Reference to the O'Fallon Decision," *American Economic Review*, suppl. 18 (1928), 196.

In addition to allocating demand costs such as generating and transmission plant by the coincident peak responsibility method, the noncoincident peak responsibility method, or the average and excess method, two other basic categories of costs must be determined: the customer cost and the energy charge. Customer cost includes costs of metering and installation on a customer's premises as well as customer accounting and expenses and facilities used for sales. Customer cost also includes those distribution plant costs that are necessary even with no load being taken. Customer cost thus varies with the number of customers in a system and is independent of the demand or energy taken. Energy cost varies with the amount of energy or KWHs taken. Energy cost will include the cost of fuel, fuel handling, and certain maintenance. Energy cost is incorporated as a charge per KWH, whereas fixed demand and customer charges may be so charged using a declining block rate. Demand charges, alternatively, may be charged per unit of load or KW when demand meters are feasible, such as with a large industrial customer.

NATURAL GAS SERVICE

Three areas must be considered in a review of natural gas pricing:

1. The well-head price for natural gas producers
2. The transmission pipeline rate
3. The utility retail gas price

All three have been regulated in different ways and by different commissions.
    Under the Natural Gas Policy Act of 1978, prices were established for the wellhead price of natural gas. Also, the incremental rates charged for nonexempt boiler fuel use of natural gas were set. At first glance, the idea of marginal cost seems to explain this action. In the case of exhaustible natural resources, Ricardian rents, not marginal costs, must be considered. A Ricardian rent amounts to the difference between the production cost at the least productive site where the resource is produced and the cost for a specific, but more productive, site. Such increments in Ricardian rents should not be included in marginal costs.[38] Rather than establishing marginal cost prices, the Natural Gas Policy Act of 1978 has attempted to fix the amount of Ricardian rent earned on natural gas. The incremental pricing creates transfer payments, as economists think of it, from certain industrial users to certain gas producers. The economics of Ricardian rents are not strictly adhered to by the practices under the act. The act includes a natural gas price escalator based upon the general price increase, rather

---

[38] E. J. Mishan, "A Survey of Welfare Economics, 1939–1959," in *Welfare Economics: Ten Introductory Essays,* 2nd ed. (New York: Random House, 1969), p. 31.

than an application of the cost of capital to the Ricardian rent.[39] The incremental price is set at the cost of residual fuel oil rather than the cost of production at the least productive site. Finally, the monopoly profits created by OPEC actions are not distinguished from the true Ricardian rents, and from remedial action taken by Congress in the act to adjust incremental price for the included monopoly profit. Such deviations from marginalist principles of pricing for wellhead and nonexempt boiler fuel natural gas create substantial second-best questions for the downstream pricing of retail natural gas sales by marginal cost methods.

Prior to the return of direct legislative price setting for wellhead gas by Congress and the scheduled 1985 deregulation, the setting of natural gas wellhead prices had been complex and changing. Before 1954, the Federal Power Commission did not believe the Natural Gas Act granted it the authority to regulate the prices charged by producers of natural gas. Excessive charges for natural gas from wells owned by pipeline transmission companies had been disallowed. Only a fair field price equal to the average price for an arms-length bargain in the same producing field was allowed. Then, in the 1954 Phillips Petroleum decision,[40] the U.S. Supreme Court held that under the Natural Gas Act independent companies selling to interstate pipelines were subject to Federal Power Commission jurisdiction, though producing and gathering gas were exempt. Immediate action in Congress attempted to exempt independent gas producers from FPC jurisdiction. After congressional passage of a bill in 1955, President Eisenhower vetoed deregulation because of questionable campaign contributions to a U.S. senator. Until the passage of the Natural Gas Policy Act of 1978, regularly offered deregulation bills failed to be enacted.

The initial response of the Federal Power Commission after the 1954 decision was to attempt to set the wellhead price of gas on an individual company cost-of-service basis. Because of complex issues and many small producers, a huge backlog of producer rate cases developed. The FPC developed an ingenious application of the cost-of-service approach to deal with the problem called the *area rate proceeding*. Rather than develop a company-by-company cost of service, a producing areawide cost of service was developed encompassing many companies. The first areawide composite cost of service was developed for the Permian Basin Area of west Texas and southeastern New Mexico. In addition, new gas received a higher price than previously flowing gas. The application of the composite cost-of-service approach in the Permian Basin cases was appealed to the courts and upheld by the U.S. Supreme Court in 1968.[41] A form of economic

---

[39] Robert M. Solow, "The Economics of Resources or the Resources of Economics," *American Economic Review*, 64, 2 (May 1974), 2.

[40] 347 US 672.

[41] 390 US 747.

price discrimination against producers was practiced to remove much of the Ricardian rent from the cost of service. This practice should not have reduced production if Ricardian rents were carefully removed. However, inexact methods of discrimination may have deterred the production of high-cost gas. A number of area rate proceedings followed until in the mid-1970s nationwide average pricing was adopted for the wellhead price of natural gas. Close on the heels of these nationwide rates, the Natural Gas Policy Act of 1978 was enacted.

The pricing of natural gas sales for resale by gas transmission systems is no less varied. The 1952 Federal Power Commission's Atlantic Seaboard decision[42] developed what came to be known as the Atlantic Seaboard formula for designing pipeline rates. Under this formula, 50 percent of fixed transmission costs were assigned on the basis of peak demand and 50 percent on the basis of commodity use. Variable costs were generally assigned 100 percent to annual commodity volumes. Two-part rate designs, a demand charge plus a commodity charge, translated the Atlantic Seaboard formula costs into the actual rate design charged to customers. The rate designs generally allow for zoned rates to attribute higher transportation costs to more distant customers.

In subsequent cases, the rates were tilted to reduce the commodity charge. Less than 50 percent of the fixed charges were allocated to the commodity charge so that natural gas would be more competitive with other fuels. Then, in the 1973 United Gas Pipe Line decision,[43] the FPC applied a "reverse tilt." In a compromise between continued use of the Atlantic Seaboard formula and the volumetric approach, which would have allocated 100 percent of fixed costs by annual commodity volume, the FPC adopted a revised cost allocation formula. Under the revised formula, 75 percent of the fixed charges were assigned to the commodity charge, and the remaining 25 percent were allocated to the demand charge.

The traditional commodity charge rolled in the higher costs of new gas supplies and based the commodity charge on the average price of gas. As curtailments of natural gas supply developed in the 1970s, the incidence of higher charges for gas from newer sources, such as synthetic or liquified natural gas, special purchases in the intrastate market, and offshore gas, became controversial. Incremental pricing to industrial users with alternative fuel capability was considered but rejected by the Federal Power Commission. The incremental pricing provision of the Natural Gas Policy Act of 1978 then mandated selective incremental pricing of natural gas by pipelines.

Retail gas distribution predates natural gas production and long distance transmission. Gas manufactured from coal was used in these distri-

---

[42] 43 PUR (NS) 235.
[43] 3 PUR 4th 491.

bution systems. The result is a retail gas rate design much like traditional electric rate designs. The three elements—customer cost, demand cost, and commodity costs—are typically incorporated into a declining block rate for general service rates. Residential and commercial users will receive gas, principally for space heating, under such a tariff. Large-volume users frequently have interruptible rates that permit interruption of service by the utility when additional gas is needed for firm customers. Rates for interruptible service generally were not allocated demand costs, on the principle that if gas main capacity or contract demand was reached, interruption could occur. Natural gas curtailments by pipelines in the 1970s brought about interruption of supply under interruptible rates because of a limited commodity supply. Retail supplies were curtailed.

Retail gas tariffs in certain states, like pipeline tariffs, include purchased gas adjustments. These adjustment charges permit increased costs for gas to be charged to consumers without raising base rates through a general rate case proceeding.

WATER SERVICE

Rates for water service traditionally have been established using fully distributed cost methods and conventional rate designs, such as flat or declining block rates. The methods of determining the customer, demand, and usage components of costs are much like those in electricity pricing. Seasonal differentials also may exist in water service.

SUMMARY

The proper mechanism for setting specific public utility rates remains unresolved. The ability of commissions to administer marginal cost pricing as well as the problem of financial losses in industries with increasing returns to scale raise questions regarding marginal cost pricing. The principal solution proposed to the latter question is the incorporation of economic price discrimination. A more recent problem, where current costs exceed embedded costs and therefore current cost revenues exceed the revenue requirement, also uses economic price discrimination to reconcile marginal cost pricing with the revenue requirement. Welfare economics has been unable to provide a secure ethical standard to buttress marginal cost pricing. Claims of efficiency and optimality rest on assumptions which cannot be substantiated—perfect foresight and knowledge, no externalities, pervasive marginal cost pricing both within and across industries, and perfect discrimination.

Enforcement of third-degree discrimination requires enforced segregation of customer classes. Utility services that are fungible, such as telephone terminal equipment, are unlikely to provide an arena within which third-degree discrimination can be enforced. So long as competition, or even resale, is permitted, discrimination can be enforced only against monopoly services, such as telephone access to the local exchange. Discrimination against many industrial users of electricity may be enforceable only to a certain degree. Large industrial customers could establish their own long distance telephone service, electric generation, and even conceivably compete for utility customers. Use of marginal cost as a floor on price to be supplemented by price discrimination is only enforceable where competition, self-provision, or resale of services is not feasible. The demand curve for customer classes with some choice may be kinked. No charge greater than the marginal current cost can be made without loss of customers. If the discriminatory charge is higher, the class will no longer exist as a utility's customer group. The price discrimination cannot be enforced without an exclusive enforceable franchise.

No *a priori* choice can be made between traditional average embedded cost pricing and marginal (minimum average) current cost pricing. Average embedded cost pricing is applied on a case-by-case basis and does not rely on all-pervasive welfare standards. Its closest welfare standard is the ideal of the "just price." Traditional pricing does directly satisfy the revenue requirement and relies upon verifiable data. Traditional utility pricing is basically a set of pragmatic tools designed for an uncertain world where change is ongoing but not easily foreseen. The use of *ex post* data enhances the authority of the commission vis-à-vis the utility.

Pragmatic versions of marginal current cost pricing also exist. Marginal cost pricing in practice varies sharply from the "textbook" version. An estimate of average current cost, coupled with the presumption of minimum average cost, is used as an estimate for marginal cost. Pervasive applications of marginal cost pricing have not occurred; rather, marginal cost estimates have been used as a surrogate for demand. Utility customers with some choice other than service by the utility are the customers to which marginal cost prices are applied in practice. For example, marginal cost pricing has been applied to industrial customers of gas and electricity—industries that have available substitute fuels, self-generation options, or are "footloose," and to the pricing of telephone terminal equipment, private lines, and certain toll services—all areas where the extant utility faces selective competition. The utility effectively faces a kinked demand curve for these services. At lower rates, the market demand curve confronts the utility. But for higher rates, the marginal current cost curve serves as the utility's own demand curve. The marginal cost pricing rule has been used to maintain the utility's market share while deriving increased profits. Relying as it does upon current cost estimates, the marginal cost places much power in the utility's hands. Increasing the utility's power to control access to cost data detracts from the commission's ability to restrain monopoly profit and prevent discrimination.

Appendix A

I. INTRASTATE RATES

Rates within Illinois   **22**

Lowest rates—
dial-direct two-minute rates

Dial-direct calls are those completed from a residence or business phone without operator assistance.

Dial-direct rates also apply on calls placed with an Operator from a residence or business phone where dial-direct facilities are not available.

On all calls, **you pay only for the minutes you talk.** The initial rate period is **two minutes** any time of day or night.

Additional savings apply evenings, nights and weekends.

	M	T	W	T	F	S	S
8 A.M. to 5 P.M.							
5 P.M. to 11 P.M.							
11 P.M. to 8 A.M.							

Dial-direct	Full (weekday) rates		Lower (evening) rates		Lowest (night & weekend) rates	
Sample rates Chicago to:	First 2 minutes	Each additional minute or fraction thereof	First 2 minutes	Each additional minute or fraction thereof	First 2 minutes	Each additional minute or fraction thereof
Bloomington	$ .60	$ .20	$ .45	$ .16	$ .40	$ .14
Carbondale	.75	.26	.60	.19	.45	.16
Centralia	.70	.24	.55	.18	.45	.16
Champaign-Urbana	.65	.22	.50	.17	.40	.14
Decatur	.65	.22	.50	.17	.40	.14
East St. Louis	.70	.24	.55	.18	.45	.16
Galesburg	.65	.22	.50	.17	.40	.14
Peoria	.65	.22	.50	.17	.40	.14
Quincy	.70	.24	.55	.18	.45	.16
Rockford	.60	.20	.45	.16	.40	.14
Rock Island	.65	.22	.50	.17	.40	.14
Springfield	.65	.22	.50	.17	.40	.14

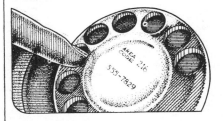

Highest rates—
operator-assisted calls

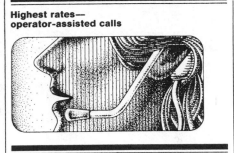

To cover the cost of operator handling, you pay an additional charge for any long distance call within Illinois requiring assistance of an operator.

In addition to the dial-direct rate (see box at left), you'll be charged:

30¢ for a station-to-station *credit-card* call you dial yourself

50¢ for a *collect, third-number* or other station-to-station call or a *credit-card* call placed by the Operator

$1.60 for a *person-to-person* call

Holiday rates
New Year's Day/July 4th/Labor Day/Thanksgiving/Christmas Day. Low evening rates apply on dial direct calls on these holidays from 11 p.m. to 8 a.m., Monday through Friday, and from 8 a.m., Saturday, to 5 p.m., Sunday. On operator-assisted calls, dial direct discount rates are in effect only on additional minutes.

Federal Excise Tax and any applicable state and local taxes are not included in rates shown. Charges are based upon rates in effect at time of connection at calling point, including calls beginning in one rate period, ending in another.

Chicago

Rates to other states

23

Lowest rates—
dial-direct one-minute rates

Dial-direct calls are those interstate calls (excluding Alaska and Hawaii) completed from a residence or business phone without operator assistance.

Dial-direct rates also apply on calls placed with an Operator from a residence or business phone where dial-direct facilities are not available.

On dial-direct calls, **you pay only for the minutes you talk.** The initial rate period is **one minute** any time of day or night.

Additional savings apply evenings, nights and weekends.
Local time where the call originates determines the rate period.

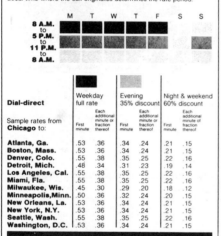

Dial-direct	Weekday full rate		Evening 35% discount		Night & weekend 60% discount	
Sample rates from Chicago to:	First minute	Each additional minute or fraction thereof	First minute	Each additional minute or fraction thereof	First minute	Each additional minute of fraction thereof
Atlanta, Ga.	.53	.36	.34	.24	.21	.15
Boston, Mass.	.53	.36	.34	.24	.21	.15
Denver, Colo.	.55	.38	.35	.25	.22	.16
Detroit, Mich.	.48	.34	.31	.23	.19	.14
Los Angeles, Cal.	.55	.38	.35	.25	.22	.16
Miami, Fla.	.55	.38	.35	.25	.22	.16
Milwaukee, Wis.	.45	.30	.29	.20	.18	.12
Minneapolis,Minn.	.50	.36	.32	.24	.20	.15
New Orleans, La.	.53	.36	.34	.24	.21	.15
New York, N.Y.	.53	.36	.34	.24	.21	.15
Seattle, Wash.	.55	.38	.35	.25	.22	.16
Washington, D.C.	.53	.36	.34	.24	.21	.15

Holiday rates
New Year's Day / July 4th / Labor Day / Thanksgiving / Christmas Day. Low evening rates apply on dial-direct calls from 8 a.m. to 11 p.m. on legal holidays. Even lower night rates apply on dial direct calls on these holidays from 11 p.m. to 8 a.m., Monday through Friday, and from 8 a.m., Saturday, to 5 p.m., Sunday. On operator-assisted calls, dial direct discount rates are in effect only on additional minutes.

Highest rates—
operator-assisted three-minute rates

Operator-assisted calls are those requiring the assistance of an Operator to complete the call. These include person-to-person, coin, collect, credit card, billed to a third number, hotel guest, and time and charge calls.

The initial period for all operator-assisted calls is **three minutes,** and the full (weekday) rates apply all days at all hours.

Additional minutes are charged at dial-direct rates, and include the same discount applicable to the time period when you call.

Operator-assisted	Station-to-station		Person-to-person	
Sample rates from Chicago to:	First three minutes	Each additional minute or fraction thereof	First three minutes	Each additional minute or fraction thereof
Atlanta, Ga.	2.15		3.30	
Boston, Mass.	2.15		3.30	
Denver, Colo.	2.25		3.45	
Detroit, Mich.	2.05	See Dial Direct tables at left under time period that applies (Weekday, Evening or Night and Weekend)	3.10	See Dial Direct tables at left under time period that applies (Weekday, Evening or Night and Weekend)
Los Angeles, Cal.	2.25		3.45	
Miami, Fla.	2.25		3.45	
Milwaukee, Wis.	1.85		2.90	
Minneapolis, Minn.	2.10		3.20	
New Orleans, La.	2.15		3.30	
New York, N.Y.	2.15		3.30	
Seattle, Wash.	2.25		3.45	
Washington, D.C.	2.15		3.30	

Calls to Alaska and Hawaii
The Operator can give rates for calls to these locations. Discounts of 30% (evening) and 55% (night and weekend) apply.

Federal Excise Tax and any applicable state and local taxes are not included in rates shown on these pages. Discount rates illustrated are rounded. Charges are based upon rates in effect at the time of connection at the calling point, including calls beginning in one rate period and ending in another.

Chicago

Appendix B

I. RESIDENTIAL SERVICE

Commonwealth
Edison Company

ELECTRICITY
For the Cities and Villages listed on
Sheets Nos. 4, 5, 6, 7 and 8
and the unincorporated contiguous territory

ILL. C. C. No. 4
6th Revised Sheet No. 9
(Cancelling 4th Revised Sheet No. 9)

RATE 1. RESIDENTIAL SERVICE

Availability.

This rate is available to any customer using the Company's electric service for residential purposes.

*Charges.

Monthly Customer Charge.

The net monthly customer charge shall be $1.00.

Energy Charge.

Summer Months.

6.556¢ net per kilowatthour for all kilowatthours supplied in the month.

Other Months.

5.330¢ net per kilowatthour for all kilowatthours supplied in the month.

For the purposes hereof the "summer months" shall be the Customer's first monthly billing period with an ending meter reading date on or after June 15 and the three succeeding monthly billing periods.

The fuel adjustment charge or credit provided for in Rider 20 shall apply to all kilowatthours supplied in the month.

Gross Charge.

The gross charge shall equal the sum for the month of the net charge and the fuel adjustment increased by five percent of the first $10.00 or less of such sum and two percent of the amount, if any, by which such sum exceeds $10.00.

Light Bulb Service.

The above charges do not include light bulb service. They will be increased 0.106¢ per kilowatthour for the first 500 kilowatthours supplied in the month for light bulb service as described in Rider 10. Light bulb service is optional with the Customer.

Minimum Charge.

The minimum monthly charge shall be the net monthly customer charge.

Term of Service.

The Customer's term of service shall commence when the Company begins to supply service hereunder and shall continue not more than ten days after notice is received to discontinue service.

Three-Phase Service.

Three-phase service is available under this rate. Where a three-phase secondary supply is not available from the Company's distribution system adjacent to the Customer's property, the necessary primary and secondary extensions will be furnished by the Company subject to the provisions of Rider 2.

General.

Service hereunder will be furnished only to a single occupancy, and where service to an apartment building is desired hereunder, each occupancy shall be treated as a separate customer; provided, however, that in apartment buildings containing six or fewer apartments, hall lights and building operating equipment, including no motor larger than one horsepower and not more than six horsepower for all motors, may be connected to the metering installation for one of the apartments, or service for such lights and equipment may be furnished under this rate to the building operator as a separate customer.

The Customer's wiring shall be arranged so that all service hereunder is supplied through a single metering installation, except that additional metering installations for service for residential purposes may be provided as optional facilities in accordance with the provisions of Rider 6. If there are two or more metering installations, the kilowatthours supplied shall be determined by adding together the kilowatthours metered at each installation.

Where a residence and a business are combined in one premises, service will not be furnished hereunder for the whole premises unless the preponderant requirement is for residential purposes.

The Schedule of which this rate is a part includes certain general Terms and Conditions and Riders. Service hereunder is subject to these Terms and Conditions and the Riders applicable to this rate.

Filed with the Illinois Commerce Commission on November 20, 1980
Issued pursuaant to Interim Order of Illinois Commerce Commission
entered November 19, 1980 in Case No. 80-0546
Asterisk (*) indicates change

Date Effective, November 20, 1980
Issued by H. H. Nexon, Senior Vice-President,
Post Office Box 767, Chicago, Illinois 60690

231

II. GENERAL SERVICE

Commonwealth
Edison Company

ELECTRICITY
For the Cities and Villages listed on
Sheets Nos. 4, 5, 6, 7 and 8
and the unincorporated contiguous territory

ILL. C. C. No. 4
5th Revised Sheet No. 24
(Cancelling 3rd Revised Sheet No. 24)

RATE 6. GENERAL SERVICE

Availability.

Except as provided in Rate 6L or Rate 22L, this rate is available to any customer using the Company's electric service hereunder for all requirements. Direct current requirements provided under another rate immediately prior to September 2, 1975, will, however, also be provided hereunder.

*Charges.

Monthly Customer Charge.

The net monthly customer charge shall be $1.86.

Demand Charge.

Net			Kilowatts of Maximum Demand for the Month
Summer Months	All Other Months		
$5.81	$4.83	per kilowatt for the first	1,000
5.29	4.37	per kilowatt for the next	9,000
4.91	4.05	per kilowatt for the next	40,000
4.44	3.64	per kilowatt for all over	50,000

For the purposes hereof the "summer months" shall be the Customer's first monthly billing period with an ending meter reading date on or after June 15 and the three succeeding monthly billing periods.

For customers without demand meters, there shall be no demand charge as such, but, in lieu thereof, such customers shall pay 2.620 cents per kilowatthour in summer months and 2.281 cents per kilowatthour in all other months in addition to the net energy charges set forth below.

Energy Charge.

Net	Kilowatthours Supplied in the Month
First 100,000 kilowatthours supplied in the month:	
4.696¢ per kilowatthour for the first	6,000
3.709¢ per kilowatthour for the next	24,000
3.072¢ per kilowatthour for the next	70,000
Over 100,000 kilowatthours supplied in the month:	
2.637¢ per kilowatthour for the first	400,000
2.296¢ per kilowatthour for the next	9,500,000
2.104¢ per kilowatthour for all over	10,000,000

except that the charge for such kilowatthours in excess of the product of 450 times the kilowatts of maximum demand shall be reduced by 0.548 cents per kilowatthour.

The fuel adjustment charge or credit provided for in Rider 20 shall apply to all kilowatthours supplied in the month.

Gross Charge.

The gross charge shall equal the sum for the month of the net charge and the fuel adjustment increased by five percent of the first $40.00 or less of such sum and three percent of the amount, if any, by which such sum exceeds $40.00.

This Rate sheet may be cancelled or revised without specific notice to you. It does not necessarily state all the conditions applicable to service under the rate.

(Continued on Sheet No. 25)

Filed with the Illinois Commerce Commission on November 20, 1980
Issued pursuant to Interim Order of Illinois Commerce Commission
entered November 19, 1980 in Case No. 80-0546
Asterisk (*) indicates change

Date Effective, November 20, 1980
Issued by H. H. Nexon, Senior Vice-President,
Post Office Box 767, Chicago, Illinois 60690

Commonwealth
Edison Company

ELECTRICITY
For the Cities and Villages listed on
Sheets Nos. 4, 5, 6, 7 and 8
and the unincorporated contiguous territory

ILL. C. C. No. 4
7th Revised Sheet No. 25
(Cancelling 6th Revised Sheet No. 25)

RATE 6. GENERAL SERVICE

(Continued from Sheet No. 24)

Minimum Charge.

The minimum monthly charge shall be the net monthly customer charge.

* **Minimum Demand Charge.**

The minimum monthly demand charge shall apply only in non-summer months and shall be 75 percent of the highest net demand charge billing (computed before application of this provision) in any summer month of the 23 months preceding the billing month, less $5,000.

Maximum Charge.

For customers with demand meters, the average cost of electricity in any month hereunder, exclusive of the Monthly Customer Charge, shall not exceed the sum of 13.715 cents net, and the fuel adjustment per kilowatthour; provided, however, that such guaranteed charge shall not operate to reduce the Customer's bill to an amount less than the minimum charge or minimum demand charge hereunder.

Maximum Demand.

The maximum demand in any month shall be the highest 30-minute demand established during such month except that, for customers served at their present premises under the Company's Rate 13 or Rate 12 on April 16, 1964 and for customers with 30-minute demands exceeding 1,500 kilowatts in three of the 12 months preceding the billing month, the maximum demand shall be the average of the three highest 30-minute demands established during such month, not more than one such demand to be selected from any one day.

Installation and Removal of Demand Meters.

The Company shall provide a demand meter for a customer when his monthly kilowatthour use exceeds 2,000 kilowatthours in each of two successive monthly billing periods or if his maximum demand or monthly kilowatthour use is estimated as in excess of ten kilowatts or 2,000 kilowatthours, respectively. The Company shall remove the demand meter of any customer whose use has not exceeded 2,000 kilowatthours and whose maximum demand has not exceeded ten kilowatts in any month of the preceding 16-month period.

Any customer for whom a demand meter is not provided by the Company may, at his request and upon payment of appropriate meter rentals, be provided therewith. In such case, meter rentals shall be payable for the period during which the Customer elects to retain the meter, but not less than 12 months, unless he becomes entitled to a demand meter prior to the end of the 12-month period.

Measurement of Demand and Kilowatthours Supplied.

Where two or more metering installations are provided on the Customer's premises, the demand in any 30-minute period shall be determined by adding together the separate demands at each metering installation during such 30-minute period except that (a) in case the demand at any metering installation is registered by a graphic type meter, the demand at such installation in each 30-minute period of any day shall be assumed to be the same as the highest demand in any 30-minute period of such day, (b) in case the demand at any metering installation is registered by an indicating or cumulative demand meter, the demand at such installation in each 30-minute period of any month shall be assumed to be the same as the highest demand in any 30-minute period of such month, and (c) the demand at any installation may be assumed to be 75 percent of the connected load if such connected load is two kilowatts or less, and such demand is to be added to a metered demand. Where there are two or more watthour metering installations on the Customer's premises, the kilowatthours supplied shall be determined by adding together the kilowatthours metered at each installation. The maximum demands and kilowatthours supplied for two or more premises will not be combined for billing purposes hereunder.

(Continued on Sheet No. 26)

Filed with the Illinois Commerce Commission on March 30, 1981
Asterisk (*) indicates change.

Date Effective, April 29, 1981
Issued by H. H. Nexon, Senior Vice-President,
Post Office Box 767, Chicago, Illinois 60690

Study Questions

1. In what way are prices considered signals by consumers and businesses? How are consumers and businesses likely to react to changes in these signals? What is the importance of "correct" signals?

2. List the four primary economic market structures. Give the characteristics of each. Which one best approximates that of the public utility? Why?

3. Consider the monopoly model with pervasive long-run economies of scale. What price provides the correct signal to the rest of the economy? If this price is set, what problems does the firm encounter? What price do regulators set? What goal of a price system does this accomplish?

4. What conceptual and practical difficulties are encountered by rate makers in marginal-cost pricing? How can these be resolved or circumvented?

5. What is peak-load pricing? What advantages does peak-load pricing have over a uniform price to peak and off-peak users? Is peak-load pricing consistent with marginal cost pricing? Why?

6. With peak-load pricing, how do shifting peaks alter the off-peak price? What should guide rate makers in this situation?

7. Are peak-load prices unfair?

8. What is price discrimination? Under what conditions should price discrimination be allowed? What is the primary economic justification for price discrimination in public utilities?

9. Is the market group receiving the higher, discriminatory price being harmed by serving the favored group? How might it be benefited in the short run? In the long run? What guidelines should be followed in setting discriminatory prices for public utilities?

10. Define incremental cost and fully distributed cost. Which should be used by regulators as the appropriate price floor? Why? Is your argument for the rationale for an appropriate price floor related to the argument for discriminatory prices for public utilities?

11. How does value of service pricing under an overall rate constraint promote development or growth of utility service? Why is the concept of value of service pricing somewhat ambiguous?

12. How do telephone and electricity pricing practices differ?

13. Give an example of value of service pricing (price discrimination) found in the telephone and electric utility industries. Give an example of peak-load pricing in each industry.

14. Refer to Appendix A, which is a partial schedule of interstate and intrastate telephone rates for Illinois Bell Telephone. What pricing characteristics (e.g., peak-load pricing) are exhibited in these rates?

15. Refer to Appendix B, which gives Commonwealth Edison's rate sheets for residential and general service.
    (a) What type of rate structures are being used in each instance?
    (b) What are the major pricing characteristics of each?
    (c) Calculate the approximate charge for a general customer using 7,000 KWH of service during a non-summer month. Compare this charge to the residential charge for the same amount of service.

Student Readings

AMERICAN GAS ASSOCIATION. *Gas Rate Fundamentals,* 3rd ed. Arlington, Va.: American Gas Association, 1978.

BAUMOL, W. J., AND A. WALTON. "Full Costing, Competition and Regulatory Practice." *Yale Law Journal,* 82, 4 (1973), 639–655.

The Bell Journal. Each issue contains at least one article relating to pricing, generally more.

BONBRIGHT, JAMES C. *Principles of Public Utility Rates.* New York: Columbia University Press, 1961, part 3.

DAVIS, O. A. "Piecemeal Policy in the Theory of Second Best." *The Review of Economic Studies,* 34 (July 1967), 323–333.

DENTON, DAVID B. "Value of Service Pricing." *Telephone Engineer and Management,* May 15, 1973, pp. 63–68, and June 1, 1973, pp. 44–50.

DIXON, PETER. "The Costs of Average Cost Pricing." *Journal of Public Economics,* 1 (1972), 245–256.

DORAN, JOHN J., FREDERICK M. HOPPE, ROGER KOGER, AND WM. W. LINDSAY. *Electric Utility Cost Allocation Manual.* Washington, D.C.: National Association of Regulatory Utility Commissioners, 1973.

FARRIS, M., AND R. SAMPSON. *Public Utilities.* Boston: Houghton Mifflin, 1973, chap. 14.

FEDERAL COMMUNICATIONS COMMISSION. Docket No. 18128, "Revision of Tariff FCC No. 26, Private Line Services, Series 5000 (Telpak)." October 1, 1976, 61 FCC 2d.

FRIEDLANDER, ANN F. "A Critique of Interstate Commerce Commission Procedures." Appendix A, *The Dilemma of Freight Transport Regulation.* Washington, D.C.: The Brookings Institution, 1969, pp. 191–194.

GRAAFF, J. DE V. "Marginal Cost and the Just Price." In *Theoretical Welfare Economics.* Cambridge: University Press, 1967, pp. 142–155.

GREENE, ROBERT LEE. *Welfare Economics and Peak Load Pricing: A Theoretical Application to Municipal Water Utility Practices.* Gainesville: University of Florida Press, 1970.

HOLMES, FRED L. *Regulation of Railroads and Public Utilities in Wisconsin.* New York: Appleton, 1915.

KAHN, ALFRED C. *The Economics of Regulation,* vols. I and II. New York: Wiley, 1971.

KAY, J. A. "Recent Contributions to the Theory of Marginal Cost Pricing: Some Comments." *Economic Journal,* 81, 322 (June 1971), 366–371.

LITTLE, I. M. D. "Output and Price Policy in Public Enterprises." In *A Critique of Welfare Economics,* 2nd ed. London: Oxford University Press, 1957, pp. 185–216.

MACHLUP, FRITZ. "Marginal Analysis and Empirical Research." *The American Economic Review,* 36 (September 1946), 519–554.

MACHLUP, FRITZ. "Rejoinder to an Antimarginalist," *The American Economic Review,* 37 (March 1947), 148–154.

MCKIE, JAMES W. "Public Utility Regulation: Structure and Performance." In *Perspectives in Public Regulation,* ed. Milton Russell. Carbondale: Southern Illinois University Press, 1973, pp. 85–107.

MISHAN, E. J. "A Survey of Welfare Economics, 1939–1959." In *Welfare Economics,* 2nd ed. New York: Random House, 1969, pp. 11–86.

NELSON, JAMES R., ed. *Marginal Cost Pricing in Practice.* Englewood Cliffs, N.J.: Prentice-Hall, 1964.

NISS, J., AND M. PLEDGE, eds. *Essay on Economic Issues.* Macomb, Ill.: Center for Business and Economic Research, Western Illinois University, 1975.

PEACOCK, ALAN T., AND CHARLES K. ROWLEY. "Welfare Economics and the Public Regulation of Natural Monopoly." *Journal of Public Economics,* 1 (1972), 227–244.

STEINER, PETER O. "Peak Load Pricing and Efficient Pricing." *Quarterly Journal of Economics,* 71, 4 (November 1957), 585–610.

TARSHIS, LORIE. "Mark-up Pricing and Marginal Pricing." In *Modern Economics: An Introduction.* Boston: Houghton Mifflin, 1967, pp. 183–197.

TEMPLE, BARKER & SLOAN, INC. *An Evaluation of Four Marginal Costing Methodologies.* Palo Alto, Calif.: Electric Power Research Institute, 1979.

TREBING, HARRY M., ed. *Essays on Public Utility Pricing and Regulation.* East Lansing: Michigan State University, 1971.

TREBING, HARRY M., ed. *Issues in Public Utility Regulation.* East Lansing: Michigan State University, 1979.

TURVEY, RALPH. *Optimal Pricing and Investment in Electricity Supply.* Cambridge, Mass.: MIT Press, 1968.

TURVEY, RALPH, ed. *Public Enterprise.* Baltimore: Penguin Books, 1968.

WISEMAN, J. "The Theory of Public Utility Price—An Empty Box." *Oxford Economic Papers,* 9, 1 (February 1957), 56–74.

8

Capital Budgeting
and Finance

Proper capital budgeting and financing decisions by both the utility and regulators are essential if the prescribed goal—adequate service at a minimum cost to customers consistent with a reasonable return to investors—is to be realized. The massive capital investment of public utilities necessitates raising funds from both internal (the utility) and external (capital markets) sources. Capital budgeting is the administrative process governing the long-term asset decisions of the firm. Both mandatory and discretionary capital projects are implemented by utilities. Often, these projects are grouped into categories to facilitate analysis. To aid in the evaluation of capital projects, several capital budgeting techniques and risk-adjustment methods are commonly used. The internal sources employed to finance these capital projects are depreciation, retained earnings, and deferred taxes. The external sources of funds are the sale of common or preferred stock and the issuance of bonds. Short-term funds are obtained from bank loans and commercial paper.

The huge financing needs of public utilities require that virtually every major source of financing be tapped. Continued need for access to the capital market and obligations to the consumer and investors require that decisions concerning the relative use of the various sources of funds (the capital structure decision) be made very carefully. The question of how much debt relative to equity greatly affects the risk and return of the utility. In addition to these topics, we will consider several common capital budgeting and financing practices in this chapter. The role of regulatory commissions in all of this cannot be ignored. Therefore, the chapter concludes with a discussion of the commission's participation in security issuance, eminent domain, and certificates of convenience and necessity.

OVERVIEW OF THE
_____ CAPITAL BUDGETING PROCESS _____

This chapter is concerned with the investment process and the financing of the public utility. To obtain an overview, consider the hypothetical balance sheet shown in Table 8.1. Note that the fixed assets and long-term financing are usually listed first in reporting for public utilities, but not for other firms.

The lefthand (asset) side of the balance sheet might be considered the firm's investment or asset package. *Capital budgeting* is the investment process involving assets with expected lives exceeding a one-year period. The capital budgeting process focuses on additions to long-term or fixed assets. The central goal in this process for the firm is to find the optimum mix of long-term assets, the bundle of assets that will maximize the value of the firm. In the next section we discuss several of the techniques firms use to determine the optimal capital budget.

The risk inherent in the level and composition of the firm's assets is called *business risk*. The earnings stream generated by these assets will fluctuate over time. Business risk is often measured by the standard deviation of the firm's basic earnings stream, earnings before interest and taxes. Figure 8.1 shows the earnings pattern over time for two hypothetical firms. Firm 2 has a markedly more volatile earnings pattern than firm 1;

TABLE 8.1 Public Utility Hypotel
as of December 31, 1981

BALANCE SHEET					
Assets			Liabilities and Owners' Equity		
Utility plant—at cost			Equity:		
Plant (net)	$ 680		Preferred stock	$ 290	
Equipment (net)	11,100		Common stock	3,000	
Land	150	$11,930	Retained earnings	1,800	$5,090
Current assets:			Long-term debt:		
Cash	11		Notes	3,000	
Marketable			Bonds	3,800	6,800
securities	12				
Receivables	33		Current liabilities:		
Inventories	10		Accounts payable		
Prepaid expenses	10	76	Taxes payable	35	
			Dividends	10	
Total assets		$12,006	Debt maturing within one	27	
			year		116
			Total liabilities and equity	44	$12,006

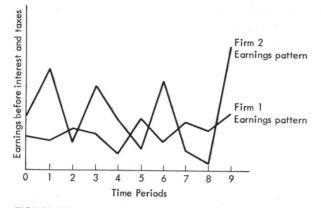

FIGURE 8.1 Pattern of Earnings for Two Hypothetical Firms

thus, firm 2 has a higher level of business risk. These fluctuations depend upon the type of assets selected (high-fixed-cost assets versus low-fixed-cost assets), supply and demand conditions in the industry, technology, and so on.[1]

The righthand side of the balance sheet may be viewed in terms of the various groups providing funds (money capital) to the firm. The firm, in turn, has certain obligations to these groups. Generally speaking, the terms of these obligations are clearly spelled out by contract—the timing and amount of interest payments, among other things, are clearly stated for bonds in the bond indenture. The *capital structure* of the firm is concerned with the relationship between long-term debt and equity of the firm—long-term debt (bonds and notes), preferred stock and stockholders' equity (capital stock and retained earnings). The *financial structure* of the firm refers to the entire righthand side of the balance sheet and reflects all the forms of financing used to purchase the firm's assets, including current liabilities. Occasionally, however, the terms "financial structure" and "capital structure" are used interchangeably. The total financial claims to the firm's assets (righthand side) must equal the total assets (lefthand side); hence the name "balance sheet."

The sources of financing for additions to assets are income from the firm's operation (that part which is retained), depreciation, deferred income taxes, and the issuance of debt, preferred, and common stock. The pattern of this financing is indicated by the changes in the balance sheet items from year to year.

Financial risk is the added risk or variation in shareholder earnings that results from the use of debt in the capital structure. The use of debt in the capital structure is called *financial leverage*. Preferred stock is treated

---

[1] This view of risk, total variability, should be contrasted with the capital asset pricing model (CAPM) approach discussed in Chapter 4, Appendix B.

as debt here because it requires only a fixed dividend payment, like interest, and for all practical purposes has the same effect as debt financing in this situation. The greater the financial leverage, the greater the financial risk. This fundamental relationship results because with greater financial leverage there is an increased probability of bankruptcy and increased variability in shareholder earnings. (This point will be illustrated more clearly later in the chapter.) The firm, acting on behalf of investors, seeks to find the capital structure that yields the lowest cost of funds to be used for financing capital investment.

The *optimal capital budget* from the investor's viewpoint is the investment package that maximizes the value of the firm. This is determined by the supply and demand for funds of the firm. Supply as used here refers to the marginal cost of capital schedule (MCC) facing the firm. The MCC schedule is the percentage rate or cost to the firm of obtaining an additional dollar of funds to be used for capital budgeting as a function of the total amount of capital investment in any given period. Demand refers to the investment opportunities, expressed as a percentage rate of return, available to the firm. A conceptual diagram of the optimal capital budget is given in Figure 8.2. It is based on the investment opportunities (IRR) schedule represented by capital projects A through G and the marginal cost of capital (MCC) schedule.

Figure 8.2 depicts seven capital budgeting projects, labeled A through G. Project A requires $1 million of funds and is expected to yield a 26 percent rate of return. This rate of return is called the internal rate of return (IRR), and its calculation will be explained below. Project B requires $2.5

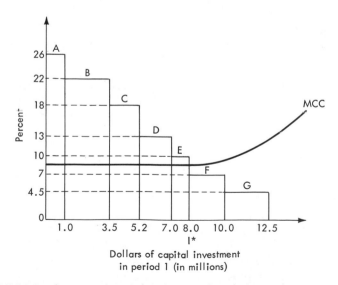

FIGURE 8.2 The Optimal Capital Budget Based on the IRR and MCC Schedules

million in funds and has an expected yield of 22 percent, and so on for the other projects. These projects are ranked according to IRR. Which projects should be accepted? This depends on the cost of investment funds to the firm—the MCC. The firm should accept projects A through E and reject projects F and G. This is because projects A through E yield a higher rate of return (IRR) than the rate (MCC) the firm must "pay" for investment funds. Projects F and G are rejected because they cost the firm more than they yield; they are unprofitable. Therefore, the optimal capital budget, the one that will maximize the wealth of the firm, is $8 million and includes projects A through E.

Capital budgeting should be viewed as an ongoing process. The first step might be called the generation of ideas. Here management might formally or informally survey the needs of the firm, which may involve planning and forecasting. The research and development of new ideas are an important part of this stage. Next, the list of proposed projects is assembled, along with relevant data needed for project analysis. Typically, projects are grouped into categories such as replacement, expansion of existing products, expansion into new product areas, and so on. This latter category might include nonrevenue-producing projects such as pollution control equipment. Then, these projects are ranked within each category, and those with an acceptable rate of return are undertaken; the rest would be rejected, at least for the time being. For some projects, the firm may not have a choice. For instance, it must undertake a given project or set of projects to maintain immediate production or to meet government pollution control standards. Finally, an audit is conducted to see if the accepted projects have performed as anticipated.

CAPITAL BUDGETING TECHNIQUES

Three commonly used capital budgeting techniques will be discussed before we consider the topic of public utility capital budgeting. These are the payback method, the NPV method, and the IRR method. These techniques are generally presented in the context of very low or no risk. In the presence of risk, however, they must be modified. We will consider adjustments for risk immediately following a description of the three techniques.

PAYBACK METHOD

The *payback period* is the number of years it takes to recoup the original investment outlay. The basic idea is that the sooner the investment is paid back the better, in the sense that risk is lower and return higher. The maximum acceptable payback period is determined by company policy. Investments with a longer payback period are rejected; those with a shorter period accepted. This rule is generally not quite this simple in practice and is augmented by judgment and experience.

Consider the simple example contained in Table 8.2. Suppose Projects A and B both require an initial outlay of $1000. *Returns* means annual net profits after taxes plus depreciation resulting from the project, or cash inflow. Project A's payback period is two, project B's is three years. If the firm's maximum payback period is two years, project A is accepted and B is rejected. Although this technique is relatively easy to use and puts a premium on early repayment, it suffers from serious drawbacks. It ignores returns beyond the cutoff period. In the example, project B's impressive cash flows after period 2 are disregarded. Moreover, the timing of the returns is not taken into account; i.e., it ignores the time value of money. For these reasons, the payback method is not a generally accepted technique. Nevertheless, it is widely used by many small firms and some large firms, often as a check on other techniques.

NET PRESENT VALUE TECHNIQUE

The *time value of money* is the notion that a dollar received today is worth more than a dollar received in the future, because it can be used in the interim. If nothing else, the dollar can be put in a savings account, which will accumulate interest. When speaking of cash flows over some span of time, it is thus inappropriate to treat a dollar received or paid out at different dates as having the same value.

These flows over time must be converted to flows of a common date for comparison. To this end, a number of discounted cash flow (DCF) techniques have been established: the net present value approach is one. The equation for the NPV is

$$\text{NPV} = \frac{R_1}{(1 + k)} + \frac{R_2}{(1 + k)^2} + \frac{R_3}{(1 + k)^3} + \cdots + \frac{R_N}{(1 + k)^N} - C$$

where R_N = the cash flow or return in period N; k = the cost of capital; and C = the initial capital outlay. To implement the technique, first estimate the various R, C, and k values for a given product and calculate the

TABLE 8.2 Payback Method Example

Years in the Future	Project A Returns	Project B Returns
1	$500	$100
2	500	200
3	0	700
4	0	300
5	0	200

Initial outlay = $1,000 for A and B.
Payback period A = 2 years; payback period B = 3 years.

NPV. The decision rule is if NPV is positive, accept; otherwise, reject the project.

The logic of the method is that we are computing the present value for the future returns (converting each of the future returns to current-period equivalents and summing) and subtracting the cost of obtaining the project, an outlay in the current period, to obtain the NPV. The difference (the NPV) between the present value of future returns and the initial cost is the addition to the value of the firm obtained by undertaking the project. Generally, we wish to accept all projects that increase the value of the firm.

Consider the following example. Project X will yield the following returns: $R_1 = \$1,000$; $R_2 = \$1,200$; and $R_3 = \$800$. The cost of the capital of the firm is 10 percent and project X costs $2200. Should the firm undertake the project? Compute the NPV:

$$NPV = \frac{\$1000}{(1 + .10)} + \frac{\$1200}{(1 + .10)^2} + \frac{\$800}{(1 + .10)^3} - \$2200$$

$$= \$909.00 + 991.20 + 600.80 - \$2200$$

$$NPV = \$301$$

Since the NPV is positive ($301) we accept the project and expect it to add roughly $300 to the value of the firm.

The diagram in Figure 8.3 illustrates how returns of future periods are converted to equivalent sums as of time period 0. R_1 ($1000) is brought back to the present (period 0) with the discount rate of .10, the present value of which is $909. The present values of R_2 and R_3 are also calculated.

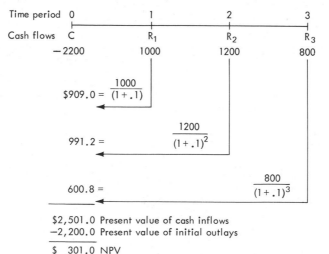

FIGURE 8.3   Net Present Value Calculation

Present value tables will aid in this computation. These individual present values are added together to obtain the present value of all future returns, which is $2501. From this, we subtract the required cash outlay in period 0 to obtain the NPV of $301.

INTERNAL RATE OF RETURN (IRR) METHOD

The internal rate of return (IRR) is the discount rate that equates the present value of the expected returns to the initial outlay. The equation is

$$\frac{R_1}{(1 + IRR)} + \frac{R_2}{(1 + IRR)^2} + \cdots + \frac{R_N}{(1 + IRR)^N} = C$$

Again we estimate the R and C values, but this time we solve for the IRR. This too is a DCF technique, but here the discount rate used is the IRR, not k.

Consider the following simple example. Suppose $C = \$1000$ and $R_1 = \$1100$, what is the IRR? $C = R_1/(1 + IRR)$ or $1000 = (1100)/(1 + IRR)$ and IRR equals 10 percent. Consider a second example. The project costs $13,500 and has returns of $5,000, $6,000, and $7,000 in years 1 through 3. The equation is

$$\$13,000 = \frac{\$5,000}{(1 + IRR)} + \frac{\$6,000}{(1 + IRR)^2} + \frac{\$7,000}{(1 + IRR)^3}$$

The solution for IRR is slightly under 15 percent. One relatively easy way to calculate this rate of return is to plug in trial values for the IRR and interpolate.

One question remains. Should the projects in these two examples be accepted? The answer depends on the cost of funds to the firm. If the cost of capital is 11 percent, the first project would be rejected because its rate of return is less than the cost of capital, and the second project would be accepted.

ADJUSTMENTS FOR RISK

All the capital budgeting models described here can be modified to take into account differences in the riskiness of the firm's projects. A review of these adjustments is contained in this section, but a more thorough treatment is found in most financial management texts.[2]

First, the NPV model can be modified in one of two ways. With the

---

[2] See, for example, John D. Martin et al., *Basic Financial Management* (Englewood Cliffs, N.J.: Prentice-Hall, 1979). For a more complete treatment of risk in capital budgeting, consult Harold Bierman and Seymour Smidt, *The Capital Budgeting Decision,* 5th ed. (New York: Macmillan, 1980), or James Van Horne, *Financial Management and Policy,* 5th ed. (Englewood Cliffs, N.J.: Prentice-Hall, 1980).

risk-adjusted discount rate method, the expected values of the project's cash flows in each period are included in the numerator of the NPV equation, while the discount rate in the denominator is adjusted for risk. A higher discount rate is used for projects with higher risk. The decision rule is the same as before: accept projects with a positive NPV. The principal difficulty with this approach is determining the appropriate risk-adjusted discount rate, which should correspond to the rate the market associates with this level of risk. Thus the approach adjusts upward the required rate of return and discount rate for projects that will increase the firm's level of risk. Of course, the converse is also true for projects of lower than average risk.

The second method of adjusting the NPV model for risk is called the *certainty-equivalent approach.* Under this approach, the uncertain cash flows in the numerator are adjusted downward depending on their riskiness, and the discount rate in the denominator is the risk-free rate. The adjustment of cash flows for risk is the troublesome step and should be accomplished so that the adjusted cash flows are just equivalent in the market's view to certain (riskless) sums. If properly calculated, the certainty-equivalent approach finds the value of a project by discounting a series of certain sums (certainty equivalents) at the risk-free rate.

The internal rate of return approach can also be modified in a number of ways. Probably the most straightforward is to calculate the IRR as discussed in the previous section and compare it with the cost of capital appropriate to the level of risk inherent in the project. Accordingly, the IRR of a project with above-average risk must be compared with a higher than average cost of capital, which contains a risk premium based on the market's assessment of that risk level. Finally, the payback method is often adjusted by simply reducing the maximum payback standard for projects of greater risk. Obviously, the difficulty with this adjustment is in the determination of the proper reduction of the payback for a given level of risk.

In conclusion, there is as yet no definitive proper adjustment for risk in capital budgeting. Other methods, such as simulation, decision trees, and portfolio approaches, do exist and are used occasionally to handle risky projects. Nevertheless, the role of judgment in adjusting for risk is paramount; none of these techniques should be applied mechanically.

PUBLIC UTILITY CAPITAL BUDGETING

As an introduction to capital budgeting in the public utility area, we consider first the sheer magnitude of utility investment. The technological features and service requirements of utilities contribute to the need for extremely heavy investment. As an example of the size of the capital budget (or construction expenditures) consider Illinois Bell Telephone, one of the 24 operating companies of the Bell System, which had a capital budget of $651.1 million in 1979 and approximately 50 employees, drawn from several departments, who worked in the capital budgeting area on collection, analysis, and evaluation of capital budgeting data. For the entire Bell System, total capital expenditures were nearly a whopping $16 billion in 1979.

A recent telephone survey conducted by one of the authors summarizes capital budgeting data for a sample of 51 privately owned electric utilities.[3] These data were compiled in May 1978 and were based on phone conversations with the director of capital budgeting (the actual titles varied) of each utility. The firms were divided into three size categories based on asset size. As may be seen from Table 8.3, the average capital budget in 1977 for all sample firms is in excess of $200 million, and the average number of employees in this area was over 20. One is struck by the magnitude of capital budgeting in public utilities. Planning and implementing these capital investments are a major activity of public utilities.

Table 8.4 shows how the average capital budget for firms in the sample is broken down using a project classification system, formerly required by the Federal Power Commission (which no longer exists and whose functions are now taken over by FERC). The generation category, which is comprised of new plants, is by far the largest, but its importance declines for smaller firms. The average percentage of capital budgeting staff time devoted to each project classification more or less follows the relative size of the category. Often, more than one classification system is used by public utilities. For example, at least two major systems are used by the Bell System. The first relates to the physical type of equipment and is used in their Construction Expenditures Report.[4] Its categories are these:

1. Land and buildings
2. Central office equipment
3. Station equipment
4. Outside plant
   a. Outside plant structures
   b. Exchange lines
   c. Toll lines
5. General equipment

The second classification system relates more to the functional use of the expenditure. Its categories and the percentage of 1979 total capital

---

[3] Keith M. Howe, "Capital Budgeting and Search in Electric Utilities," paper presented at the Financial Management Association meetings, Boston, October 11, 1979.

[4] AT&T, *Engineering Economy* (New York: McGraw Hill, 1977), p. 66.

TABLE 8.3 Profile of Capital Budgeting Survey of Electric Utilities

ASSET SIZE OF FIRM*	NUMBER OF FIRMS	1977 CAPITAL BUDGET*				NUMBER OF EMPLOYEES ON CB STAFF				EXPENDITURES ON CB STAFF**			
		Group Average	Low	High	Std Dev	Group Average	Low	High	Std Dev	Group Average	Low	High	Std Dev
Small $10–$950	22	$49.9	$1	$121	$36.6	7.6	1	50	10.0	$188.0	$14	$377	$105.5
Medium $950–$2000	13	$199.9	$94	$359	$68.6	22.7	2	100	25.1	$576.5	$40	$2500	$381.2
Large $2000–$7000	16	$442.4	$175	$1000	$78.7	32.6	5	175	43.4	$875.9	$50	$2625	$524.8
All sample firms $10–$7000	51	$211.3	$1	$1000	$208	20.1	1	175	30.0	$502.3	$25	$2625	$662.6

* In millions of dollars.

** In thousands of dollars.

SOURCE: Telephone survey of 51 electric utilities conducted April and May, 1978.

TABLE 8.4 Summary of Capital Budgeting Survey of Electric Utilities
(by Size of Firm and Project Classification)*

PROJECT CLASSIFICATION	AVERAGE PERCENTAGE OF CAPITAL BUDGET IN CLASSIFICATION				AVERAGE PERCENTAGE OF STAFF TIME IN CLASSIFICATION			
	Firm Size				*Firm Size*			
	Small	Medium	Large	Total	Small	Medium	Large	Total
Generation	51.0	66.1	72.4	67.3	43.0	51.5	60.0	50.1
Transmission	15.5	10.8	8.8	13.2	20.2	19.5	17.8	19.4
Distribution	26.4	17.0	14.2	20.2	33.0	22.0	17.0	25.8
Other	7.1	6.2	4.6	5.1	3.8	7.0	5.2	4.7

* Note firm size is defined in Table 8.3.

SOURCE: Telephone survey conducted April and May, 1978.

expenditures for the Bell System are these:

1.	Growth	52.0%
2.	Modernization	21.2
3.	Customer movement	20.5
4.	Plant replacement	6.3
	Total	100.0%

The classification systems help organize and facilitate the systematic analysis of projects. They are also used for reporting purposes.

The vast amount of public utility investment is remarkable. The huge expenditures obviously have implications for public utility financing. Moreover, the individual projects must be evaluated to see if the expenditure is warranted. With most projects, especially the smaller ones, economic evaluation is routine. With large, unusual, or particularly risky projects, detailed analysis is required. The techniques used for this purpose are not unlike those used by other firms. However, differences do exist.

TECHNIQUES FOR EVALUATION OF UTILITY INVESTMENT

For public utilities, projects are often said to be mandatory or discretionary, depending on whether or not they are necessary to maintain adequate service. With mandatory projects, there may be only a single reasonable alternative and therefore, given its mandatory nature, there is really no decision—the project is undertaken. Similarly, a breakdown of a piece of equipment may result in a complete stoppage or inferior service. This must be fixed immediately, and again there is no decision involved. This is a fairly common occurrence, and the decision technique used is sometimes referred to as the *urgency criterion*. However, inherent in many mandatory projects is a choice among alternatives. That is, there is more than one way or one project which will accomplish the task. Because the revenues in any of the alternatives are the same, they are usually ignored; the focus is on

249

costs. One technique frequently used in this situation is the present value of annual cost method. This is a discounted cash flow method that seeks the least cost alternative; that is, it selects the project that has the lowest present value of revenue requirement, which, in turn, is based on its costs. A simplified example of this technique will help make its use clear. To simplify, corporate income taxes are ignored. Data for alternatives A and B are presented below. Both projects have a service life of four years.

	Alternative A	Alternative B
Initial cost	$7,000	$10,000
Net salvage value	600	700
Operating costs	1,500	750

Assuming the cost of capital equals 10 percent

$$\text{PV}_A \text{ of costs} = 7,000 + \frac{1,500}{(1 + .1)} + \frac{1,500}{(1 + .1)^2} + \frac{1,500}{(1 + .1)^3} + \frac{1,500 - 600}{(1 + .1)^4}$$

$$= 7,000 + 1,500(3.1699) - 600(.6830) = \$11,345.$$

$$\text{PV}_B \text{ of costs} = 10,000 + \frac{750}{(1 + .1)} + \frac{750}{(1 + .1)^2} + \frac{750}{(1 + .1)^3} + \frac{750 - 700}{(1 + .1)^4}$$

$$= 10,000 + 750(3.1699) - 700(.6830)$$

$$= \$11,899.$$

Based on the present value of annual cost criterion, alternative A is preferred because it has the lowest present value of annual cost, even though B has much lower operating costs. It is also clear that if the revenues will be the same under the two alternatives, it is safe to eliminate them from the calculation because the net result of including them is zero (PV$_A$ of revenues − PV$_B$ of revenues = 0).

A second technique which is used to determine the best project is a modification of the internal rate of return approach. The IRR approach described in an earlier section must be modified if it is used to decide among two competing alternatives. The chief difference is that cash flow differences or incremental cash flows are used. This method is often called the *incremental IRR approach*. A simple example will illustrate. Suppose we have two mutually exclusive investments. Project C initially costs $100 and has cash costs of $70 and $85 in periods 1 and 2. Project D initially costs $120 and has cash flows of $60 and $70 in periods 1 and 2. The relevant calculation is the IRR based on incremental cash flows of projects C and D (D minus C). Thus, the initial outlay of D is $20 greater than for C, $10 less in period 1 and $15 less in period 2. The IRR formula is

$$0 = -20 + \frac{10}{(1 + \text{IRR})} + \frac{15}{(1 + \text{IRR})^2}$$

Using trial and error values for IRR, we find that about 15 percent is the solution discount rate, or IRR. The decision rule is that we accept project D if the incremental ROR is greater than the cost of capital; otherwise, we reject D and accept C. Thus, if the cost of capital is 10 percent, we would adopt project D. Apparently, the higher initial outlay is more than compensated for by the operating savings of alternative D.

Turning now to discretionary capital projects, we find that the utility operates very much like an unregulated firm. The tendency is to use one or more of the techniques discussed above (the NPV, IRR, or payback methods). Also popular is the accounting rate of return approach, which is computed as the ratio of average profits over the project's life to average investment.[5] Occasionally, a breakeven approach, reflecting the project's revenues and costs as a function of output, is used. The "profits" (the excess of total revenues over total costs) in the breakeven approach are considered a contribution and are used to offset other utility costs.

When used for discretionary projects, the present value of annual cost method must be modified to take into account any revenue changes which may occur. Thus, the PV of annual cost method becomes identical to the NPV method. Examples of discretionary projects for telephone utilities include vertical equipment, such as various types of telephones (the Princess or Trimline) and extensions for residences and a variety of terminal equipment for businesses, radio signaling, mobile services, data terminals, and so on.

A recent survey by Brigham indicates that electric utilities rarely use the common adjustments for risk which are fairly prevalent in the unregulated sector.[6] Specifically, very few of those surveyed adjusted the cost of capital (as in the risk-adjusted discount rate approach) or cash flows (as in the certainty-equivalent approach) for the level of risk inherent in a project. The primary type of explicit analysis commonly employed is sensitivity analysis. Approximately 42 percent of the respondents in the Brigham survey used sensitivity analysis. Sensitivity analysis simply reworks the capital budgeting problem under differing assumptions regarding cash flows, expected project lives, and discount rates. The idea is to see how sensitive the expected outcome is to the assumptions employed. Another 42 percent of the respondents made no formal risk analysis whatever, but rather relied on judgment. A few utilities made an arbitrary downward adjustment in the expected life of a project that appeared to be unusually risky. Sophisticated analysis of risk does not appear often in the electric utility industry.

A recent book written by AT&T's construction plans department, while an otherwise thorough and extremely competent treatment of capital budgeting, gives the problem of risk short shrift.[7] Though somewhat un-

---

[5] The average rate of return approach was discussed in Chapter 4.

[6] "Capital Budgeting by Utilities," *Financial Management*, 3 (autumn 1973), 11–22.

[7] *Engineering Economy*, 3rd ed. (New York: McGraw-Hill, 1977).

certain, it appears that the treatment of capital budgeting risk in the telephone industry is similar to that in the electrics, with adjustments for risk
less common than for the unregulated sector. What is sometimes done in
telephone utilities is simply to apply higher cutoff rates to projects or
categories of projects that are perceived to be of greater risk. This approach,
if formalized, could be consistent with other risk-adjustment techniques,
such as the IRR approach adjusted for risk or the risk-adjusted discount
rate approach.

INFLATION AND OTHER PROBLEM AREAS

Rising operating costs and revenues during periods of inflation should be
reflected in the cash flow estimates of the various capital budgeting models.
To be consistent, if a nominal cost of capital is used as a discount rate,
then nominal flows should be used in the numerator, not flows in terms
of current dollars. Owing to inflation, the cost of capital for utilities has
increased significantly in recent years. However, the added forecasting
and planning problems encountered because of these inflation-related factors are not unique to public utilities, and several other regulatory problems
related to inflation were discussed in Chapter 4.

One common argument suggesting regulatory failure is relevant to
capital budgeting and inflation. First, it is recognized that public utilities
must make the investment necessary to provide adequate service to their
franchise area. Second, as certain costs increase at a steady rate because
of inflation, their realized rate of return may drop below the allowed rate.
If so, a rate hearing is initiated and utility rates are adjusted eventually.
But for a period, the utility's rate of return is less than its cost of capital.
Typically, the utility is not compensated for this shortfall in revenues;
rather, the brunt is borne by capital suppliers. The "fuel adjustment"
clause of electric and gas utilities ameliorates this condition somewhat by
permitting the utility to increase electricity and gas rates immediately to
reflect higher fuel costs. Also, some jurisdictions permit the utility to file
for a temporary rate increase, which permits the utility to collect revenues
at the higher rate until a formal hearing is held.

In a 1975 article by Joskow and MacAvoy, the financial prospects of
the U.S. electric utility industry are analyzed and forecast for the late 1970s
and early 1980s, given the high rates of growth in demand and continued
inflation.[8] Their principal conclusion, based on a financial model, is that

> . . . the nation's investor-owned utilities (providing over 90 percent of gen-
> erating capacity) are not likely to be able to raise the required amounts of
> capital. Increases in construction costs, fuel costs, and interest charges have

[8] "Regulation and the Financial Condition of the Electric Power Companies in the
1970's," *American Economic Review*, 65 (May 1975), 295–301.

recently outstripped revenue growth, and expectations that this trend will continue have made utility investments unattractive. The suspicion is that regulatory procedures have recently caused price increases to lag behind cost increases, resulting in earned rates of return below the cost of capital. If this continues, capacity to meet increased demands . . . will not be achieved.[9]

Thus, these authors projected severe financial difficulties with associated capacity shortages if allowed rates are not significantly increased.

Next, we turn to the current predicament of the electric utility industry to see if these projections are accurate. The headline of a *Wall Street Journal* article of February 2, 1981, read: "Big Financial Problems Hit Electric Utilities; Bankruptcies Feared." The article noted that many electrics are no longer able to generate sufficient cash earnings to pay for dividends. Rather, they finance their dividends from other sources such as depreciation, borrowings, or common stock sales. Though bankruptcy is currently unlikely, safety margins have narrowed substantially and financial analysts are now at least considering the possibility. Perhaps the biggest problem, the *WSJ* article contends, is the astronomical growth of construction costs in recent years. Numerous cost overruns occur because of rising costs owing to inflation; the complexity of projects, which taxes builders' abilities; and building delays resulting from actions by environmentalists or the tightening of credit. In short, while the *WSJ* headline may be exaggerated, all is not well in certain firms in the electric utility industry.

An important problem area, as perceived by electric utility managers, is the difficulty of obtaining regulatory approval for new generating plants (especially nuclear) from environmental protection agencies and the AEC.[10] Numerous plants under construction have been stalled or even abandoned in reaction to regulatory efforts and actions by conservationist groups. Certainly, the incident at the Three Mile Island Nuclear Power Plant has greatly heightened concern over the dangers of nuclear power production. When planning their capital expansion program, utility managers are aware of these delays. This source of uncertainty is extremely difficult to handle in the quantitative analysis of capital projects. Still, the effects of regulatory delay and construction modifications may be anticipated to some extent. To account for these factors, the utility manager may use more pessimistic estimates of a project's useful life, completion date, and cash flow stream, among other things.

One other problem area for utilities is related to what economists call "externalities." An externality occurs when voluntary economic action affects the interests of others outside recognized avenues of compensation. In this regard, outside recognized rights of compensation generally means outside the price system. Social costs and social benefits are externalities.

---

[9] Ibid., p. 295.

[10] Brigham and Pettway, "Capital Budgeting by Utilities," pp. 11–22.

Social costs are costs borne by society as the result of a firm's activities that are not properly priced in the market. Examples include pollution in the form of harmful emissions, visual nuisances such as transmission lines, noise pollution, and the dangers of nuclear leakage and storage and monitoring of spent nuclear fuels that are still radioactive. It is a generally recognized principle that to be efficient, an economic agent (perhaps a utility) generating a positive (beneficial) externality ought to be induced to engage in this process even more than its private interests would dictate. Conversely, production of a negative externality with associated social costs should be discouraged.

With regard to public utility capital budgeting, benefit and cost calculations ought to reflect the positive and negative externalities generated by the undertaking. Typically, these social costs and benefits are not in fact part of the utility's capital budgeting calculus. To provide proper inducements for the utility to undertake the socially desirable level and type of capital investment, numerous proposals have been advanced. We will mention three. First, prices charged by utilities may be increased to cover full costs, both the usual internal costs and the external costs (social costs) that would reduce consumption. But this method provides a windfall profit to utilities and may not affect the utility's decision regarding the specific type of process used. Second, commission orders may be issued to control certain negative environmental impacts. Higher rates reflecting higher costs and reduced consumption may accompany these direct orders. However, these orders are not uniform and generally do not reflect a consistent policy. Third, pollution taxes have been proposed. Firms that have equipment and plant which would easily permit the installation of pollution control equipment to meet standards at a lower cost than the tax itself would install the equipment. Other firms would simply pay the tax. In both cases, utility prices are increased and consumption is reduced. Pollution taxes make it fairly easy for utility rates to reflect the social costs of pollution, through the tax or the increased cost of pollution control equipment. Still, there is the formidable task of setting and adjusting standards for all major pollutants. Although there is no general consensus regarding the appropriate regulatory treatment of externalities, it is commonly believed that the social benefits and costs of capital projects ought to be included in the utility's capital budgeting analysis.

SUMMARY OF PUBLIC UTILITY CAPITAL BUDGETING

Larger, well-managed public utilities seem to follow the general capital budgeting process used by nonutilities. However, several nuances should be mentioned. First, the size of public utility investment is massive. Second, utilities must pay more attention to the community's needs for service. They are required by law to provide adequate service to all who are willing to pay for it. This means they must monitor and forecast population growth, customer movements, consumer incomes, and the like so that adequate capacity is installed to satisfy demand. Planning and budgeting studies are very important. Third, as the utility undertakes projects in any given period with a rate of return exceeding the allowed rate of return, the regulators under effective regulation will lower the utility's prices, although with some lag, to keep overall rates in line with costs. This of course diminishes a project's rate of return. Fourth, electric utilities face some difficulty increasing capacity to meet projected demand because of rapidly increasing costs and problems in obtaining financing. Another problem may arise with depreciation. For nonutilities, accounting depreciation is a sunk cost and should not affect the decision to replace old equipment with new. (The tax effect of depreciation, however, is a cost that must be included in the capital budgeting calculation.) For public utilities, however, depreciation enters the rate-making equation as a cost of service and may influence the decision, depending on the regulatory treatment.

But for the most part, public utilities employ capital budgeting techniques much the same as any other firm. For smaller, routine projects, less effort and less sophisticated techniques are employed. But with larger capital investments with greater risk, more elaborate studies and capital budgeting analysis may be undertaken prior to embarking on the project. However, risk analysis appears to be given somewhat less consideration by utilities than by their counterparts in the unregulated sector.

PUBLIC UTILITY FINANCING

As indicated by their massive capital budgets, the financing needs of public utilities are enormous. Of the total securities (bonds, notes, preferred and common stock) issued by corporations in 1978 and 1979, public utilities accounted for 35 percent.[11] Public utilities dominate major U.S. financial markets. Access to these markets is critical to the continued provision of adequate utility service. The necessary funds come from a variety of sources, which will be surveyed shortly. The question of the appropriate mix of these sources of capital is important and was briefly discussed in Chapter 4. The problem of an optimal capital structure in a general sense is considered below. It is followed by a discussion of public utility financing practices and forms of public utility financing.

THE EFFECT OF FINANCIAL LEVERAGE

The firm analyzes a number of factors including sales volatility, asset composition, profitability, market conditions, and the like and then sets a target

---

[11] U.S. Department of Commerce, *Survey of Current Business*, April 1980.

capital structure, which implies some degree of financial leverage. Let us look at the effect of financial leverage on financial risk, stockholder earnings, and the firm's cost of capital.

With its level and composition of assets already decided, suppose a firm is contemplating the following alternative financial structures:

Plan A		Plan B		Plan C	
0% Financial leverage		50% Financial leverage		80% Financial leverage	
Total debt	$ 0	Total debt	$ 500	Total debt	$ 800
Equity	1000	Equity	500	Equity	200
Total liabilities		Total liabilities		Total liabilities	
and equity	$1000	and equity	$1000	and equity	$1000

Further, suppose the firm pays an average rate of 8 percent on its debt, and the price per share of stock is $10. With these assumptions, we compute the stockholders' earnings per share under varying economic conditions. The results are presented in Table 8.5.

These computations indicate that the use of financial leverage magnifies the effect of a change in economic conditions on stockholders' earnings. Thus the earnings per share and the rate of return on equity are much more variable than the underlying movements in economic conditions. For example, with a change in economic conditions from the indifference level to a good year and the associated change in the rate of return on total assets of 8 to 15 percent, the earnings per share moves from $0.40 to $0.75 if no leverage is used, but it moves from $0.40 to $2.15 with financial leverage of 80 percent. This magnification process works in the other direction as well. With a change from the indifference level to a bad year, earnings per share moves from $0.40 to $0.20 if no leverage is used and from $0.40 to a negative $0.60 if financial leverage is 80 percent. The greater swings in rate of return on equity are also evident in this example.

Greater financial leverage thus increases the risk to common stockholders. But this added risk is accompanied by a greater expected earnings per share if expected rate of return on assets exceeds the cost of debt (8 percent in the above example). With favorable leverage (with the rate of return on assets exceeding the cost of debt), the higher the leverage, the higher the expected rate of return on equity. Note the indifference level— if the rate of return on assets equals the cost of debt, the rate of return to equity is invariant under the different leverage alternatives. We observe, then, a tradeoff between risk and return to shareholders. How this tradeoff is valued in the marketplace for common stock depends in part on the attitudes and alternatives of investors. The optimal capital structure the firm would select is the particular debt-equity combination that maximizes the value of the current owners' stock. At any given level of capital investment, stockholders' value varies inversely with the cost of capital.

A series of graphs help illustrate the argument. Figure 8.4 presents

TABLE 8.5 The Effects of Financial Leverage

	Bad Year	Indifference Level	Good Year
Rate of return on assets	4%	8%	15%
Earnings before interest and taxes (EBIT)	$40	$80	$150
With Plan A, 0% Leverage:			
EBIT	$40	$80	$150
Minus interest	0	0	0
Taxable income	40	80	150
Taxes at 50%	20	40	75
Earnings available to common stock	$20	$40	$ 75
Earnings per share (100 shares)	$0.20	$0.40	$0.75
Rate of return on equity	2%	4%	7.5%
With Plan B, 50% Leverage:			
EBIT	$40	$80	$150
Minus interest	40	40	40
Taxable income	0	40	110
Taxes at 50%	0	20	55
Earnings available to common stock	$ 0	$20	$ 55
Earnings per share (50 shares)	$0.00	$0.40	$1.10
Rate of return on equity	0%	4%	11%
With Plan C, 80% Leverage:			
EBIT	$40	$80	$150
Minus interest	64	64	64
Taxable income	(24)	16	86
Taxes at 50%	(12)	8	43
Earnings available to common stock	$(12)	$ 8	$ 43
Earnings per share (20 shares)	$(0.60)	$0.40	$2.15
Rate of return on equity	(6%)	4%	21.5%

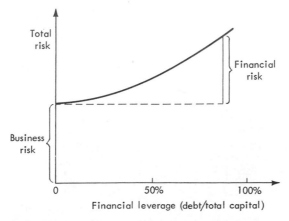

FIGURE 8.4 Risk as a Function of Financial Leverage

a graph indicating that the use of financial leverage increases the risk faced by shareholders above the level of business risk. As a result of this added risk, existing and potential equity investors in the firm require higher rates of return on investments in the firm's stock. This risk takes the form of more volatile earnings per share and an increased probability of bank-ruptcy. Investors must be compensated with a higher expected rate of return if they are to accept the higher level of risk. In Figure 8.5, the required rate of return is depicted as the sum of the risk-free rate, a pre-mium for business risk, and an added premium for the level of financial leverage the firm assumes. The required rate of return on common stock is the most important determinant in computing the cost of equity capital and in fact equals the cost of equity capital in several instances. (For ex-ample, k_e is the cost of capital if the only new equity capital is retained earnings.)

In the computations showing the effects of financial leverage (Table 8.5) it was assumed that the cost of debt capital is 8 percent regardless of financial leverage selected. Though it simplified the illustration, the as-sumption of a constant cost of debt no matter what the level of financial leverage is unrealistic. Lenders of debt capital realize that the likelihood of bankruptcy rises with level of debt. As the level of debt increases, there is an increased chance that the higher fixed interest payments on debt will not be covered by current earnings, and thus the rate required by lenders increases to compensate for the added risk. As a result, the cost of debt capital also rises with leverage. This is the assumption employed in Figure 8.6, which combines the cost of debt and the cost of equity capital to obtain the average cost of capital (upper graph) and shows that the minimum average cost of capital corresponds to the maximum of the value of the firm's stock (lower graph).

In the upper graph of Figure 8.6, as more of the lower-cost debt is

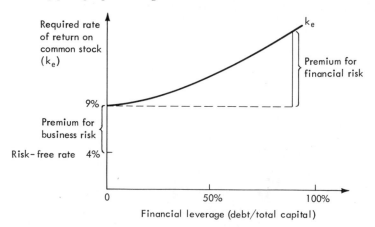

FIGURE 8.5 Required Rate of Return on Common Stock

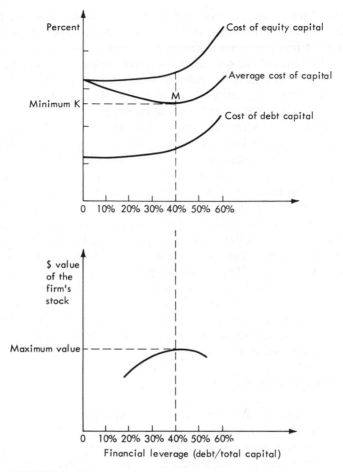

FIGURE 8.6 The Optimal Capital Structure

combined with the cost of equity capital, the average cost of capital, weighted by the proportions of each type of capital, falls up to the point M. To illustrate, at 0 percent financial leverage (debt ratio), the average cost of capital equals the cost of equity capital, since the percentage weight in the debt component is zero. Suppose the average cost of capital at this point is 13 percent. Now suppose at a debt ratio of 20 percent the cost of equity increases to 13.8 percent and the cost of debt is 8.5 percent. The important average cost of capital is reduced from 13 percent to 12.74 (K_0 = .2(8.5%) + .8(13.8%) = 12.74%). This reduction continues until the minimum average cost of capital is reached (point M). After this point, rising debt and equity costs "pull" the weighted average of these costs up. The minimum average cost of capital corresponds to the maximum value of the firm's stock for a particular level of investment. These relationships

259

are consistent with much of the existing research in finance and represent the dominant view in this area. But the research on which these views are based is only suggestive, not definitive.

Once the optimal capital structure is determined, it is used as a target for future financing. This is because the firm's assets may be financed most efficiently by employing this capital structure. As conditions change over time, the target ratio will have to be adjusted. The principal determinants of the optimal capital structure often cited are the stability of sales, the asset structure, the market structure of the industry, the firm's growth rate, the tax structure, profitability, and lender attitudes.

Finally, the primary link between the capital structure and capital budgeting will be restated. Given the optimal capital structure, the marginal cost of capital schedule used earlier to determine the optimal capital budget may be derived. With a given financial leverage ratio, additional increments of money capital after some point may be obtained during the period only at a higher cost. That is, the cost of capital increases with the size of the capital budget. Thus, the marginal cost of capital may be constant over an initial range of investment funds obtained but then may begin to rise. The marginal cost of capital (MCC) is the correct cost to use in capital budgeting. Thus, to determine the optimal capital budget, we compare the MCC with the IRR schedule or compute the NPV of projects, using the MCC at the projected level of investment.

PUBLIC UTILITY FINANCING PRACTICES

Out of the average dollar spent on capital expenditure by utilities, about 35 cents is raised in financial markets. In 1979, all utilities spent over $60 billion on plant and equipment. The Bell System spent nearly $16 billion. For the decade of the 1980s, estimates of capital spending for the electric utility industry alone run as high as $700 billion. The sheer magnitude of these figures is astounding.

The business risk of utilities, as measured by the variability in earnings before interest and taxes, tends to be lower than that for industrial firms. This is largely due to their stable growth, insulation from competition in their primary service area, and the basic nature of utility industries. Because their earnings are relatively stable, utilities are able to use more long-term debt in their capital structure without excessive fear of insufficient earnings to cover interest payments. This is evident in Table 8.6.

Table 8.6 indicates that electric and telephone utilities have adopted larger long-term debt ratios than manufacturing firms. This merely reflects the fact that firms whose earnings are relatively stable can carry more long-term debt than businesses with more volatile earnings. But as pointed out above, firms cannot continue to add to their financial leverage without limit. As they increase their debt, they increase their financial risk. Though

TABLE 8.6 1979 Capital Structure Percentages

	FPC Privately Owned A and B Electrics*	Bell System*	All Manufacturing
Short-term debt	10.9%	11.9%	27.0%
Long-term debt	44.6	39.3	22.8
Preferred stock	11.0	2.1	
Common equity	33.5	46.7	50.2
Total	100.0%	100.0%	100.0%

* Ignores deferred items.

SOURCE: *Moody's Public Utility Manual*, Moody's Investor Service, Inc., New York, 1980; *Statistics of Privately Owned Electric Utilities in the United States 1979*, FPC, Washington, D.C.; *Quarterly Financial Report for Manufacturing, Mining and Trade Corporations, Fourth Quarter 1979*, Federal Trade Commission, Washington, D.C.

increasing financial leverage over some initial range lowers the cost of capital to the firm, after some point the cost of capital to the firm begins to rise because of the greater likelihood of default on interest payments and the increased variability in earnings available to common stock. The optimal capital ratio for utilities includes more debt than for most other firms.

Another striking contrast between utilities and nonutilities is their relative payout ratios, the percentage of earnings available to common stock that are paid out as dividends. The payout ratios of utilities are much higher than those of manufacturing firms. The payout ratios in 1975 for FPC A and B electrics and the Bell System were 69 and 66 percent, respectively, and only 39 percent for all manufacturing. This means, among other things, that utilities must rely even more heavily on new capital financing of investment. But utility investors have come to rely on relatively high dividend payouts, so a major reduction would most likely affect the financial markets.

In general, once the firm's target capital structure is determined, the firm moves incrementally toward this structure and will tend to oscillate about this structure. For example, the utility will usually let short-term debt build up for a period of time until it is economical to come out with a bond issue. The transaction costs per dollar of proceeds are lower for larger issues. The new bond issue will replace almost all short-term debt and any long-term debt that is being retired, and any amount in excess will be placed in marketable securities until needed. The short-term debt of the utility after the bond issue will be near zero, the current ratio will be high, and the debt ratio may be higher than the target for a period of time. As another example, the firm may plan to issue long-term debt during some quarter, but market conditions dictate against it for a quarter or two, so the long-term debt ratio is below the target ratio until the firm finally comes out with the issue. The financial procedures and practices are in some measure a matter of managerial experience and judgment, but over the long haul the impact of financial markets and regulatory conditions determines the range of possibilities.

Typically, utility managers think in terms of target debt ratios. Financial executives design their financing to fluctuate within limits around this target. Some think of the optimal capital structure in terms of a range. For example, John Scanlon, former vice-president and treasurer of AT&T, described his company's policy in terms of a range: "All of the foregoing considerations led us to conclude, and reaffirm for a period of many years, that the proper range of our debt was 30% to 40% of total capital."[12] The target for AT&T increased somewhat in the late 1970s. Among the factors cited as primary considerations in the determination of this target capital structure are: (1) maintenance of the quality of the firm's credit position (bond ratings), (2) current level of business risk (the degree of volatility in earnings), (3) protection of existing debt suppliers, (4) maintenance of access to capital markets under almost all conditions, (5) provision of an adequate borrowing cushion or reserve, and (6) advantages of financial leverage (lower cost and tax advantage). The Bell System's stated capital structure objective is to seek a balance between consumers' and investors' interests by employing a debt ratio slightly less than that necessary to maintain a high-quality credit rating, thereby always assuring access to capital markets.

Continued access to capital markets requires a good credit rating. Utility bonds are rated by services such as Standard and Poor's and Moody's. Bond ratings range from AAA, the highest, down to D, the lowest, which is reserved for bonds in default. Bonds rated BB and below are considered speculative. Generally speaking, the higher the rating, the lower the required rate of return. Several factors that rating agencies cite as important in bond ratings are the use of financial leverage, firm size, use of subordinated debt, variability of earnings, and profitability of operations. Interest coverage ratios are believed inferentially to be an important measure of leverage considered by bond rating services. These rating services do not give specific rating criteria and, in fact, may have no fixed and predetermined criteria. In recent years, utility bond ratings have progressively deteriorated. Almost every telephone company carried bonds with an AAA or AA rating in the early 1970s. Many of these companies found their bonds rated at AA and A (or below) in the early 1980s. Consider the plight of U.S. electric utilities: Only 4 percent of their bonds were rated BBB, the lowest investment grade rating, in 1970. In 1980 nearly 30 percent were rated BBB. These lower ratings and the higher required rates of return associated with them reflect the assessments of the bond rating agencies and the financial markets.

---

[12] "Bell System Financial Policies," *Financial Management*, 1 (summer 1972), 16–26.

FORMS OF PUBLIC UTILITY FINANCING

Public utilities use several types of securities and sources of funds for financing. Though such securities and sources are used by business in general, utilities make greater relative use of senior securities and mortage bonds than industrial firms. However, small businesses rely upon debt, especially bank loans, even more heavily than public utilities. Also utilities have available consumer-contributed capital such as the tax savings from accelerated depreciation and the investment tax credit. The capital intensity, the monopoly power, and the ability to pass taxes on to consumers makes such consumer-contributed capital a significant source of capital. Here, however, we will look at investor-contributed capital such as short-term debt, long-term debt, and equity.

Senior securities such as debt and preferred stock provide much of the financing used by utilities. Short-term debt is a temporary part of capitalization; that of long-term debt is permanent. In addition, common stock equity finances the remainder of utility assets. As an illustration, see the balance sheet presented in Table 8.1.

Short-term debt finances construction and temporary working capital needs. Construction financing is refinanced by issuance of long-term securities after completion of the project. Bank loans and commercial paper are two significant sources of short-term debts. Commercial and industrial loans by banks to public utilities, communications, and transportation companies at year-end 1980 were 13.8 percent of outstanding loans.[13] Such bank loans may take two forms: lines of credit and specific loans. A *line of credit* commits a bank to supply funds up to a maximum amount. As the utility draws on its line of credit, the amount is added to the utility's outstanding loan. Upon maturity, the outstanding loans made under the line of credit are paid. Compensating balances may be required of utilities by banks providing the lines of credit. Of course, any regularly maintained deposit goes toward covering the compensating balance and reduces the additional cost caused by compensating balances. *Specific loans* may be negotiated between the utility and the bank. The interest rate utilities pay on bank loans is often at or near the prime rate charged by banks.

Another source of short-term debt for large public utilities is commercial paper, an unsecured negotiated note issued in bearer form by the utility. The term of the note may be from a few days up to nine months. Commercial paper generally has a lower rate than the bank prime rate and does not require the maintenance of compensating balances. At times, however, a line of credit is required to support commercial paper issues.

As noted earlier, public utilities use much larger proportions of long-

---

[13] Board of Governors of the Federal Reserve System, *Federal Reserve Bulletin*, 67, 1 (January 1981), A22.

term debt financing than industrial corporations. Since utility long-term debt tends to be permanent, all issues are refinanced as due through new issues. Some utilities, particularly very small ones, may retire debt through sinking funds and periodic redemptions. A sinking fund requires an annual payment that allows for the periodic retirement of the debt issue. It eliminates the potential danger of repayment problems at the maturity date if the firm then is faced with temporary financial distress. Most utility long-term debt is in the form of mortgage bonds. Industrials, on the other hand, make wider use of debentures, bonds supported by the general credit standing of the firm. Some utilities do rely on debentures. For example, the major source of long-term debt for American Telephone and Telegraph and many of its subsidiaries is debentures. But generally, utilities issue only a limited number of debentures.

Utility mortgage bonds are secured not only by the creditworthiness of the utility, but also by a lien on specific assets. Only first mortgages are widely used. Should a default of the interest or principal payments on the mortgage bond occur, the mortgage holders have first claim to the proceeds from the sale of the mortgaged assets. Any remaining shortage then has equal status with other unsecured notes and bonds.

A contractual agreement exists between the debtor and the utility. This agreement, the *indenture*, sets forth the terms and conditions of the outstanding bonds. Among the terms and conditions are restrictive convenants, a description of any property mortgaged, the amount and place of payments, and call privileges. A trustee, acting as an agent for the bondholder, polices compliance of the debtor with this indenture. The term of utility bonds is commonly 25 to 30 years, though shorter and longer periods have been provided, with interest being paid twice annually. The open-ended mortgages permit subsequent property additions to be used to support new series of mortgage bonds, series with different interest rates and maturities. The amount of new mortgage debt that may be issued relative to the property additions may be limited by restrictive covenants in the bond indenture. Commonly, issuance of new series of senior or equivalent securities is restricted if certain coverage ratio tests, generally a pre-income-tax interest-coverage ratio test, are not met. Various funds, such as replacement or maintenance funds, require that either cash payments or capital and operating expenditures be made by the utility. The *call privilege* gives the utility issuing the security the right to redeem the bond or other security at a specified price. The call of a bond may reduce the cost of capital to a utility if the saving in interest cost compensates for any premium paid when exercising the privilege. Indentures are only a private contract between creditor and debtor and as such cannot bind a third party, a utility commission. Unreasonably restrictive covenants, such as post-tax interest-coverage tests, have been set aside by commissions in determining a fair rate of return.

Utilities, in early years, used few leases and still use leases only occasionally. Some utilities, particularly some electric utilities, have paid little,if any, income taxes in recent years because of low income levels and accelerated depreciation and investment tax credits. Sale leasebacks and leveraged leasing have been used to convert a potential income tax savings into a lower effective cost of financing. Therefore, these leases are not particularly attractive for some electric utilities today.

Preferred stock, though a senior security, has a claim junior to the utility's debt but is more widely used by utilities than by industrials and is a larger proportion of utility capitalization as well. Preferred stock, carrying a higher rate than bonds, permits the utility to not pay a dividend without defaulting. Most utility preferred stock dividends are cumulative, so that past unpaid preferred stock dividends must be paid before any common stock dividends can be declared. To some extent, this protects preferred stockholders from omitted preferred dividends. However, dividends on preferred stock have not been omitted since the Great Depression. In recent years, some utilities have issued *preference stock*, which has a lower priority claim to earnings for payment of dividends than traditional preferred stock.

Preferred stock, issued because it is less costly than common stock, may be at the same time easier to issue than debt because of bond indentures or tight credit. The preferred stock of most utilities has no maturity date, though issues that mature or are callable do exist. The issuance of preferred stock can impose certain conditions and terms on the utility similar to though less strict than those imposed by a bond indenture. Restrictive covenants may restrict the payment of common dividends or the issuance of future preferred stock or senior securities under various conditions. Voting rights may be granted if a specified number of preferred dividends is not paid.

Public utilities commonly have only one class of common stock. Again, exceptions among small or new utility corporations do exist. The common stockholders have a residual claim on the earnings of the utility. The common stock in publicly traded public utilities is more widely held by small investors and less widely held by institutional investors. Many utilities, unlike industrials, issue new common stock on a regular basis.

The common stock can be accounted for in three parts—common stock, paid-in capital, and retained earnings. In addition to paying cash dividends, utilities from time to time have made stock splits or paid stock dividends. As a matter of accounting treatment, a stock split does not raise or lower the total amount of common stock, paid-in capital, or retained earnings, but only distributes it over more shares. A stock dividend, however, reduces total retained earnings by transferring an amount to common stock or paid-in capital.

The public utility, when issuing securities, uses both public and private placement of primary issues. Private placements usually tailor, by negotiation, the rates and conditions and terms of the security to the needs of the utility and a particular investor, frequently an insurance company for senior securities. Public issues are subject to detailed requirements and procedures. Underwriting of public security issues requires an investment bank that is compensated for its services. The underwriter will advise the utility on the type of security to issue and help prepare the information required for a prospectus and by regulatory agencies such as the Securities and Exchange Commission. Usually, the underwriting syndicate guarantees a price to the utility. Upon distribution to the public, the market price received produces the profit or loss for the underwriting syndicate.

Other methods are used by utilities to issue new securities. *Rights offerings* that permit existing shareholders to purchase, at a discount below market price, a *pro rata* share of new common or preferred stock have been used. If shareholders choose to, the rights may be sold to prospective investors who in turn will purchase the securities. American Telephone and Telegraph Company had generally, before the 1970s, relied upon rights offerings to issue new common equity. Presently, *dividend reinvestment programs* are popular among public utilities. Rather than receiving a cash dividend, an investor may purchase shares of common stock at a price slightly below market price. Public utilities, particularly telephone utilities, have occasionally used other methods of issuing securities. Convertible bonds and preferred stock or warrants for the purchase of other securities have been a right available on certain issues of senior securities. Mergers and acquisitions, made through pooling of interests and direct purchases, have required the issuance of new securities.

An important point of this section is that because of their immense capital needs, public utilities tend to tap virtually every major financial market for funds. Probably the most notable features of public utilities are their regular issuance of new securities, their heavy reliance on mortgage debt and other senior securities, and their practice of permanent financing of utility capitalization. Such features are not unique to public utilitities, though the preponderance of these features in the public utility industry makes the industry's financial structure unique.

THE PARTICIPATION
——————— OF REGULATORY COMMISSIONS ———————

Public utilities do not have a free hand in their capital budgeting and financing decisions. Capital investments and financing are subject to review by utility regulatory commissions and other governmental bodies. Imprudent costs are not charged to customers, but are charged "below-the-line"—i.e., charged against investors' equity. A determination of prudence is part of a cost of service determination. Other reviews by commissions take place prior to financing or capital investment. The commission's authorization must be secured before certain transactions occur. As we will see below, three such transactions are reviewed by many commissions and agencies: securities issuance, use of eminent domain powers, and certificates of convenience and necessity.

SECURITIES REGULATION

Massachusetts first regulated security issues by public utilities. New York, in a 1907 statute, undertook the regulation of utility security issues. In 1978, the District of Columbia and some 44 states regulated security issuance by public utilities.[14] The Federal Energy Regulatory Commission and the Securities and Exchange Commission also regulate security issuance by public utilities. In order to assure utility customers and investors access to financing, security regulation was introduced. Protection against overcapitalization and undercapitalization, and the assurance that security issues secure capital and not just income, are functions of security regulation.

Equity and debt capitalization can approximately equal utility assets, but overcapitalization can occur when the capitalization exceeds the asset value. Undercapitalization, on the other hand, occurs when asset value exceeds capitalization. Since debt and preferred stock are fixed income securities, overcapitalization leads to a lowered return on common equity, while undercapitalization leads to an increased return. Because the fair rate of return is applied to a utility's rate base, rather than to capitalization, overall equity earnings rise and fall with under- and overcapitalization, respectively. For example, assume $1 million in rate base upon which a 10 percent return is earned. With capitalization also of $1 million, of which debt is 60 percent, and a cost of debt of $8\frac{1}{3}$ percent, the return to common equity is 12.5 percent. The utility would be overcapitalized if instead $1.2 million worth of securities were issued. Then, for 60 percent debt at $8\frac{1}{3}$ percent and a 10 percent return on the rate base, the earnings available to common stock are reduced to $40,000 on $480,000 of common equity. The overall return on common equity declines to $8\frac{1}{3}$ percent.

Overcapitalization could hinder the ability of utilities to secure capital in two ways. Since utilities traditionally have high dividend payout ratios, the net income available to pay dividends is reduced to at or below the level of the dividends themselves. Also, indentures are entered into by utilities upon issuance of debt and preferred stock. These indentures gen-

---

[14] National Association of Regulatory Utility Commissioners, *1978 Annual Report on Utility and Carrier Regulation* (Washington, D.C.: National Association of Regulatory Utility Commissioners, 1979), p. 447.

erally will set forth interest coverages and other tests that must be met before new debt can be issued. Likewise, if preferred stock dividends have not been paid, issuance of senior securities and preferred stock is prohibited. Overcapitalization can lower interest coverage and reduce net income available to pay preferred stock dividends. The issuance of new senior securities by the utility is forbidden. Not only may the fixed-income security holders be denied a return, but the utility's ability to finance is restricted. Overcapitalization occurred early in the history of utilities. It was the result of issuance of securities (1) based upon goodwill and franchise value, (2) to buy out competitors and purchase new service territory, (3) for overpriced property, and (4) as a bonus to purchasers of senior securities.

Securities should be issued to secure capital, not income. Securities, if generally issued to cover operating expenses, would increase net income available for dividends while increasing future financial obligations. The rate on securities issued should also be reasonable. A lack of arms-length transactions can result in a rate that exceeds the rate necessary to secure capital. The higher rate provides income, but not additional capital. Of course, the intent of securities regulation is not to guarantee imprudent or extravagant interest and dividend rates or other considerations, such as the provisions of indentures, to investors. Moreover, securities regulation may not be sufficient to ensure a prudent capital structure. Public utilities still may reduce the financial risk, at a given return, by increasing equity unnecessarily through retained earnings. Hypothetical capital structures, as discussed in Chapter 4, are a cost of service method used to ensure that only the lower costs of efficient financing are paid by consumers.

Uniform accounts, accounting compliance audits, and recording assets at original cost did much to enforce the equality of assets and capitalization as well as prevent the issuance of securities to secure income rather than capital. Various commissions also require competitive bids from underwriters of securities to ensure minimum issuance costs. The consolidation of the electric and gas systems from the late 1910s through the 1920s by holding companies led to the most significant example of securities regulation. Under the Public Utility Holding Company Act of 1935, a "death sentence clause" limited holding companies to three levels, the grandfather level and two subordinate levels of subsidiaries; created contiguous and integrated power systems; and effectively limited a holding company to the control of only one utility system. The Public Utility Act of 1935 also authorized the Securities and Exchange Commission to reorganize the capital structure of the electric holding companies.

The holding company held as assets a controlling interest in the voting securities of a subsidiary. That subsidiary in turn held as assets controlling securities in its subsidiaries. And, in turn, each level of the pyramid held controlling interests in its own subsidiaries. Further, at each level, the separate holding company level issued fixed-income securities such as debt and preferred stock, whose payment depended upon dividends paid ultimately by operating subsidiaries. A diagram of this pyramid is presented in Figure 8.7. The holding company, through service company subsidiaries, often provided services and sold capital assets to operating subsidiaries at overstated prices. The SEC was also authorized to eliminate such writeups from capital.

The pyramids resulted in excessive leverage in the capital structure. When the depression of the 1930s reduced the return of the operating utilities, the holding companies were prohibited from securing additional capital because of losses or failure to meet indenture requirements. Assuming a four-level holding company pyramid had a 6 percent return and the following capitalization, reductions in operating returns to 4 and 2 percent led to substantial reductions in returns and interest coverage, even losses, at the top of the pyramid. These results are shown with a numerical example in Tables 8.7 and 8.8. By about 1950, the utility reorganizations were completed. Surviving, but reorganized, holding companies in the electric industry are, unless exempt, still required to seek prior approval of securities issuance from the Securities and Exchange Commission.

TABLE 8.7 Capital Ratio

Operating level		6.0%	4.0%	2.0%
Interest rate	3%			
Times: Debt ratio	50%			
Less: Cost of debt		1.5%	1.5%	1.5%
		4.5%	2.5%	0.5%
Divided by: Equity ratio		50.0%	50.0%	50.0%
Parent level return		9.0%	5.0%	1.0%
Interest rate	3%			
Times: Debt ratio	50%			
Less: Cost of debt		1.5%	1.5%	1.5%
		7.5%	3.5%	(0.5%)
Divided by: Equity ratio		50.0%	50.0%	50.0%
Grandfather level return		15.0%	7.0%	(1.0%)
Interest rate	3%			
Times: Debt ratio	50%			
Less: Cost of debt		1.5%	1.5%	1.5%
		13.5%	5.5%	(2.5%)
Divided by: Equity ratio		50.0%	50.0%	50.0%
Great-grandfather level return		27.0%	11.0%	(5.0%)
Interest rate	3%			
Times: Debt ratio	50%			
Less: Cost of debt		1.5%	1.5%	1.5%
		25.5%	9.5%	(6.5%)
Divided by: Equity ratio		50.0%	50.0%	50.0%
Holding company equity return		51.0%	19.0%	(13.0%)

Level

A: Great-grandfather level

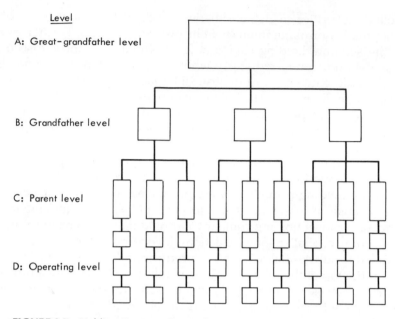

B: Grandfather level

C: Parent level

D: Operating level

FIGURE 8.7 Holding Company Pyramid

EMINENT DOMAIN

Eminent domain is the right of the state to take property for public use. The authority to exercise eminent domain is legislative, but the legislature can delegate the power to agencies such as utility commissions or to private businesses such as public utilities. Electric power, gas, telephone, and water utilities are widely held to fulfill a necessary public use and have use of the eminent domain power. Utility commissions, legislatures, statutes, and courts have granted eminent domain to public utilities in various states. The utility and agency must establish public use and necessity, follow constitutional due process, and provide reasonable compensation for the taking of the property.

The U.S. Constitution requires just compensation for property taken when the sovereign power of eminent domain is exercised. Just compensation returns to the ex-owner a pecuniary position equivalent to the owner

TABLE 8.8 Post-Tax Interest-Coverage Ratios

Operating return	6%	4%	2%
Operating level	4×	2.67×	1.33×
Parent level	6×	3.33×	0.67×
Grandfather level	10×	4.67×	*
Great-grandfather level	18×	7.33×	*

* Negative.

still having the property. The owner's loss generally determines the compensation. One useful standard of owner's loss is the market value of property taken.

Eminent domain may be used by utilities to acquire sites for power plants and telephone plants, and to acquire rights-of-way and easements for gas and water pipelines and mains, electric transmission and distribution lines, and telephone lines. The utility, of course, may purchase such land and rights of way on the open market; but if obstructed in completing the project, the power of eminent domain may be used to acquire the property.

The power of eminent domain restricts the monopsony power of property owners. Without such power, property owners could require the utility and its customers to accept "all-or-nothing" agreements and require excessive compensation. The constitutional requirements protect the property owner where the property is not necessary and reasonable alternatives could be used, and by restoring the pecuniary worth of the property owner when the property is taken.

CERTIFICATES OF CONVENIENCE AND NECESSITY

Let us look at power plant siting. The energy crisis, power blackouts, and environmental concerns drew attention to power plants, and involvement by state government in power plant siting increased substantitally during the 1970s. The 1965 and 1977 blackouts in New York City, as well as the issues of nuclear power and storage of nuclear waste, helped focus nationwide interest on electric power system planning.

About half the states require prior approval from utility commissions or other designated agencies before an electric utility can construct a generating plant. Even in states where the utility commission does not make the siting determination, the commission or its commissioners are usually involved in the decision-making process. This prior approval became necessary when state legislation was passed in the 1970s. Frequently, one-stop proceedings are used to avoid conflicts among different government decisions in licensing power plants.

Three considerations enter into a power plant siting decision:

1. Demand forecasting
2. Plant size and location
3. Environmental effects

Of the three, demand forecasting and environmental effects have received the greatest attention at the agency level. But the costs of appropriate plant size and location have not been ignored.

Demand forecasting involves forecasting of both load (kilowatts) and

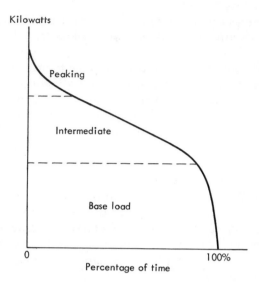

FIGURE 8.8 Load Duration Curve

energy (kilowatt hours). The load forecast will establish the need for capacity. The energy forecast is related to the load forecast by a load duration curve, the cumulative time that certain levels of load are demanded. The area under the load duration curve will equal the energy demand, as Figure 8.8 shows.

Until quite recently, many load and energy forecasts were simple trend lines, such as

$$KW_t = KW_o \times (1 + g)^t$$

where g = growth rate, and t = time. In the last decade, more sophisticated time series and econometric forecasts as well as end-use models have been used. The more sophisticated time series related load and energy to their own history. A statistical method called autoregressive moving-average analysis relates data to their own history. An econometric forecast, on the other hand, can relate load or energy demand to the price of electricity, consumer income, and prices of alternative energy sources. This relationship will depend on an accurate estimation of the short-run and long-run price elasticities, income elasticity, and cross-elasticity of load or energy with other energy sources, as well as projections of prices and income. End-use models disaggregate load or energy information into the end use in each consuming sector, such as residential, commercial, and industrial customers. Various factors, such as customer growth and changes in per customer use, affecting demand growth in each sector are analyzed, and a growth rate for each sector is estimated. Individual forecasts for each sector are added together to arrive at total load or energy end-use forecasts.

Plant size and location can be determined next. The forecasts of increased load and energy demand establish a need for further electric generation, generation which can take the form of base load, intermediate load, and peaking capacity. Forecasts of stable and continuous use suggest that base-load capacity should be planned for, while unstable and limited use at peaks suggest peaking capacity. Base-load capacity presently includes coal-fired generation and, to an extent, nuclear-powered generation. Peaking capacity includes fast-starting oil-fired turbines. Intermediate load may be met by a variety of sources, including downgrading of smaller, less efficient base-load units. The size of generation units depends on another consideration, the reliability of the capacity chosen. Additional capacity, often in the form of other generation units, is needed to ensure that load is met even if major units fail. A common reliability objective is that capacity be sufficient to permit an outage only during one day in ten years. Fifteen percent or more excess capacity has been maintained by utilities to reach this objective. Reliability in transmission and distribution must, of course, be maintained.

Choice of location is considered an influential part of cost. For example, the delivery of coal would cause an important location cost; transmission line costs also depend on locational choice. The locational choice can be restricted significantly by noncost factors such as availability of cooling water, existing transportation facilities, the previous use of the site for generation, and transmission routes.

Environmental decisions must also be made. In the areas of air and water quality, statutes and environmental agency rules generally establish minimum physical performance standards. For example, a maximum level of sulfur dioxide emissions is set. The operation and design of the plant must be such that these standards are met. For example, the burning of low-sulfur coal and the use of stack scrubbers reduce sulfur dioxide emissions. Other environmental concerns include endangered and threatened species, esthetic qualities, and land use. Transmission lines that connect the plant site to the grid also require solutions to environmental problems. These problems include standard clearances to ensure safety and the esthetic design and placement of transmission poles and towers.

The regulatory commission, an agency reviewing power plant siting, must reflect carefully on a project that could cost many millions or even billions of dollars, serve the public for upward of 25 years, and affect the environment in many ways. It is hoped the agency's expeditious review and determination of the low-cost power plant will meet forecasted demand as well as environmental standards and needs. But clearly, this plant siting process restricts the utility's capital budgeting decision. It is far from the simple case of comparing the internal rate of return on a project to its cost of capital.

Power plant siting regulation is only the most significant recent example of an authority that many commissions have, the power to grant or deny *certificates of public convenience and necessity*. During earlier periods, other expanding utility services received much more attention in proceedings to determine public convenience and necessity. For example, during the late 1930s, the 1940s, and the 1950s, advances in welding technology made possible long-distance pipelines that could transport natural gas from fields in Texas, Louisiana, and other states to distant urban and industrial centers. In even earlier decades, during the developmental phase of most utility industries, commission reviews of public convenience and necessity focused on unnecessary duplication of services. Large fixed costs of investment in central electric stations, in gas manufacturing plants, and in distribution systems for water, electricity, and gas, if duplicated by competing utilities, greatly increased the unit costs of service while the utility's customers and revenues declined. Competing utilities then engaged in rate wars to recover the lost customers, revenues and economies of scale. Unfortunately, the collapse of companies and services to various customers followed. The historical results from such competition resembled closely the instability described in our discussion of social overhead capital in Chapter 2. Unstable competitive utilities were replaced by grants of monopoly and certificates of public convenience and necessity.

Statutory or constitutional authority permits the regulatory commission to exercise the legislative power to issue certificates of public convenience and necessity. The commission has reasonable latitude in deciding substantive issues, but is required to provide procedural due process to parties in its review of an application. Prior to the utility providing service, in most jurisdictions it must receive a certificate of public convenience and necessity from the commission. Utilities that existed prior to the enactment of certificate requirements are generally exempted, and their existing service territory protected. Public convenience and necessity are defined jointly; absolute or indispensable public need is not a prerequisite. Only public expedience, reasonable benefit, or prevention of detriment to the public is required.

The commission will ascertain if the utility is ready, willing, and able to provide the service to benefit the public—the public as a whole, both current and future consumers, not just the applicant for the certificate. In doing this, commissions have inquired into:

1. The costs of construction and operation
2. The ability to meet expected demand
3. Efficient operation and prevention of waste, such as productive use of natural gas replacing simply burning off the gas or manufacturing lamp black
4. The company's ability to finance the project

5. The safety, engineering, and construction practices of the project
6. Probable rates
7. The ability of an existing utility to provide the service

The commission may find that the public convenience and necessity will be served by the utility requesting the certificate. Alternatively, the commission may reject the application or establish conditions to be carried out by the applicant before the certificate is authorized. The certificate may or may not carry a time limit within which the utility must begin providing service.

SUMMARY

Capital budgeting and financing decisions are crucial to the successful operation of a public utility. Its massive requirement for new capital, particularly in inflationary times, forces the utility not only to employ internal sources of funds (retained earnings, depreciation, and deferred taxes), but also external funds. Virtually every major source in the capital market is tapped, including issuance of common stock, preferred stock, and bonds of various types. Careful consideration of the utility's capital budget and its financing is essential for regulators and utility management alike.

Capital budgeting is the administrative process that governs the selection of long-lived assets, whereas financing deals with the procurement of funds needed to finance the capital projects at the lowest cost to the firm. The primary link between the asset structure and the financial structure of the firm is the cost of capital. The cost of capital is used as a standard in the principal capital budgeting methods; it is a major factor in asset selection. But the cost of capital, in turn, is influenced by the relative use of the various financing sources—i.e., the financial structure of the firm. Typically, the lower the risk in the firm's pretax earnings stream, the more financial leverage (use of the lower-cost debt), with its associated financial risk, can be tolerated. Thus, public utilities tend to use more debt financing in their financial structures.

Generally, similar capital projects are grouped into categories to facilitate comparison and analysis. With some projects, called mandatory projects, very little choice is involved. For example, the project may be urgently needed to continue production. With discretionary projects, a choice must be made. To help in evaluation, a number of capital budgeting techniques and risk-adjusted methods are used. Among them are the NPV (or present worth of expenditures), IRR, and payback methods. Public utilities tend to use the available risk-adjustment methods less frequently than their counterparts in the unregulated sector. Some problem areas in the capital budgeting process are dealing with inflation, estimating and incorporating social benefits and costs, and obtaining approval from environmental protection agencies.

To finance its assets, the utility employs almost every major source of financing. The mix of these sources determines the utility's capital structure. The capital structure that provides the needed financing at the lowest cost is the one desired. Public utilities tend to think in terms of target capital structures. Their financing patterns will tend to fluctuate about this preferred capital structure. Utilities not only have higher debt ratios, but also higher dividend payout ratios than manufacturing firms in general. Higher dividend payouts mean that more external financing is required.

Finally, it must be recognized that the regulatory commission plays a role in utility capital budgeting and financing. This participation is illustrated by our discussion of securities regulation, which deals with the problems of over- and undercapitalization; eminent domain, which relates to a utility's right to take property for "public use"; and power plant siting, which shows that the issues relating to major capital project decisions are far more involved and complex than we usually realize.

Study Questions

1. Define the following terms: (a) assets, (b) liabilities, (c) bonds, (d) common stock, (e) capital structure, (f) business risk, (g) financial risk, and (h) financial leverage.

2. Show graphically the optimal capital budget.

3. Define and briefly discuss the NPV, IRR, and payback techniques of capital budgeting. Which is conceptually superior?

4. Suppose a utility needs a certain project that has a negative NPV to continue to provide adequate service. Should the firm undertake the project? Why? What are the consequences?

5. How might the degree of risk be incorporated into capital budgeting analysis?

6. Explain the effect of financial leverage on risk. How does financial leverage affect the earnings per share of common stock?

7. If the debt-equity ratio of the firm is increased, what will be the effect on the cost of equity capital? On the average cost of capital?

8. What is the weighted average cost of capital if the cost of equity is 14 percent, the cost of debt is 10 percent, and the debt-equity ratio is two-thirds?

9. Since the cost of debt capital is always lower than the cost of equity

capital, why doesn't the firm use near 100 percent debt? Would regulators let a firm use 95 percent debt?

10. What factors determine the target ratio of debt to equity?

11. How does the fact that utilities have a relatively low business risk affect the amount of financial leverage they employ?

12. How does the growth rate of public utility investment affect the utilities' cost of capital?

13. Why are public utilities' payout ratios greater than those for other firms? What is the effect of a high payout on external financing?

14. What are the primary sources of capital employed by public utilities?

Student Readings

AT&T's Construction Plans Department. *Engineering Economy*. New York: McGraw-Hill, 1977.

BIERMAN, HAROLD, AND SEYMOUR SMIDT. *The Capital Budgeting Decision*, 5th ed. New York: Macmillan, 1980.

BRIGHAM, E., AND R. PETTWAY. "Capital Budgeting by Utilities." *Financial Management*, 3 (autumn 1973), 11–22.

FARRIS, M., AND R. SAMPSON. *Public Utilities*. Boston: Houghton Mifflin, 1973, chap. 13.

JOSKOW, P., AND PAUL MACAVOY. "Regulation and the Financial Condition of the Electric Power Companies in the 1970's." *American Economic Review*, 65 (May 1975), 295–301.

LATIMER, H. A. "Competition in Regulated Industries: Rate of Return and Financing Needs." *Essays on Economic Issues*, eds. J. Niss and M. Pledge. Macomb, Ill.: Center for Business and Economic Research, Western Illinois University, 1975, pp. 105–128.

MARTIN, J. D., et. al. *Basic Financial Management*. Englewood Cliffs, N.J.: Prentice-Hall, 1979.

PHILLIPS, CHARLES F., JR. *The Economics of Regulation*, 2nd ed. Homewood, Ill.: Irwin, 1969, chap. 6.

VAN HORNE, JAMES. *Financial Management and Policy*, 5th ed. Englewood Cliffs, N.J.: Prentice-Hall, 1980, chaps. 5–10.

WESTON, J. F., AND E. F. BRIGHAM. *Managerial Finance*. Hinsdale, Ill.: Dryden Press, 1975, chaps. 10, 11, 18, 19, 21.

Index

DATE DUE